A Practitioner's Approach

and Interpretation

of

The Party Wall etc. Act 1996

Dr. Philip Antino Ph.D.

Second Edition

Gotham Books

30 N Gould St.
Ste. 20820, Sheridan, WY 82801
https://gothambooksinc.com/

Phone: 1 (307) 464-7800

Published by Gotham Books (December 6, 2022)

ISBN: 979-8-88775-132-0 (sc)

ISBN: 979-8-88775-133-7 (e)

PREFACE

It is just over ten years since the first edition was published. What a journey it has been, culminating with obtaining my Ph.D. on the 14th June 2021 and the first in the world on this specialist subject of party walls. It is time to update the first edition and, in some instances have changed my previous position, opinions and interpretations. The exponential growth in litigation has influenced this second edition, not least because the true measure of the ongoing conflicting interpretations and approaches amongst the party wall community and those who operate on the periphery such as Solicitors, Barristers, and Judges, reiterates the authors concern's that the Act is not being implemented correctly. Clearly, the conflict is caused by the dissemination of information, through various mediums, not least of all various organisations and associations that seek to promote themselves as an authority on the Act. Unfortunately, their goal to assert themselves as the authority often complicates matters with inconsistent and conflicting advice rather than removing the fog that surrounds the Act. Unless clarity and consistency on the strict interpretation of the Act is achieved, the growth in disputes will continue to draw the Act into the abyss of litigation, litigation, and more litigation. This is plainly contrary to Parliament's and indeed Lord Lytton's intentions, but good for the barrister's bank accounts.

When the Act received Royal Assent, it was considered a substantive piece of legislation and a substantial step forward within the built environment. Very sadly after 26 years nothing seems to have changed. If the Act were a car, it would be considered a classic with its finest days behind it, is it now time to repeal the Act? I believe it is.

I have changed the format to improve the expression, clarity and understanding of what I, in my humble opinion, suggest is the correct interpretation and approach to the Act. Whether my opinions are accepted, ultimately rests with the readers desire to adopt an open or closed mind when reading this book. Where appropriate I am critical (and justifiably so) of those that I consider have not contributed to the Act and or indeed the Law, through inconsistent and erratic judgements and approaches.

Dr Philip Antino Ph.D., BSc (Hons), MSc, MRes, FCABE, MCIArb.

DOCTORAL JOURNEY

Having completed my undergraduate degree in Building Surveying at the respected Heriot Watt University, and prior to graduating with a BSc (Hons), I was invited to read for an MSc in Construction and Project Management. Towards the end of my post-graduate degree, I began taking an interest in research and was offered an opportunity to remain at Heriot Watt and continue with a Ph.D. However, having spent the previous four years in student poverty, and without at that time having a clear research topic in mind, I decided to enter the real world and work for a living, with the intention of returning within a few years. But life took over and time passed by until in much the same way as other building surveyors, I engaged with the Act. Mistakenly, if not having a naïve belief that the Act did what the packaging said, enabling specific building works without creating or interfering with an adjoining owner's property rights. For the first six-months or thereabouts, together with the vast majority of the party wall community, we muddled along on the basis that at the time those operating within the P&T were the experts and had all the answers to the difficult questions that construction works created when triggering the Party Wall etc. Act 1996. I soon realised that was not the case.

Therefore, after many years of experiencing unnecessary and wholly avoidable disputes arising out of conflicting interpretations in some instances blatant dishonesty and substantial gaps in knowledge, some very interesting if not bizarre judgements, I decided to commence my doctoral journey with a two-year part time MRes (Master in Research) at Salford University under the supervision of Paul Chynoweth[1] (now Dr). I had intended to continue my doctorate at Salford. However, a Ph.D. is not for the feint hearted, and taking on board the logistics, time, cost of temporary accommodation, and commuting to Salford from Essex on a regular basis created unnecessary additional logistical issues. I therefore transferred with Paul's recommendation to Anglia Ruskin University ("ARU") and on 14th June 2021 very proudly received my Ph.D.

---

1 Paul Chynoweth is senior lecturer in Construction and Property Law, and programme leader for the professional doctorate, in the University of Salford's 'School of the Built Environment'. By profession he is a solicitor with a building surveying degree, and accredited commercial mediator. He is the editor of the International Journal of Law in the Built Environment and the coordinator of CIB Working Commission (W113) on Law & Dispute Resolution. His many publications include The Party Wall Casebook and a number of award-winning peer-reviewed journal articles on the future of expert evidence in rights to light litigation. He is also a co-author of the best-selling student textbook, Law and the Built Environment.

Research Aims and Outcome of the Authors Doctoral Research

(1). The author is the first person in the world to have researched the Party Wall etc Act 1996 at Ph.D. level;

(2). A Ph.D. is the highest academic qualification in the UK;

(3). The research identified numerous gaps in knowledge and the common area of dispute specific area;

(4). Demonstrates that the Act is flawed;

(5). Demonstrates that a reinforced concrete basement box is a special foundation;

(6). Demonstrates that the Chaturachinda v Fairholme judgement is wrong;

(7). All reinforced concrete basements constructed under the premise that Chaturachinda was correct are unlawful;

(8). That the section 7(4) veto applies; and

(9). The adjoining owner's permission for projecting special foundations must be obtained;

TABLE OF CONTENTS

LIST OF FIGURES

LIST OF TABLES

TABLE OF CASE LAW

Adams v Marylebone Borough Council [1907] 2 KB 822
AMEC Capital Projects Ltd v Whitefriars City Estates Ltd [2004] EWCA Civ 1418, [2005] 1 All ER 723.
AM Shipping Ltd v TTMI Ltd [2006] 1 Lloyd's 374
American Cyanamid v Ethicon Ltd [1975] AC 396.
Antino v Reeves (2016) Barkingside Magistrates Court.
Antino v Stirling Properties Ltd (2016) Barking Magistrates Court.
Antino v Burke & Johnny (2016) Barking Magistrates Court.
Ash v Trimnell- Richard [2019] County Court at Central London F20CL088.
AT & T Corp v Saudi Cable Company [2002] ALLER (Comm) 625.
AWG Group Ltd v Morrison [2006] 1 ALL ER 139

Bansal v Myers [2007] Romford County Court Unreported.
Barnard v National Dock Labour Board [1953] 2 QB 18.
Bennett v Harrod's Stores Ltd (1907) The Builder, Dec 7 P.624
Bennett v Rowlins and Rowlins [2021] County Court at Brighton (G00BN668)
Blake v Reeves [2009] EWCA Civ 611.
Block 6 Ashley Gardens Ltd v David Franses, Simon Franses, S Franses Ltd, James Ramsay and the Bouyges v Dahl-Jensen (1999) EWHC (Receiver of Basement Flat, Block 6 Ashley Gardens, Thirleby Road, London).

Capper, M (1) and Capper, R (2) v Macey, B (1) & Antino, P. (2) – (2021) The County Court at Central London H20CL135.
Cardiff Rating Authority v Guest Keen Baldwin's Iron and Steel Co Ltd [1941] KB 485.
Car-Saunder v Dick McNeil Associates Ltd [1986] 1 WLR 922.
Canary Riverside PTE Ltd -v- Dr & Mrs Schilling, LTL 8/6/2006.
Chandler v Thompson (1811) 3 Camp.
Chaturachinda v Fairholme (2015) TCC County Court at Central London
Cofely Ltd v Anthony Bingham and Knowles Ltd [2016] EWHC 240 (Comm).
Colls v Holmes and Colonial Stores (1894) 3 Ch. 659.
Conaghan & Conaghan v Abdul (2022) County Court at Edmonton.
Continental Property Ventures Inc -v- Mr. & Mrs White, LTL 21/3/2006.
Crosby v Alhambra Co Ltd [1907] 1 Ch 295.
Crowley v Rushmore Borough Council [2010] EWHC 2237
Cubit v Porter (1828) High Court, Kings Bench, [1824-34] All ER Rep 267.
Cutts v Head [1984] Ch. 290

Dalton v Angus (1881) 6 APP.CAS 740 at 792.
Davies & Sleep v Wise [2006] Barnet County Court.
Deakins v Hookings [1994] 14 E.G., 133.

Delva Patman Redler LLP v D Franses (2020) - County Court Money Claims Centre G09YJI98

Dimes v Grand Junction Canal Proprietors (1852) 3 HL Cas 759.

Dodosh v Bibizadeh & Bibizadeh [2014] County Court at Romford.

Dodosh v Bibizadeh & Bibizadeh [2015] Central London County Court

Dury v Army & Navy Auxiliary Cooperative Supply Ltd (1896) 2 QB 271.

Duke of Westminster v Guild [1985] 1 Q.B. 688 at 700 E.

Dust v Marioni Greenaway & MacNulty (2004) County Court at Clerkenwell HHJ Collins CBE.

Edmond, Edmond & Mulligan v Denham & Seekings-Denham (2021) County Court at Central London (J20CL075).

Ellenborough Park [1956] Ch. 131.

Emms v Polya [1973] 227 EG 1659.

Evans v Paterson, (1) McGeevy-Harris (2), Newton (3) & McAllister (4) [2021] In the County Court at Central London G20CL068

Farrs Lane v Bristol Magistrates Court (2016) EWHC.

Ferguson Court Residents Association Ltd v Mr. S Fisher (2015) Romford County Court.

Ferguson & Ferguson v Lloyd-Baker (2017) County Court at Central London.

Findlay v United Kingdom (1997) 24 EHRR 221, 244, para 73

Fishenden v Higgs and Hill Ltd (1935) 153 LT 128.

Flannery v Halifax Estate Agencies Ltd [2000] 1 WLR 377, 381.

Franco Rusciani v Kamal Kumar and Rajesh Sharma (2013) Chelmsford County Court.

Garritt v Sharp (1835) 3 A & E.

Gaunt, J.Q.C. and Morgan, P.C.C. (2002) *"Gale on Easements"* 7th Edition Sweet & Maxwell Ltd.

Gillies v Secretary of State for Works and Pensions [2006] EWCA Civ 392; [2006] 1 ALLER 731 at [38].

Goodhart v Hyett (1884) 25 Ch.D. 182.

Goodmans Autos Ltd v Maverstone Properties Ltd & Byoot Develop Ltd (2021) County Court at Central London H02CL868

Grand v Gill [2011] 1 WLR 2253.

Gray v Elite Town Management Ltd (2015) County Court at Central London.

Grey v Pearson [1857] 6 HL.C. 61

Gyle-Thompson v Wall Street (Properties) Ltd 1 WLR 123 [1974] 1 ALL ER 295.

Halsbury's Laws of England Fifth Edition, Volume 95, paragraph 1143.

Haslam, S., and O'Connor, L. (2013) *"Specialist Domestic: Underpinning and Subsidence "*.

Hobbs, Hart & Co v Grover [1899] No. 1 Ch 11.

Irvine -v- Moran [1991] 1 EGLR 261.

Jaggard v Sawyer [1995] 1 WLR 269.
Jones v Pritchard [1908] 1 Ch. 630.
Jones & Lovegrove v Ruth & Ruth [2011] EWHC Civ 804.
JSA Properties (UK) Ltd v Gary Harvey Waldman – G20CL109 (unreported).

K/S Norjarl A/S v Hyundai Heavy Industries Co. Ltd CA [1991] 1 Lloyd's Rep. 524
Kelliher v Ash Estates Ltd and Normand Developments Ltd [2013].
Khan v Genesis Ruan (2017) Central London County Court Claim D20CL053 2017
Kioa v West (1985) 159 C.L.R. 550 at 583, High Court (Australia).
Kultar & Sohanpal v Humble & Humble (2020) County Court at Central London.

Lacy V Baker (2019) County Court Central London D20CL111 & E20CL228
Leadbetter v Marylebone Corporation [No. 1] [1904] 2 KB 893.
Leadbetter v Marylebone Corporation [No. 2] [1904] 2 KB 893.
Lehmann v Herman [1993] 1 EGLR 172.
Longmire v Maldura [2015] County Court at Central London Sonantal.
Loost v Kremer [1997] County Court at West London 12 May (Unreported).
Louis v Sadiq [1997] 1 EGLR 136; (1998) 59 Con LR 127.

Maddow v Fernandez (2020) TCC.
Manu v Euroview Investments Ltd [2008] 1 EGLR 165.
MacLachlan v Patel (2019) - County Court at Central London HHJ Luba (injunction).
Macey v Capper & Capper (2019) County Court at Central London F20CL063
Manu v Euroview Investments Ltd [2008] 1 EGLR 165.
Midland Bank plc v Bardgrove Property Services Ltd [1991] 2 EGLR 283.
Mills & Mills v Savage & Savage [2016] County Court at Central London (Case No 1).
Mills & Mills v Sell & Sell [2016] County Court at Central London (Case No 1).
Mohamed & Mohamed v Takhar, Takhar, & Takhar [2016] County Court at Central London.
Mohamed & Mohamed v Antino & Stevens [2017] County Court at Central London.
Mohamed & Lahrie v Takhar & Takhar & Takhar (2021) in the County Court of Central London TCC List G20CL122
Montgomery, Jones & Co v Liebenthal & Co [1898] QB 487.
Morgan v Fear [1907] AC 429.

Nelson's Yard Management Co v Eziefula [2013] EWCA Civ 235.

Nutt V Veda Road Ltd & Podger [2021] County Court at Central London.

Onigbanjo, v Pearson [2008] BLR 507 The Mayors and City of London Court.

Partridge v Partridge [1894] 1 Ch 351.
Peter J Edmond v Nicholas Bartholomew Denham & Helen Julie Seekings-Denham (2021) H00PE335
Patel & Patel v Peters, Peters, at al [2014] EWCA Civ 335.
Patel v W.H. Smith (Eziot) Ltd [1987] 1 wlr 853 [2014] EWCA Civ 335.
PC Harrington Contractors Ltd v Systech International Ltd [2012] EWCA Civ 1371.
Phillis Trading Ltd v 86 Lordship Road Ltd [2001] 2 E.G.L.R 85; [2001] EWCA Civ 350.
Phipps v Pears [1965] 1 QB; [1964] 2 WLR 996; 2 All ER 35.
Pincus v Singh (2022) The High Court of Justice Chancery Division Property, Trust and Probate List (2022) Claim no. PT-2022-000711
Porter v Magill [2001] UKHL 67.
Prudential Assurance Co Ltd v Waterloo Real Estate Inc (1999) 2 EGLR 85.

Ramzan v Brookwide Limited [2010] EWHC Civ 2453 (Ch).
R v Cambridge University [1723].
R v Deputy Industrial Injuries Commission, Ex-parte More [1965] 1 QB 856 at 487 – 488
R v Sussex Justices Exp McCarthy [1924] 1KB256 at 259
Re Medicaments and Related Classes goods (No. 2) [2001] 1 WLR 700 (CA).
Rees v Skerrett [2001] 1 WLR 1541.
Regan v Paul Properties Ltd [2006] EWCA Cir 1391.
Reeves v Blake [2009] EWCA C iv 611.
Reeves v Young, Young & Antino [2017] County Court at Central London.
Riley Gowler Ltd v National Hospital Board of Governors [1969] 3 ALL ER 1401.
Rupra & Sohanpal v Humble & Humble (2020) TCC unreported
Rusciani v Kumar and Sharma (2012) County Court at Chelmsford (unreported).

Sachs v Jones [1925] AER 514
Schmid v Hulls & Athanasou [2016] TCC County Court at Central London
Seef-v-Ho [2011} EWCA Civ 186.
Selby v Whitbread & Co [1917] 1 KB 736.
Sell & Sell v Mills & O'Callaghan (2014) County Court at Kingston Upon Thames A00KT940.
Shah v Ken Power Lee Kyson [2022] EWHC 209 (QB) Mr Justice Eyre
Shelfer v City of London Electric Lighting Co [1895] 1 Ch 287.
Shrager v Basil Dighton Ltd [1924] 1KB274 at 284.

Simper v Foley (1862) 2 J&H 555.
Skerrits of Nottingham Ltd v Secretary of State for the Environment, Transport and the Regions and Harrow LBC (No. 2) [2002] 2 PLR 102.
Speedwell Estates Ltd and Covent Garden Group Ltd v Daziel [2001] EWCA Civ 1277 per Rimer J; McDonald v Fernandez [2003] 4 A11 ER 1033, CA
Spiers and Son Ltd v Troup (1915) 84 LJKB 1986.
Standard Bank of British and South America v Stokes (1878) L.R 9 Ch. D.
Southwell & Southwell v Burrows [2021] County Court at Central London H20CL102
Sunsaid Property Company Ltd v Omenaka & Omenaka.
Systec International Ltd v PC Harrington Contractors Ltd [2012] EWCA Civ 1371

Thurrock Gray's & Tilbury Joint Sewage Board v E. J. & W. Goldsmith (1914) 79 J.P. 17.

Watson v Gary (1880) 14 Ch. D 192 at 194.
Woodhouse v Consolidated Property Corp 1993, 1 EGLR 174.

Yawar Khan v Genesis Ruan (2017) County Court at Central London Claim D20CL053 2017.

Zaher & Zaher v Patel (2019) - County Court at Central London HHJ Luba.
Zaman v Zala (2020) County Court at Central London HHJ Parfitt.
Zissis v Lukomski & Carter [2006] EWCA Civ 341.

TABLE OF STATUTORY INSTRUMENTS

TABLE OF NOTATIONS

AC	Advisory Committee
ADR	Alternative Dispute Resolution
AOS	Adjoining Owners Surveyor
ANLA	Access to Neighbouring Land Act 1992
APA	APA Property Services Ltd
AS	Agreed Surveyor
ASUC	The Association of Specialist Underpinning Contractors
ARU	Anglia Ruskin University
All ER	All England Reports
BA	Basement Assessment
BCA	Bristol Corporation Act 1926
BIA	Bristol Improvement Act 1847
BLR	Building Law Reports
BOS	Building Owners Surveyor
BRE	Building Research Establishment
BSc (Hons)	Bachelor of Science degree with Honours
BSI	British Standards Institute
CA	Court of Appeal
CABE	Chartered Association of Building Engineers
CCA	County Courts Act 1984
Ch App	Chancery Appeals
Ch D	Chancery Division
CIArb	Chartered Institute of Arbitrators
CIAT	Chartered Institute of Architectural Technicians
CITB	Construction Industry Training Board
CMC	Case Management Conference
COP	Certificate of Posting
CPBRC	Council Planning and Building Regulations Committee of the Council
CPD	Continuing Professional Development
CPR	Civil Procedure Rules
DPC	Damp Proof Course
DSN	Dangerous Structures Notice
EDA	Exploratory Data Analysis
ER	English Reports

EWHC	England and Wales High Court
FPWS	Faculty of Party Wall Surveyors
GPDO	Town and Country Planning (General Permitted Development) Order 1995
GDPR	General Data Protection Regulations
GLC	Greater London Council
HL	House of Lords
HGCRA	Housing Grants, Construction and Regeneration Act 1996
HHJ	His or Her Honour Judge
ICE	Institute of Chartered Engineers
ICIOB	Incorporated Member of the Chartered Institute of Building
IPWS	Institute of Party Wall surveyors
JCB	Manufacturer of heavy construction machinery
JCT	Joint Contracts Tribunal
KB	Kings Bench
KC	Kings Counsel
LBA	London Building Amendments Act 1939
LBC	London Borough of Camden
LCC	London County Council
LGR	Local Government Reports
LPA	Law of Property Act 1925
LR	Law Reports
LVT	Leasehold Valuation Tribunal
MBA	Metropolitan Building Act 1855
MCA	Magistrates Court Act 1980
MCIArb	Member of the Chartered Institute of Arbitrators
MRes	Masters in Research
MSc	Masters of Science Degree
NHBC	National House Building Council
PDP	Planning and Development Policies
PhD	Doctor of Philosophy
PII	Professional Indemnity Insurance
PNJ	Principles of Natural Justice
PPS	Planning Policy Statements
PPG	Planning Policy Guidance Notes

GLOSSARY OF TERMS

Ad infinitum	Again and again in the same way; forever
Appellant	A person who applies for a High Court for a reversal of a decision.
Audi alteram partem	No man shall be condemned unheard.
Award	To give a judicial determination; to assign or apportion, after careful regard to the nature of the case; to adjudge.
Chambers	Term used to refer to Judges and Barristers offices.
De minimis	The law cares not for small things. A legal doctrine by which a Court refuses to consider trifling matters.
De novo	From the beginning; anew.
Forthwith	Immediately; without delay.
Functus officio	Without legal standing.
Injunction	A judicial order restraining a person from beginning or continuing an action threatening or invading the legal right of another or compelling a person to carry out a certain act.
in lieu	instead of or replacement of.
inter alia	Amongst other things.
Mala Fides	a sustained "bad faith" form of deception.
Nemo judex in causa sua	No man shall be a judge in his own cause.
Nuisance	When a land owner carries out an act on his own land which affects another person's use or enjoyment of their own neighbouring land or of some right that is connected with that land.

| Obiter dictum | a judge's expression of opinion uttered in Court or in a written judgment but not essential to the decision therefore not legally binding as a precedent. |

Obiter dictum — a judge's expression of opinion uttered in Court or in a written judgment but not essential to the decision therefore not legally binding as a precedent.

Omne majus continent in se minus — The greater contains the less

Otiose — serving no practical purpose or result.

Quasi-judicial — Non-judicial body (role) that can interpret law.

Raison d'etre — The most important reason or purpose for someone or something's existence.

Reify — make (something abstract) more concrete or real.

Res judicata — A matter that has been adjudicated by a competent Court and therefore may not be pursued further by the Same parties.

Respondent — Against whom a petition is filed, especially one in the appeal of a case.

Right of access — A right to go on to someone else's land to access specific parts of your own property which are inaccessible from anywhere within your own land

Ultra viries — An act that requires legal authority but is executed without it.

Without prejudice — Without detriment to any existing right or claim.

CHAPTER 1

1.0   INTRODUCTION

1.1   STRUCTURE

There is an abundance of written material purporting to provide guidance on how to approach, interpret and administering 'The Party Wall etc. Act 1996' ("The Act") some of this advice is incorrect and is of questionable accuracy. Case law has also moved matters forward however, in my opinion not always for the good of the Act or indeed the law. I began my approach to this second edition by restructuring the format to achieve greater clarity, ease of referencing and understanding. I have also updated/revised some of my earlier opinions, views, and interpretations and introduced new information and case law. I am not a lawyer and therefore my views, understanding, and interpretation of the law is that of a reasonably well-informed professional operating within a quasi-judicial function. If greater clarification and/or further detailed explanations on the law are required, I advise the reader to obtain legal advice (although choose your counsel carefully) especially if the clarification is related to a live issue that may be or is intended to go before the Court.

I have introduced an extended overview of the Act's historical evolution and context and introduced additional topics that I believe are relevant to the surveyor's development and global understanding of how to conduct party wall matters and the issues that flow from its administration.   The subsequent chapters address various sections of the Act out of sequence, in order to provide clarity and to reflect on the importance and inter-relationships between the sections. Not unsurprisingly, I have introduced a chapter that deals specifically with basements and the issues created by the section 7(4) veto.

1.2   The Party Wall etc. Act 1996

How did the current Act evolve into its current configuration? Firstly, it is a bi-product of Part VI of the London Building (Amendment) Act 1939 ("LBA") which in turn evolved from much earlier legislation and legal concepts. It was introduced as a private member's bill into the House of Lords by Lord Lytton, then a practising surveyor as a statutory instrument designed to facilitate the execution of specific works notifiable building works that may potentially impact upon an adjoining owner's property right. This is achieved by imposing rights and liabilities on all the various owners/occupiers by stepping over pre-existing common law principles. The Act is intended to provide an efficient framework and procedure that enables building works to be put in hand promptly and on a fair and reasonable basis.[2] Coming into force on the 1st July 1997 subject to transitional provisions[3] it was anticipated to be the panacea to all the historical common law obstacles that restricted certain works, unfortunately it has added to the frustration and confusion.

Although previously treated as a subsection of the LBA, the most significant difference is the increased geographical jurisdiction now incorporating the whole of England and Wales.[4] Thus, taking it beyond the earlier limitations of the Greater London Council ("GLC") jurisdiction and other locations such as Bristol which had its own unique party wall legislation 'The Bristol Improvement Act 1847' ("BIA") under the Bristol Corporation Act 1926 ("BCA").

The reiteration of the majority of the LBA content is a recognition of the benefits that the LBA format had previously provided. However, having seen the growth in disputes and litigation it is fair to say that it is undoubtedly, one of the most contentious and aggressive areas of surveying that currently exists.

But what is the Act actually all about? Essentially it is a form of Alternative Dispute Resolution ("ADR") which ironically creates/invites a dispute that may never have arisen in the first instance, and then introduces a process to resolve the dispute with a first instance binding Award that can only be challenged by appeal[5] or a Courts' declaration of invalidity.

1.3   Parliaments Intent

It was anticipated that by extending the quasi-judicial process/jurisdiction, the new legislation would benefit the built environment as a whole, with the benefit of reducing an overloaded and underfunded Court system in much the same way as ADR has. However, one only has to undertake a cursory investigation into the considerable litigation that has arisen since 1997 to recognise that the Act is highly contentious, creating even more work for the Courts. On that clear analysis alone the administration of the Act should be considered a failure.

---

2 Antino, P. (2012) "A Practitioner's Approach and Interpretation of the Party Wall etc. Act 1996" Xlibris Corporation P.27.
3 The Party Wall etc. Act 1996 (SI 1997/670 and 1.25).
4 Bickford-Smith, et al (1997).
5 See Chapter 11, section 11.17.

1.4   Antecedents

If the reader has an interest in researching the antecedents further, I would recommend another publication[6] and my doctoral thesis.[7] Accordingly, I do not intend to delve substantively into the history save as to give the briefest outline of what created the need for legislative control relating to ownership of shared walls as tenants in common. Whilst the basis of party wall law in London can be traced back to the twelfth century Assize of Buildings[8] formal party wall agreements have existed since 1724[9]. Notwithstanding, the most significant single event that impressed the need for specific legislation was the 1666 Great Fire of London.

The conflagration demonstrated the potential risk that fire posed to the populace and the built environment due predominantly to the use of combustible building materials when building onto and/or close to another building. It was recognized that pro-active rather than re-active measures were required and The Rebuilding of London Act 1666, ("RBL") was drawn up by Sir Matthew Hale. This introduced certain regulations, controls and authorized the City of London Corporation to reopen and widen roads. Encouraged by Charles II, radical rebuilding plans for the devastated city were proposed with surprisingly much of the old street plan being retained but with improvements in sanitation and fire safety. Wider streets with accessible wharfs and unobstructed access to the river Thames constant water supply to fight future fires was paramount to avoiding/limiting another conflagration. More importantly, walls between buildings were required to be constructed from brick and stone rather than combustible timber to create fire breaks. However, the cost of masonry/stone was extremely high in comparison to timber, and to overcome/avoid these costs walls, were either constructed in shared ownership or enclosed upon, some by agreement and some covertly[10] thus creating the legal concept of 'tenants in common' over a shared wall.

1.5   Birth of an industry

Whilst party wall legislation is not a new concept and was traditionally administered by a very close-knit group of self-appointed elitist surveyors. That all changed in 1997 with the impact of the national legislation turning the

---

6 Bickford-Smith, et al (2017).

7 Antino P. (2020) "Interpretating the Party Wall etc. Act" and The Implications of building below ground" PhD Thesis Anglia Ruskin University.

8 Whittick, K. G. (2007) "The Party Wall a Short History" Faculty of Party Wall Surveyor P.6.

9 Chynoweth, P. (2001) "Impartiality and the Party Wall Surveyor" Construction Law Journal No. 2 © Sweet and Maxwell Ltd and Contributors.

10 Which still occurs in the present day.

provisions into a country-wide regime[11] capturing virtually every building project.[12] Not unsurprisingly there were simply not enough trained/experienced party wall surveyors to satisfy the demand. The principles of supply and demand encouraged professionals from wide professional[13] and/or non-professional backgrounds to take up the role of party wall surveyor. The majority of which were armed with no more than a copy of the Act and without any formal training and/or understanding of the complexities behind the statutory regime began to offer their purported "expert" services as a party wall surveyor.

1.6   The party wall community

Prior to 1997 party wall surveyors were simply surveyors administering party wall services, in much the same way as they would administer landlord and tenant matters, or undertake a building survey. 'Party Wall Surveyor' services have now evolved into a stand-alone title distinct from other professional titles, such as Surveyor, Engineer, and Architect. Now surveyors promote themselves as 'party wall surveyors' and with the party wall community growing organically, it is not unsurprising that the surveyors that had been operating under the earlier legislative process's historic approaches and interpretations clashed with new entrants who developed new concepts, interpretations and approaches.

Of particular importance is the surveyor's appointment[14] which is unique and diametrically opposite to the traditional client/surveyor role which falls away once appointed or selected.[15] However, this should not create an opportunity for the surveyor to simply do what they want, when they want, and how they want, although invariable it does. They owe an implied, if not explicit duty of care to all the owners[16] to remain objective and impartial and must follow the Act even when it goes against their owners' objectives.

For example, it is not uncommon for a building owner to appoint their architect as their party wall surveyor, thus creating a multi-professional role, but is that appropriate given that the appointed surveyor's duty is to assess and where necessary challenge the notifiable work?[17] Would an architect be as objective and critical of their own design as an independent party wall surveyor would obviously not hence a conflict arises?

---

11 Antino, P. (2012) "A Practitioner's Approach and Interpretation of The Party wall etc. Act 1996.
12 Commercial and Residential.
13 Architects, Engineers, Surveyors, Builders, Landscape gardeners etc.
14 See Chapter 2.9.
15 Building Owners Surveyor, Agreed Surveyor, Adjoining Owners Surveyor, Third Surveyor.
16 Chapter 1 subsection 1.7.
17 Design/specification.

The legality of this dual role has been addressed to a limited extent,[18]

> HHJ Cowell: "…. the mere fact that he has acted as architect does not, in my judgment mean that he must disqualify himself…….. he changes in his capacity from being simply an agent to a quasi-arbitrator and he has to bear in mind those are his duties……that is all there really is to this point."[19]

Regrettably there have been a number of cases in recent years where a clear conflict of interest have arisen (Reeves v Young & Young, and Sell v Mills & Mills). The Sell case was particularly frustrating given that Mr. Mills was the building owner and a RIBA qualified Architect who failed to serve notice and became the recipient of an injunction.[20] Thereafter, serving notice the situation was further complicated when Mr. Mills appointed a surveyor and then replaced him with their father/father-in-law[21] which is bizarre given that he was also the building contractor that had trespassed onto and caused damage to the adjoining owner's (Sell's) property. The difficulties did not end there, whilst the party wall issues were ongoing Mr. Kevin O'Callaghan (father-in-law) decided to purchase the property from Mr. Mills. This created an incapacity to act as the building owner cannot represent themselves and another replacement party wall surveyor had to be appointed.

The Reeves case was slightly different in that the building and adjoining owners had each appointed a surveyor that worked for the same company. With one of the surveyors being an employee of the other, any reasonably informed independent observer (applying the test) would recognise the risk of a perceived or an actual bias (the two being the same). Unfortunately, given the broad definition of surveyor[22] there is nothing within the Act that prevents this situation arising. It does however create significant moral and professional ethical issues that should be addressed by the surveyors and their respective professional associations. It is astonishing that one of these surveyors did not deem himself incapable of acting on any one of the following grounds: -

    (a) Conflict of interest with his employee/employer;
    (b) No independent assessment of reasonable fees;
    (c) Section 10(1)(a); and
    (d) Unreasonable duplication of Professional Fees.

---

18 Loost v Kremer [1997] West London County Court 12 May (Unreported).
19 Chynoweth, P. (2003) 'The Party Wall Case Book,' Blackwell Publishing Ltd.
20 See Chapter 19.
21 Mr. Kevin O'Callaghan.
22 See Chapter 1, subsection 1.8.

But that is the current state of play with the law.

1.7   Surveyors immunity from negligence fact or fiction

Immunity is an exemption from penalties, payments or legal requirements, granted by authorities or statutes. Generally, there are four areas that can generate an immunity: -

(a) A promise not to prosecute for a crime in exchange for information or testimony in a criminal matter, granted by the prosecutors, a judge, adjudicator, arbitrator a jury or an investigating legislative committee;
(b) Public officials' protection from liability for their decisions (like a judge, magistrate, or member of a public hospital board);
(c) Governmental (or sovereign) immunity, which protects government agencies from lawsuits unless the government agreed to be sued; and
(d) Diplomatic immunity which excuses foreign ambassadors from most criminal laws.

If certain occupations did not have immunity, it is unlikely that any one would take on a specific role for example the role of Judge, Arbitrator and/or Adjudicator. Why? because ultimately their decision is going to please one party and upset another and, in some instances, both parties. Without the immunity the disgruntled party would vent their anger at the Judge, Adjudicator and/or Arbitrator.

This does raise the question of whether immunity should be extended to the party wall community? They are providing quasi-judicial roles and determinations as the Court of first instance which is no different to a Judge. Their jurisdiction is significantly different to any other aspect of the surveyors work such as advising on landlord and tenant law, owe their client a duty of care.

1.7.1   Immunity from negligence

Party wall surveyors have been operating under a misconceived belief that they have immunity and are exempt from negligence claims when administering the Act. This is flawed because there is nothing within the Act that grants such immunity unlike other statutory instruments such as Arbitration/Adjudication.[23] Therefore, on the natural and correct reading of the Act, there is no implied right of immunity granted to a party wall surveyor. If Parliament had intended

---

23 Paragraph 26 of the Scheme for Construction Contracts (England and Wales) Regulations (as amended).

there to be immunity, then Parliament would have been expressed their position in clear terms within the Act.

Other statutory instruments such as the Housing Grants and Construction and Regeneration Act 1996 ("HGCR") incorporate immunity as an explicit right -

> "The contract shall provide that the adjudicator is not liable for anything done or omitted in the discharge or purported discharge of his function as adjudicator unless the act or omission is in bad faith, and that any employee or agent of the adjudicator is similarly protected from liability".[24]

The author can confirm having been instructed on six occasions as CPR Part 35 expert witness in regard to advancing negligence claims against several party wall surveyors, and they have all been successful. The test is not whether they have acted in bad faith[25] but whether on the balance of probability the services they provided as the party wall surveyor did not meet the appropriate test being 'the skill and knowledge of the ordinarily competent party wall surveyor'.

In five of the six cases settlement was reached with the surveyor's professional indemnity insurers accepting liability but insisting on a non-disclosure clause. However, in Brian Macey v Mark van Blommestein ("MVB") Chartered Surveyor,[26] the settlement did not include a non-disclosure clause. The building owner's surveyor had served notice under section 6(1). Mr. Macey had dissented and appointed MVB, who joined with the building owner's surveyor and served an Award which wrongly (i) authorised section 1 (5) works, (ii) unlawfully authorised scaffolding on the adjoining owner's property; and (iii) trespassing projection of foundations beneath the adjoining owners dwarf boundary wall.

There were no rights to build on the line of junction under section 1(5) and no rights of access and/or to erect scaffold on the adjoining owner's land because section 1(5) notice had not been served. The two surveyors were functus officio in that regard. Mr. Macey, was justly concerned and sought clarification from Mr Antino (as he was then), both surveyors, asserted somewhat surprisingly that the section 6 (1) notice allowed the building of a wall to be built on the line of junction without the need to serve a section 1(5) notice. Secondly, the projecting foundations without any notice under section 1 (6)

---

24 Section 108 (4).
25 As required under section 108 (4) of the HGCR.
26 Surveyor's name withheld to avoid embarrassment.

were claimed to be underpinning the adjoining owner's 300 mm high dwarf garden wall not a party wall.

The absence of a notice under section 1 (5) and/or 1 (6) removed any such rights. Furthermore, the projection of the foundations was unnecessary, which is the qualifying test for allowing a projecting foundation (see Figure No 9). The foundation could have been moved over in line with the outer face of the wall avoiding any projection on to the adjoining owners' land. Mr. Macey took the authors' advice and made an application for a declaration that the Award was invalid. Before the hearing took place the two surveyors served a second Award setting the wall back from the line of junction and the positioning foundations on the line of junction therefore removing the projection. The placing of scaffolding on the adjoining owners land had also been removed.

However, by this time Mr. Macey had incurred considerable fees for both expert[27] and legal advice[28] in respect of the application to appeal the primary Award. A claim was also raised against the adjoining owner's surveyor's MVB practice to recover these costs. Settlement was reached with the surveyors PI insurers paying the claim in full.

1.7.2   Accepted liability

In another case, Mr. Yawar Khan[29] commenced building works without the service of notice and was threatened with an injunction. He stopped works, appointed a surveyor, his surveyor then failed to progress matters properly. After many months of delay and two requests under section 10 (7) to bring the matters to a natural conclusion, Mr. Antino had no option but to serve an *ex parte* Award. Mr. Khan appealed the Award, but as Counsel's arguments were exchanged, it became clear to Mr. Khan that his surveyor had not operated with due diligence and the skill of an ordinarily competent surveyor and the appeal would fail. A settlement was reached whereby Mr. Khan settled the costs following an agreement with his surveyor to reimburse Mr. Khan. Accordingly, any party wall surveyor that operates within the statutory legislation must do so on the understanding that they are not immune from negligence or liability to costs[30].

1.8   De minimis works

De minimis[31] is the term used by the law where it does not take account of trifling matters, or matters of little importance. In other words, there is a

---

27 Dr P Antino
28 Mr. Ashley Bean and Mr. David Mayall.
29 Yawar Khan v Genesis Ruan (2017) Central London County Court Claim D20CL053 2017.
30 See Chapter 11, section 11.10.10.
31 See Glossary of Terms and Chapter 5, subsection 5.6.6.

threshold beneath which the law, in all its intellectual might and procedural majesty does not deign to concern itself. In the absence of any explicit reference within any enactments[32] and/or any evidence of any explicit qualification setting out what does or does not qualify as de minimis works, it is open to interpretation. Barristers who recognise their case is weak will often claim the breach of the Act is de minimus and outside the jurisdiction of the Act. Mr. Isaac (2014) in his book[33] at paragraph 1 – 26 raises the following question: -

> "If one wants to drill a hole to hang a picture or
> remove a patch of unkeyed plaster or repoint a
> party wall, do these bring the Act into play?"

Mr. Isaac suggests the first of these activities would certainly fall into the de minimis category. But does it? It is a bold statement which does not take into account any number of factors such as the construction of the wall, its thickness, or indeed where the hole is to be drilled, all of which could have devastating implications upon the adjoining owners use of the wall as a tenant in common.

For example, would drilling into a 4-inch (112.5 mm) party wall be substantively more hazardous than perhaps drilling into a traditional solid 9-inch (225 mm wall)? Possibly therefore, in my view it is not as cut and dry as Mr. Isaac suggests. Each construction activity must be assessed on its own merits and if someone decides that the works are 'de minimis' to avoid service of notice, they take the risk that if it causes damage there is an exposure to a claim for damages, negligence and a breach of the Act's statutory procedures.

Mr. Isaac also suggests that the activity of removing plaster has been traditionally viewed by party wall surveyors as falling into the category of de minimis works. In a 2013 case[34] the question of whether the removal of the plaster could fall within section 2(2)(f)[35] of the Act went before HHJ Bailey, who in my opinion correctly expressed an opinion that it depended on how the work was executed. Accordingly, if the plaster was in poor condition and could be removed easily with hand tools, it would not fall within the Act, why because the operative is not cutting in the wall. In the alternative, where it is well adhered and required percussive machinery to remove it, HHJ Bailey held that the Act is engaged: -

> "As soon as an operative, holding an electric or
> other Bosch tool whether with a drill end or a
> spade end, so attacks the plaster that he goes

---

32 Halsbury's Laws of England Fifth Edition, Volume 95, paragraph 1143.
33 Isaac, N. (2014) "The law and Practice of Party Walls" Property Publishing.
34 Kelliher v Ash Estates Ltd and Normand Developments Ltd [2013].
35 See Chapter 5, subsection 5.6.1.

> into even the very edge of the brickwork,
> comprising the party wall, he is then in a
> position where as I see it, he is cutting in to a
> party structure, for any purpose and in this of
> course the removal of plaster, which is covered
> by section 2(2)(f) of the Act".

The following are factual scenarios that will assist with understanding the argument of 'de minimis' works.

1.8.1   Scenario I

When preparing drawings for the removal of the chimney breast at ground, first and roof void and cutting chasings into the remaining wall floor level, the architect had not unreasonably assumed that a party wall between two terraced properties (built by the local authority in the 1950's) was a traditional 9-inch (225 mm) wide for its full height. The building owner's surveyor when preparing the notices was advised that there was an intention to chase into the party wall and run electrical cables up into the roof void.

Are these de minimis works or should they be included in the notice? The building owner's surveyor exercised caution and served a notice under section 2(2)(f). When notices were received the adjoining owners, surveyor[36] was able to advise that the party wall above the ground floor ceiling level was only 4-inch (112.5 mm) brickwork. The proposed cutting into the wall to insert conduits for various electrical cables, (which in construction terms is a common activity) became a substantially more complicated process. Indeed the 4-inch (112.5 mm) wall already had conduits for electrical cables, sockets, and switches cut into the adjoining owner's side of the party wall. If someone had drilled/cut into the wall, at the same location (albeit innocently) they might have easily drilled into one of the neighbour's conduits buried within the wall. The building owner was able to relocate his proposed conduits onto the surface of the wall within the roof void thus avoiding a catastrophe. However, this was only possible because the building owner's surveyor had served notice which alerted the adjoining owner's surveyor to the risk. The benefits of serving notice are clear.

1.8.2   Scenario II

Using 'de minimis' as a defence to avoid compliance with the Act and/or to extricate a client from an injunction is becoming a common defence by certain

---

barristers. In two recent cases[37] the same building owner had commenced excavations in breach of their statutory duty to serve notice. Both claimants (adjoining owners) on advice from their surveyor[38] sought an injunction, and were represented by Counsel and Solicitor.[39] Mr. Patel had commenced excavations and reduced the ground levels in preparation of a reinforced concrete slab and had commenced steel lined reinforced concrete piles without serving notice. When challenged the advice of his surveyor[40] was to claim the works were 'de minimus'. Two separate injunctions were obtained, at the return date hearing Mr. Patel instructed Mr. Isaac Q.C., who suggested to the Judge that driven steel lined piles were (i) not notifiable because forming a hole by driving a tube into the ground was not an excavation and/or (ii) the driven piles and excavation for the reinforced concrete slab were 'de minimis' works. It was accepted that the excavations had gone below the adjoining owners' foundations to boundary walls, patio, and block paving, all of which Mr. Isaac (2014) advises (in his book at para 5 – 24) (1 – 8) are structures and therefore, would require notice.

The 'de minimis' defence claimed by Mr. Isaac, involved the removal of approximately 15 tonnes of earth and rubble from each property (total 30 tonnes) and the introduction of 15 tonnes of concrete and steel for each property (total 30 tonnes). These works were designed by a structural engineer and subject to building control approval. In my view, if a building activity is captured by building regulations or requires a skilled engineer to design the foundations, the works cannot on any rationale understanding Mr. Isaac's submission be de minimis. Why? Because building regulations does not address trivial matters, which is the same test applied by the Courts.[41] HHJ Roberts was dismissive of Mr. Isaac's submission referring to them as 'all very Alice in Wonderland'.

1.8.3   Scenario III

Does cutting into a plasterboard ceiling fixed directly to the underside of the timber floor joists to install new recessed spotlights and cables notifiable under section 2(f) or does it qualify as de minimis works? A floor separating two properties is a party structure and the plaster board is an important element of the party structure, providing for example fire protection and acoustic performance. Any interference that changes the dynamics and performance capabilities of the structure would be a breach of building regulations. Accordingly, there can be no logical grounds to suggest that these works are de

---

37 Zaher & Zaher v Patel, [2020] Central London County Court, MacLachlan v Patel, [2020] Central London County Court. (unreported).
38 Dr P Antino.
39 Mr. David Mayall and Mr. Ashley Bean.
40 Mr. Simon Dove MRICS.
41 See Chapter 1, subsection 1.8.

minimis and therefore a party structure notice under section 2(2)(f) must be served.

1.8.4   Scenario IV

Would cutting into a suspended (secondary) decorative ceiling directly beneath the underside of the party structure timber floor joists to install new recessed spotlights and cables qualify as de minimis works? Providing the suspended ceiling has not been installed as part of the party structure's function to comply with building regulations, fire resistance and/or acoustic performance these works would not require notice.

1.8.5   Scenario V

Would cutting into or replacing floor boards laid over timber floor joists of a party structure between two properties require notice? The same approach discussed in scenario III above would apply. However, where the works relate to laying or removing a laminate wood flooring or tiles over the existing floor boards, which does not form part of the party structure's building regulation function, they would not require notice.

1.9   Rules of natural justice

It is all too easy for the dissatisfied party to comb through a Party Wall Award for any procedural irregularity[42] and to challenge an Award based on allegations of 'excessive jurisdiction' or 'breach of the rules of natural justice'. Therefore, it is important that the surveyors understand the limit of their jurisdiction[43] and fully appreciate the importance of ensuring that justice is not only seen to be, but is executed fairly and transparently. The Principles of Natural Justice ("PNJ") has been succinctly[44] explained by Dyson, L J as follows: -

> "The common law rules of natural justice or procedural fairness are twofold. First, the person affected has the right to prior notice and an effective opportunity to make representations before a decision is made. Secondly, the person affected has the right to an unbiased tribunal."

---

42 Maddow v Fernandez (2020) TCC.
43 See Chapter 11, subsection 11.13.1.
44 AMEC Capital Projects Ltd v Whitefriars City Estates Ltd [2004].

1.9.1 Right to be heard

Right to be heard[45]: the first principle entitles all parties to the right to participate and to be heard, has been enshrined in English Law for centuries[46]. Of course, a party can refuse to participate, but to do so would be a serious error of judgment, withholding information or relying on a position to cry foul play at a later date is misconceived[47]

1.9.2 Right to an unbiased tribunal

Right to an unbiased tribunal[48]: the second principle requires the judge/tribunal to be independent of all parties. The test does not require the dissatisfied party to demonstrate actual bias, the perception of bias is sufficient to bring a successful challenge to a decision-makers continued involvement as the judge/tribunal. It must therefore be obvious that in any fair system of decision-making, no person can judge a dispute in which he/she has a personal interest or a conflict of interest such as a friendship with a party.

1.10 Bias: actual and/or perceived

At the heart of any dispute resolution process[49] is the willingness of the parties to entrust the resolution of their dispute into the hands of private citizens or third parties. To trust the process, the parties must be able to have confidence in the professional and ethical conduct of the individual or the tribunal. This is an essential requirement of the dispute resolution process that will ensure the impartiality and neutrality of the person and/or persons acting within the decision-making tribunal so that decisions are made without *fear* of bias.

But what is meant by "bias"? It can be described as a predisposition on the part of the decision-maker (conscious or sub-conscious) to decide for (or against) one party without proper regard to the true merits of the dispute. In such circumstances the decision-maker should be live to the fact that their Award or Judgment may be overturned on that very point.

All dispute resolution methods[50] aim for an appropriate level of fairness and natural justice. Fairness and natural justice are central to the concept, acceptance and enforceability of each method of the dispute resolution procedure.

---

45 Audi alteram partem.
46 R v Cambridge University [1723].
47 Manu v Euroview Investments Ltd [2008] 1 EGLR 165.
48 Nemo judex in causa sua.
49 Party wall, arbitration, adjudication.
50 Litigation, Arbitration, Adjudication, Mediation, PWA et al.

Natural justice is an "umbrella term" used to denote the centrality of the concept of fairness and absence of bias. When people talk of natural justice they are, in technical terms, referring to the rules that entitles a disputant or accused being entitled to a fair hearing and for the matter to be heard by an unbiased, neutral, independent third party (whether that is a Judge, arbitrator, adjudicator, third surveyor, or some other dispute resolution provider or decision-maker).

> "It has been recognised in the context of administrative decision-making that it is more appropriate to speak of a duty to act fairly or to accord procedural fairness."[51]

Primarily, the rules of natural justice have been expressed as encompassing; -

The bias rule – that a person may not be a Judge in his or her own case (or that everyone is entitled to have their matter determined by an unbiased/neutral decision maker).

The hearing rule – that every party to a dispute has a basic right to be heard.

The evidence rule – that a decision must be based on evidence relevant to the issue to be determined[52].

The principle upon which the bias rule has been founded in modern times flows from Lord Hewart's statement that *'justice should not only be done, but seen to be done[53].'*

In the same year Aitkin LJ clearly supported this doctrine and similarly remarked that *next to the tribunal being in fact impartial is the importance of it appearing so[54]*. It is clear that on these expressed views that appearances are important to justice and should not only be fair but it should appear to be fair.

Some ADR procedures specifically address for example section 33(1) of the Arbitration Act 1996, that the tribunal[55] must act "impartially". It is clear and implied that in any dispute an Arbitrator must both act and also appear to act

---

51 Kioa v West (1985) 159 C.L.R. 550 at 583, High Court (Australia).
52 Lord Diplock in R v Deputy Industrial Injuries Commission, Ex-parte More [1965] 1 QB 856 at 487 – 488.
53 R v Sussex Justices Exp McCarthy [1924] 1KB256 at 259.
54 Shrager v Basil Dighton Ltd [1924] 1KB274 at 284.
55 The tribunal can comprise of one or a number of professionals who act as the decision makers.

impartial[56]. If there are justifiable doubts as to his/her/their impartiality this will provide a *ground for removal* by the Court under section 24(1)(a) of the Arbitration Act 1996.

Whilst the PWA does not incorporate a similar section, it is nonetheless implied that the surveyors and specifically the Third Surveyor when acting as a decision-maker in respect of a referral under section 10(11) must be both impartial and seen to be impartial. When challenged

The importance of the appearance of impartiality is becoming increasingly linked to public conflicts, not only in the Courts, but in all other forms of decision-making to which the bias rule applies and that would include a referral to the Third Surveyor, Arbitrator, Adjudicator, Mediator etc.

The bias rule also aligns with the objective test by which it is now governed, being the mythical fair minded and informed observer (whose opinion governs the bias rule) and who is clearly a member of the general public. Holding the views attributable to the general public provide the justification for and content of the bias rule. The requirement of impartiality which lies at the heart of the bias rule is often confused with the related issue of independence, but there is a clear difference between the two.

Impartiality is regarded as a reference to the objectivity of the decision-maker and the absence of bias, and is an aspect of the wider duty to act fairly. Alleged, perceived or actual bias or impartiality usually arises out of the relationship between an Arbitrator, Adjudicator and a Party Wall Surveyor or Counsel.

Impartiality concerns absence of bias or the predisposition of the decision-maker or dispute resolution provider towards one of the parties. The two common forms of bias are familiarity with the dispute/disputant, or prior conduct such as a legal opinion for other parties which is contrary to one parties' interest. It is of course an abstract measure, that a state of mind that can only be proved through facts and a mental attitude is clearly harder to evaluate.

Independence concerns the connection or relationship between the decision-maker resolution provider and any of the parties or their counsel: personal, social, and financial. It is an objective and factual measure – to determine relationships between decision-maker and party in question. The key is the proximity between both and depends on past and/or current relationships with parties which should be catalogued and verified.

---

56 K/S Norjarl A/S v Hyundai Heavy Industries Co. Ltd CA [1991] 1 Lloyd's Rep. 524.

Independence is usually reference to: -

> ".... An absence of connection with either of the parties in the sense of an absence of any interest in, or of any present or prospective business or connection with, one of the parties, which might lead the decision-maker to favour the party concerned."[57]

Baroness Howe in the House of Lords drew attention to the distinct and related nature of impartiality and independence: -

> "Impartiality is not the same as independence, although the two are closely linked. Impartiality is the tribunals approach to deciding the cases before him. Independence is the structural or institutional framework which secures this impartiality, not only in the minds of the tribunal members but also the perception of the public."[58]

The underlying point of this reasoning is that impartiality is a concept generally directed to specific instances of decision-making, while independence is an institutional concept that governs the wider structures within which decision-makers act.

Nevertheless, the concepts are entrenched in the ADR processes. The Party Wall etc. Act 1996 is undeniably a dispute resolution procedure and therefore does **not** escape the same stringent obligations required under the natural rules of justice. This obligation also appears as a requirement of every institutional rule. For example, article 11 of the CIArb Arbitration rule provides; -

> "When a person is approached in connection with his or her possible appointment as an Arbitrator, he or she will disclose any circumstances likely to give rise to justifiable doubts as to his or her impartiality or independence. An Arbitrator, from the time that his or her appointment and throughout the Arbitral proceedings, shall without delay disclose any such circumstances to the parties

---

57 AT & T Corp v Saudi Cable Company [2002] ALLER (Comm) 625.
58 Gillies v Secretary of State for Works and Pensions [2006] EWCA Civ 392; [2006] 1 ALLER 731 at [38].

and the other Arbitrators unless they have already been informed by him or her of these circumstances."

Under these rules, **impartiality and independence are tested against** *circumstances likely to give rise to justifiable doubts as to the Arbitrators impartiality or independence.*

The circumstances referred to are those that may **impute** bias. Bias can take the form of actual bias, imputed bias, apprehended or apparent bias. Actual bias is usually very difficult to prove in practice while imputed bias, once shown will result in a decision being void without the need for any investigation into the likelihood of real possibility of bias.

Thus, the concept of apparent or apprehended bias i.e., *the whiff of bias that may affect the decisions-makers impartiality, becomes important.* In all forms of ADR, the parties have consented to a process and a part of that process is the agreement that the issue in dispute will be determined by, or a resolution will be facilitated by, a person who does not have and/or will **not be perceived** to have, an interest in the outcome. This notion is therefore central to most forms of ADR.

1.10.1 What is the bias Test

The test bias in England was laid down by the House of Lords in *Porter v Magill*[59] which finally laid to rest the historic test that there had to *be a real danger of bias* by endorsing (with modification) the formulation adopted by the Court of Appeal[60] that a *real danger* is now to be read as *a real possibility.*

The relevant question for determining bias has been *whether the fair-minded observer, having considered the facts, would conclude that there was a real possibility that the tribunal was bias.*

In Porter v Magill, Lord Hope said: -

> "There is a close relationship between the concept of independence and that of impartiality. In Findlay v United Kingdom[61] the European Court said: -

---

59 [2009] 1 UKHL 67; [2002] 2 WLR 37; [2002] 2 AC357.
60 Re Medicaments (No. 2) [2001] 1 WLR700.
61 Findlay v United Kingdom (1997) 24 EHRR 221, 244, para 73.

> "The Court records that in order to establish whether a tribunal can be considered as *independent* regard must be had *inter alia* to the manor of appointment of its members and their term of office, the existence of guarantees against outside pressures and the question of whether the body presents an appearance of independence.
>
> As to the question of impartiality, there are two aspects to this requirement. First, the tribunal must be subjectively free from personal prejudice or bias. Secondly, it must also be impartial from an objective viewpoint, that is, it must offer sufficient guarantees to exclude any legitimate doubt in this respect.
>
> The concept of independence and the objective impartiality are closely linked ….".
>
> In both circumstances the concept of bias requires not only that the tribunal must be truly independent and free from any bias, proof of which is likely to be very difficult, but also it must not appear in the objective sense to be bias or that leads essential qualities."

To ensure impartiality and neutrality, the decision maker is required to disclose all and any circumstances that may impact upon the decision makers impartiality and independence. Professional bodies[62] have published codes of professional and ethical conduct which addresses inter alia the conduct of its members when acting or seeking to act as neutrals in alternative dispute resolution processes.

The pivotal point to bear in mind about a perceived or actual conflict of interest is that it must be considered from all relevant points of view. Obviously, the most important of these are those of the decision-makers. However, the wise decision-maker will not forget that such a concern may come before a Court, and they should always take the possibility into account before ignoring any alleged conflict.

---

62 RICS, CIArb, CABE etc.

The decision-makers situation is not dissimilar to that of a Judge. In one case the Judge[63] noticed in his pre-reading of the bundle that he knew a witness that was to be called by the Claimant. The Judge immediately alerted the parties to this fact. The Claimant noted (conceded) that this witness was peripheral to the case and undertook not to call him, but the Defendants objected. The Judge took careful note of all the points put to him and decided there was insufficient cause for him to withdraw.

1.10.2 Court of Appeal reverses Judgment

In a recent Arbitration matter[64] it was found by the Courts that an Arbitrator erred in continuing to act, as the Claimants principal witness and the Arbitrator (acting as advocate) had both been involved in another wholly unrelated Arbitration in which this witness had been accused of fraud. The Arbitrator had been the advocate regarding a preliminary matter (that had been settled) and stated in Court that he had no knowledge of the alleged fraud.

In a 2021 Adjudication[65] the Adjudicators decision was appealed by PC Harrington Contractors Ltd because the Adjudicator was employed by Systec, one of the parties in the Adjudication. It transpired that the Adjudicator had failed to disclose the relationship and therefore had not acted in a proper manner and that his Award was invalid. This was due to a clear breach of the rules of natural justice insofar as a party cannot be a judge of their own matter and the relationship between the Adjudicator and Systec, was so intimate and obvious, that it could be inferred from the Adjudicators involvement that any reasonably informed independent observer would consider that this relationship gave rise to a real risk of perceived if not actual bias.

1.10.3 Will a Directorship create actual or perceived Bias?

Mr. Alex Frame FRICS is both the President and a Director of the FPWS and Mr. Alan Bright FRICS is both a Regional Chairman and a Director of the FPWS. These two gentlemen often engage in party wall matters where for example: Mr. Frame is selected either by agreement or pursuant to section 10(8) as the third surveyor. Both gentlemen are also members of the RICS, they may even be members of the P&T. Would their joint memberships reach the threshold of a perceived or actual bias? However, their FPWS directorships[66] introduces another dimension arising from their legal obligations under the Company's Act 2006 and the duties and responsibilities they both have as directors creates a clear financial/commercial relationship. This raises an

---

63 AWG Group Ltd v Morrison [2006] 1 ALL ER 139.
64 AM Shipping Ltd v TTMI Ltd [2006] 1 Lloyd's 374.
65 Systec International Ltd v PC Harrington Contractors Ltd [2012] EWCA Civ 1371
66 PC Harrington Contractors Ltd v Systech International Ltd [2012] EWCA Civ 1371.

important question, would a fair-minded and informed independent observer (the test) conclude that there was a real possibility, or a real danger, (the two being the same) of perceived or actual bias? In my opinion they would and of course this scenario would apply to all the directors and/or any commercial relationship. It does not matter if the surveyors conduct themselves with the utmost probity, it's the perception, and in my opinion, this does satisfy the test. In fact, this relationship is substantially more obvious than perhaps the Dimes v Grand Junction case[67]

1.10.4 Employer/employees on opposite sides

In a 2017 case[68] the issue of perceived bias related to the adjoining owners' surveyor and the building owner's surveyor company[69]. The third surveyors[70] Award was critical of the two surveyors' (relationship as employer and employee) and attempts to unlawfully authorise the removal of the adjoining owner's boundary fence and to place trespassing scaffolding on their land to facilitate the construction of a wall situated some 350 mm away from the boundary (line of junction). In addition, the surveyors threatened the adjoining owners with reporting them under section 16, if they objected.[71]

Counsel[72] for Reeves appealed the third surveyors Award on the bizarre basis that he had not been selected under section 10(1)(b) and therefore did not have jurisdiction. Despite the two surveyors having recorded Mr. Philip Antino as the third surveyor in the Parent Award. It was now being conveniently claimed (or was the court being misled) that there had been an earlier discussion between the two surveyors (employer/employee) where they had discussed selecting Mr. Alistair Redler as the third surveyor. Mr. Frame claimed the alleged conversation created a binding selection under section 10(1)(b) although it was never conveyed in writing (a mandatory function of section 10(2)) to any party and/or indeed to Mr. Redler. This alleged conversation was only raised after a referral had been made to the Third Surveyor.

HHJ Bailey astonishingly ruled that the discussion about selecting Mr. Redler satisfied section 10(2) requiring all appointments/selections 'shall be in writing'. HHJ Bailey ruled that Mr. Antino was not validly appointed. The potential for the building owner to use this alleged conversation to avoid the consequences of their unlawful actions did not feature in HHJ Bailey's thoughts! he was blind to the possibility that this was a manufactured

---

67 See Chapter 1, section 1.10.
68 Reeves v Young, Young & Antino [2017] Central London County Court.
69 Vincent Brown & Associates Ltd.
70 Mr. Philip Antino.
71 See Chapter 15.
72 Mr. S Frame.

discussion or was he just bias towards Mr. Antino? The correct and proper questions that HHJ Bailey should have asked to do but failed to are: -

> (1) Did the employer/employee relationship give rise to a perceived if not an actual bias with regards to this alleged conversation;
> (2) If so what weight (if any) could or should be given to this alleged conversation that Mr. Redler was selected;
> (3) If the alleged conversation took place, how did it satisfy section 10(2) where all appointments/selections must be in writing;

If an appointment or selection is not recorded in writing, under the Act the surveyor is not validly appointed/selected. On the literal reading of section 10(2) any reasonably independent observer would conclude that the alleged conversation did not create a valid written appointment and HHJ Baileys' ruling was simply wrong in law. A grievous decision on a clear point of law that HHJ Bailey will have to live with. Given that the Parent Award, relied upon by the building owner to build her extension recorded Mr. Antino as the third surveyor had not been appealed. It is difficult to apply any rational logic to HHJ Baileys' Judgement. Accordingly, we come full circle to the whether he was blind to the possibility that this was a manufactured discussion or was he just bias towards Mr. Antino?

1.10.5 Inconsistent information

In a 2021 party wall case Mr. Kevin Turner FRICS was appointed by the building owners and served party[73] wall notices, Dr Antino was appointed by the adjoining owner, neither surveyor could agree on the third surveyor. During an exchange of suggested names to try and reach an agreement, Mr. Turner without disclosing his intention to do so, made a covert[74] application to the local authority[75] to appoint a third surveyor wrongly asserting the councils' authority arose under section 8 to select a surveyor.

The appointing officer was a solicitor and had stated that she had read the Act and was satisfied that she had jurisdiction to select a third surveyor under section 8 and subsequently appointed Mr. Alex Frame without notifying Dr Antino. Dr Antino was only informed of the appointment[76] of Mr. Frame several days later and immediately requested full disclosure of all documentation between Mr. Turner and the local authority. On disclosure it became apparent that the appointing officer was ignorant of the Act advising in writing *'I have never come across this before'* and had simply relied upon Mr.

---

73 See Chapter 11, subsection 11.8.
74 RICS rules of professional competency require there to be transparent/
75 Spelthorne Borough Council
76 A Third surveyor is only ever selected not appointed.

Turner's incorrect reference to appoint a third surveyor under section 8. Clearly, Spellthorne Council's solicitor did not check the Act otherwise she would have realised (i) that section 8 related to rights of access, (ii) a third surveyor is only selected and not appointed and (iii) more importantly Spellthorne Council's jurisdiction arises under section 10(8).

Dr Antino raised concerns firstly that Mr. Frame had not been validly selected. Mr. Frame took exception to this claiming that it was so obviously a typing error, but was it? In various correspondence Mr. Turner repeats the reference to section 8 as the provision for appointing the third surveyor. A typing error is something that is done once, repeating the same error suggests the person is ignorant of the correct provisions under section 10(8) of the Act. There were justified concerns, not only with the fact that this was a purported section 8 selection of a third surveyor but the covert way in which it had been done. Dr Antino requested that both Mr. Frame and Mr. Turner give full disclosure of all communications between them, not an unreasonable request given the circumstances, and plainly due diligence of Dr Antino to ensure that there had been no ex parte communications between the two surveyors creating a perceived or actual bias.

In response Mr. Turner[77] confirmed that he had a conversation with Mr. Frame[78]. Mr. Frame's response and stated that he had **not** had any conversations with Mr. Turner? Clearly, the information being provided by both surveyors was inconsistent. Clearly, these two surveyors had not got their storeys straight, and this raises an important question about whether a third surveyor bc engaging covertly with one surveyor? Obviously, they should not.

1.10.6 Non-disclosure of documents

The party wall surveyor should remain independent of the owners in much the same way as an expert in litigation matters. Accordingly, the surveyors owe both parties an implied and explicit duty of care to give full disclosure of all relevant documentation at the appropriate times and/or when requested to facilitate the execution of the notifiable works. Unfortunately, it is becoming a common activity for surveyors[79] to deliberately ignore this duty of care and indeed purposely withhold relevant documentation. This is not acceptable conduct or behaviour. Full disclosure must be given of all relevant facts.

---

77 Building owner's surveyor.
78 Third surveyor.
79 See Chapter 6, sub-section 6.6.

1.10.7 Summary of bias

The overriding principle is whether a relationship will affect a decision-makers impartiality or independence in any material way, and whether the decision-maker will treat the parties equally and maintain a neutral stance in the decision-making process.

It is clear from case law that the importance of the perception of bias is as fundamental to the proper discharge of the rules of natural justice as actual bias. The application of the test is extremely broad going beyond the any relationship or circumstance with the parties and/or their advisors and can include witnesses and any previous historic circumstances.

The test is not how the decision-maker considers their relationship with any, but how a reasonable independent observer would *perceive* the relevant facts as to whether a perceived or actual bias arises. If any matter might be reasonably considered as a conflict of interest the decision-maker should declare it. If the decision-maker believes a matter constitutes a conflict-of-interest or bias **withdrawal is the only option**, unless both parties expressly agree that the decision-maker should continue.

If, however, the decision-maker considers the incident or relationship immaterial then he/she should still give full disclosure and advise the parties and hear their respective submissions.

1.11 Res judicata

'Res judicata' is the legal doctrine that prevents a matter that has previously been adjudicated by a competent Court/Tribunal[80] from being revisited by the same parties. Some construction projects can last many years and require numerous Awards and there are occasions where the tribunal of surveyors may change.[81] The new tribunal simply continues and ultimately concludes matters with Addendum Awards if required. However, where issues have previously been determined in an Award, they cannot be revisited by the new tribunal. A comparison is found within section 108(3) of the HGCR where an adjudicator is bound by any previous decision. If a party wall Award has not been appealed[82] (even if it contains strikingly obvious defects) the legal principal *'Res Judicata'* bites. Regrettably HHJ Bailey did not follow this principle[83]

---

80 Adjudicators, Arbitrators, and Party Wall Surveyors.
81 See Chapter 10, subsections 10.6 and 10.9.
82 See Chapter 10, subsection 10.14.2.
83 Reeves v Young, Young & Antino [2017] County Court at Central London.

1.12   Delegated authority

Historically organisations structure their operations around a hierarchal chain, such as upper, middle, and lower management with instructions being passed down the hierarchal chain. This is the process of transferring responsibility for a task to another employee to ensure the business can function economically, efficiently and profitably. This is predicated upon the principle of delegated authority, which is the legal doctrine that allows a person or company to undertake activities as if they were 'standing in the shoes of that person/organisation' and anything done by that person in that capacity would be legally binding upon the company. Delegated authority is regularly used by insurance companies when instructing loss adjustors to settle the claim in accordance with the terms of the policy.

How would 'delegated authority' feature within the Act and how should a surveyor deal with delegated authority situation? It's very simple, it should be ignored, all correspondence should be sent to the appointed surveyor. If they fail to engage either through silence or suggest that a junior staff member can deal the statutory provisions in their name, then a section 10 (6) or (7) request[84] must be served on the appointed surveyor requesting that the appointed surveyor deals with the enquiry/issue personally. The 'tribunal of party wall surveyors has a quasi-judicial role, as the Court of First Instance, it is clear from the judgements of Lord Justice Denning and Lord Justice Romer in a Court of Appeal Case[85] that a holder of a judicial or quasi-judicial office or a person exercising judicial or quasi-judicial powers **may not**, except in exceptional circumstances delegate his responsibilities.

> Lord Justice Denning said: "While an administrative function can often be delegated, judicial functions rarely can be. No judicial tribunal can delegate its judicial functions unless it is enabled to do so expressly or by necessary implication".
> and;
> Lord Romer holding a similar view "A judicial function is one which from its very nature, is incapable of being delegated."

In Longmire v Maldura,[86] Mr. & Mrs Longmire[87] had appointed Mr. John Gillies as their surveyor. An Award was agreed, although it was ultimately

---

84 See Chapter 11, subsection 11.7.
85 Barnard v National Dock Labour Board [1953] 2 QB 18.
86 Longmire v Maldura [2015] Central London County Court HHJ Bailey.
87 adjoining owners.

signed by Mr. Johnathon Gillies, (the son of Mr. John Gillies) also a surveyor and working within his fathers' practice. Mr. Longmire appealed the Award on the grounds that it was not signed by his appointed surveyor because it was an unlawful delegation of the statutory authority. The error was immediately accepted and surveyors served another Award with the correct signature. It is not clear whether the Court's decision was assisted by the Barnard v National Dock case and their Lordships Denning and Romer Judgement upheld the principle that delegated authority does not exist within the statutory legislation. Furthermore, given the explicit wording of section 10(2) delegated authority cannot be transferred to an assistant.

1.13   Quasi-judicial authority

The following narrative is interesting, if you have an interest in legal science (jurisprudence). What has jurisprudence got to do with administering the Act? The administration of the Act falls within common law, but what is common law and how did it evolve into its current structure? The foundations of common law undoubtedly reach back to the feudal model that existed prior to the Norman invasion of 1066. In the 12th century a system of Royal Courts formed the basis of English law with the introduction of the Magna Carta in 1215, wherein it was declared that common pleas[88] would be heard by a permanent group of judges in London, and this continued until the 19th century without any significant reform. Of course, there were important changes in procedures and substantive law; but the structure remained the same.[89] Indeed, juries were a common part of all legal cases until the 20th century when they were removed from non-criminal cases.[90] Thereafter, the role of fact finding fell to the Judges, and their duty to give reasons for decisions as a function of natural justice commonly referred to as due process. The duty to include decisions is predicated upon the premise, that without reasoning, it is impossible to establish whether the Judge has got the law right or wrong. Thus, the losing party would altogether be deprived of a chance to appeal, unless the Appeal Court would entertain an appeal based on the lack of reasons itself.[91]

Every surveyor should assume that their Award will be appealed, and it would be naïve to think otherwise, because the surveyors are the Court of first instant the award is a quasi-judicial decision based on fact finding of the circumstances of each party wall matter. Just like Judges, the surveyors owe a duty to give reasons for their decisions as a function of natural justice i.e., due process. If the surveyor does not include reasons, then it is highly likely that the Judge will use his powers to make a finding of fact and reject or amend the Award

---

88 All disputes.
89 Samuel, G. (2013) "A Short Introduction to Common Law" Edward Elgar Publishing Limited.
90 Defamation and Fraud are exceptions.
91 Flannery v Halifax Estate Agencies Ltd [2000] 1 WLR 377, 381.

accordingly.[92] It is therefore important to the production of a valid Award that the surveyors include reasoning. When giving reasons for the decisions, the surveyor should be mindful that the Award should also be written in a concise and structured way so as to be informative and understandable to the layman. Avoid using unnecessary technical jargon and/or including every bit of information and/or reference to the documentation because this will not support the premise that the Award would withstand criticism.

The more issues or points included will create opportunities that: (i) the losing party, the Court of appeal, and/or any future readers of the Award will be able to identify the crucial matters which swayed the surveyor; and (ii) the Award will contain something that the unsuccessful party can legally take issue and appeal. It is a fine balance and indeed there is an art to writing a solid Award.

1.14   Schedule of Condition

This is not a statutory requirement but it is good practice to record a schedule if possible. However, the building owner's agreement should be obtained before doing so because there are cost implications. The benefits of a schedule should be explained to the owners, because it is a double-edged sword that cuts both ways and can protect the building owners from false claims for damage that pre-existed the commencement of the notifiable works and the adjoining owners by establishing that a particular crack did not exist. A limited number of surveyors believe that the schedule should be limited to the areas that are within a reasonable distance from the proposed works and that it is unreasonable to record the whole of the property. I do not support or encourage that approach, given that the surveyors are already at the property to record a schedule of some areas, it should not take too much time to inspect the whole of the property. If any serious issues are observed they should be recorded with digital cameras as a minimum approach. The schedule should ideally include a narrative and be cross-referenced with the photographs, some surveyors are extremely reluctant to do this, which is either laziness or ignorance. If a building owners' surveyor refuses to agree to a full schedule of condition, the request should be made in writing and the response duly recorded.

However, not all adjoining owners will participate[93] and it is not possible to obtain access. If the adjoining owner's refuse to co-operate, the surveyors should fully inform the adjoining owners in writing that their refusal could prejudice any potential claim for any alleged loss and/or damage. A full record of all requests and refusals should be properly documented.

---

92 See Chapter 10, subsection 10.14.2.
93 See Chapter 11, section 11.5

The consequence of failing to record a full schedule was at the forefront of the Takhar dispute[94] which has been rumbling on since 2015 and now in its 9th year. The building owners' first surveyor had indeed refused to agree to a full record a schedule of condition, when requested by the adjoining owner's surveyor. When substantial damage was caused the adjoining owner's surveyor had estimated these works at circa £250,000 + vat plus professional fees. The building owner's replacement surveyor[95] engaged a quantity surveyor who estimated the cost of repairs at £2000.00 + vat. The surveyor also claimed that a lot of the damage pre-existed the commencement of the notifiable works. An independent expert was appointed to resolve the dispute. The Mohammed's did not agree with his award and in 2021 attempted to appeal the award on damages, legal and professional costs. Had there been a full schedule then any pre-existing damage (if such existed) would have been recorded, but it was not, because the first building owner's surveyor refused to include those areas out side the distances under section 6 (2).

---

94 Mohamed & Lahrie v Takhar & Takhar & Takhar (2021) in the County Court of Central London TCC List G20CL122
95 Mr. Alistair Redler FRICS.

CHAPTER 2

2.0   SECTION 20: - Interpretation

2.1   Introduction

I have continued my earlier approach of having the section 20 definitions at the front of the book due to the encouraging responses that I received from surveyors/practitioners reading my first edition. Understanding the language and the specific meanings of certain words is fundamental to understanding the Act's intent and the unique vocabulary adopted therein. I have also expanded my personal definitions[96] which I hope will remove some of the fog that surrounds the Act and increase clarity and understanding of the Act or create further debate which is never a bad thing.

2.2   Adjoining Owner and Adjoining Occupier

"Adjoining Owner" and "Adjoining Occupier" respectively mean any owner or occupier of land, buildings, storeys, or rooms adjoining those of the building owner and for the purposes only of section 6 within the distances specified in that section.

The Act does not differentiate between the proprietary rights of the adjoining owner and/or tenants/leaseholders who are referred to as an occupier. Providing their occupation of the property complies with the definition of an owner[97]. The inclusion of the word "any" illustrates that where there are multiple owners/occupiers each have individual property rights who are also entitled to notice.

2.3   Building Owner

"Building owner" means an owner of land who is desirous of exercising rights under this Act

Although the Act uses the term to a building owner (in the singular) it applies in the plural. Importantly, one owner cannot operate independently of any joint owners and cannot stand in the shoes of another unless there is an explicit agreement to do so.[98] Therefore, a failure to include all building owners in the process will invite a jurisdictional challenge. In 1993, Mr. & Mrs. Lehmann[99]

---

96 See Chapter 2, subsection 2.11.
97 See Chapter 2, subsection 2.4.
98 See Chapter 1, subsection 1.12.
99 Lehmann v Herman [1993] 1 EGLR 172.

received a notice from Mr. Herman, they contested the validity of the notice on the grounds that Mrs Herman had not been included within the notice. They reasonably requested that Mrs Herman should undertake to treat herself as bound by the notices in order to regularise the situation. Mrs Herman refused, arguing that it was not necessary citing Crosby[100] claiming that Mr. Herman was the person undertaking the works and was therefore the building owner and the only person required to serve notice. Mrs Herman further advised that she would do nothing other than to make a *"cup a tea"* for the builders. However, the Court drew a clear distinction between the two cases concluding that the circumstances within the Crosby case were substantially different to the Lehmann case. The former relating to the receipt of notices by one of 'joint tenants' and was held an effective service of a notice, whereas the service of a notice by one of two building owners upon joint owners was not. The Court[101] held: -

> "Simply in practical terms it would be very odd if the statute provided for one of the two joint/owners to deal with an adjoining owner without the other joint owner being involved. In real property law terms, the concept of one joint owner being able to deal with the property without the other being a party to the transaction has been foreign to English law since the 1925 property legislation. It is therefore important that all building owners are properly identified within the notices"[102]

2.4   Owner

Owner includes: -
(a)   a person in receipt of, or entitled to receive, the whole or part of the rents or profits of land;
(b)   a person in possession of land, otherwise than as a mortgagee or as a tenant from year to   year or for a lesser term or as a tenant at will;
(c)   a purchaser of an interest in land under a contract for purchase or under an agreement for   a lease, otherwise than under an agreement for a tenancy from year to year for a lesser term.

This definition does not draw a distinction between the freehold and/or leasehold interests that are commonly found with the United Kingdom's built environment where it is common for numerous leases and sub-leases to exist

---

100 Crosby v Alhambra Co Ltd [1907] 1 Ch 295.
101 Lehmann v Herman [1993] 1 EGLR 172.
102 Chynoweth, P. (2003) 'The Party Wall Case Book,' Blackwell Publishing Ltd P.22.

within a single property.[103] As this definition confirms that the beneficiaries of those leases will all qualify as owners and are therefore entitled to receive notice and this can have substantial cost implications for the building owner.

2.4.1   Potential ownership

The definition helpfully recognises three types of owners, although it is silent on a party that is in the process of purchasing a property. If contracts have been exchanged, they will satisfy the definition of owner because they now have a legal interest in the property. Accordingly, they are entitled to serve and/or receive notice in relation to any intended works. Service of notice prior to completion of the purchase and/or assignment of a lease is not unusual, although perhaps more common in commercial situations where a developer may want to commence the statutory procedures as soon as possible after signing the contracts to avoid delays to any proposed building works.

However, this approach has not been without pitfalls and the importance of getting the timing right was demonstrated[104] when contractors engaged by the building owners to develop an investment property, simultaneously began negotiations to agree a 99-year lease on one of the development properties. In anticipation of reaching an agreement, Spiers & Son jumped the gun and served a notice as the building owner. It was held that because the negotiations and exchange of the lease had not been concluded; Spiers did not have a legal interest in the property. Therefore, they were not owners and the notice was invalid. Accordingly, it is only after the exchange of contracts or an intent to assign of a lease that the purchaser/lessee have a legal interest in the property. Thereafter, both the vendor and purchaser are technically joint owners as tenants in common until completion of the contract when the ownership fully transfers to the new owner.

2.5   Foundation and special foundation

2.5.1   Foundation

means: - in relation to a wall, means the solid ground or artificially formed support resting on solid ground on which the wall rests;

On the literal and natural reading this seems reasonably clear, regrettably as with a large proportion of the Act the devil is in the detail. There are two important criteria within this definition that the surveyors must be satisfied that the proposed foundation design demonstrates in order to be classified as the foundation under the Act, they are: -

---

103 Residential, Industrial and Commercial.
104 Spiers and Son Ltd v Troup (1915) 84 LJKB 1986.

(i) The wall must be physically 'resting on' the artificially formed support claimed; and

(ii) The artificial formed support must be 'resting on' solid ground.

Figure No 1 satisfies the definition although may not necessarily be notifiable works.

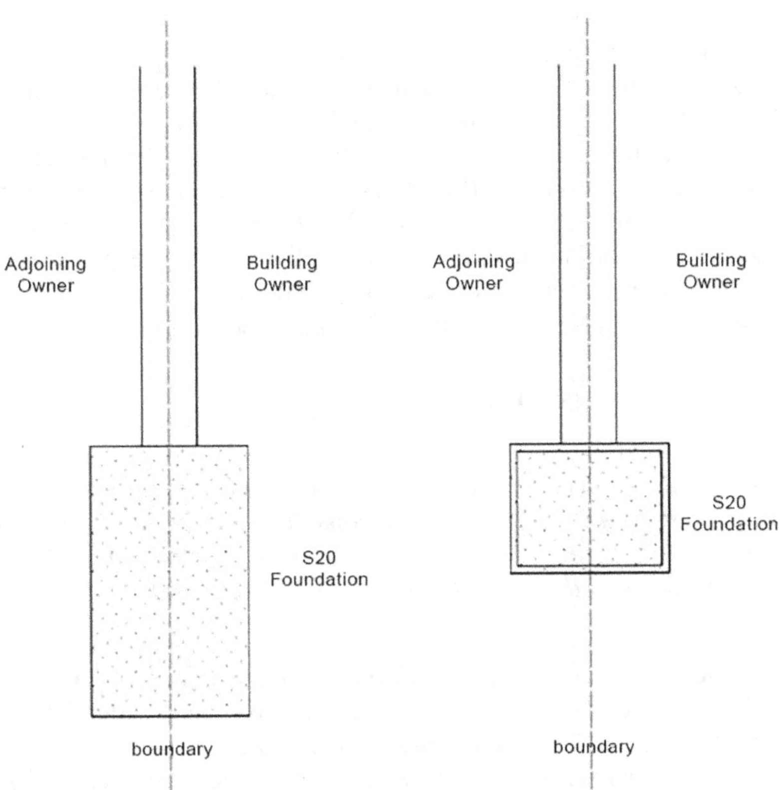

Figure 1 Example of Foundation on the Left and Special Foundation on the Right

2.5.2   Special foundations

Special foundations mean foundations in which an assemblage of beams or rods is employed for the purpose of distributing any load: and

The devil is in the detail requiring two criteria that the special foundation design must demonstrate: -
<blockquote>
(i)   include an assemblage of beams or rods;[105] and
(ii)   or for the distributing any load.
</blockquote>

It is surprising that such a clear and concise section of the Act has caused so much controversy and/or conflict between the legal and party wall community. Particularly, when used in basements[106] and therefore I have included chapter 18 specifically address this point. Given the significance of getting it wrong (2020 multi-million-pound collapse of residential Chelsea Property), surveyors must be fully informed about the criteria that determines what falls within this definition. On the natural meaning of the definition, if the proposed design includes any reinforcement, irrespective of whether it is an assemblage of roads or beams such as a steel mesh, it is by definition a special foundation.

2.6   What is a party fence wall

Party Fence Wall means a wall (not being part of a building) which stands on lands of different owners and is used or constructed to be used for separating such adjoining lands, but does not include a wall constructed on the land of one owner the artificially formed support of which projects into the land of another owner.

This applies to a freestanding wall astride the boundary (line of junction)[107] and therefore both the building and adjoining owners have legal title. The location of the boundary in relation to the width of the wall, is irrelevant. As long as a part of the wall is across the boundary that part of the wall is captured by the Act's definition giving the owners legal rights as 'tenants in common' over the full width of the wall, with the benefits and liabilities associated with the wall.

---

105 Reinforcement.
106 Antino, P. [2020] Interpreting the Party Wall etc. Act 1996 and The Implications for Building Below Ground "Anglia Ruskin University, PhD Thesis.
107 Not necessarily the same thing.

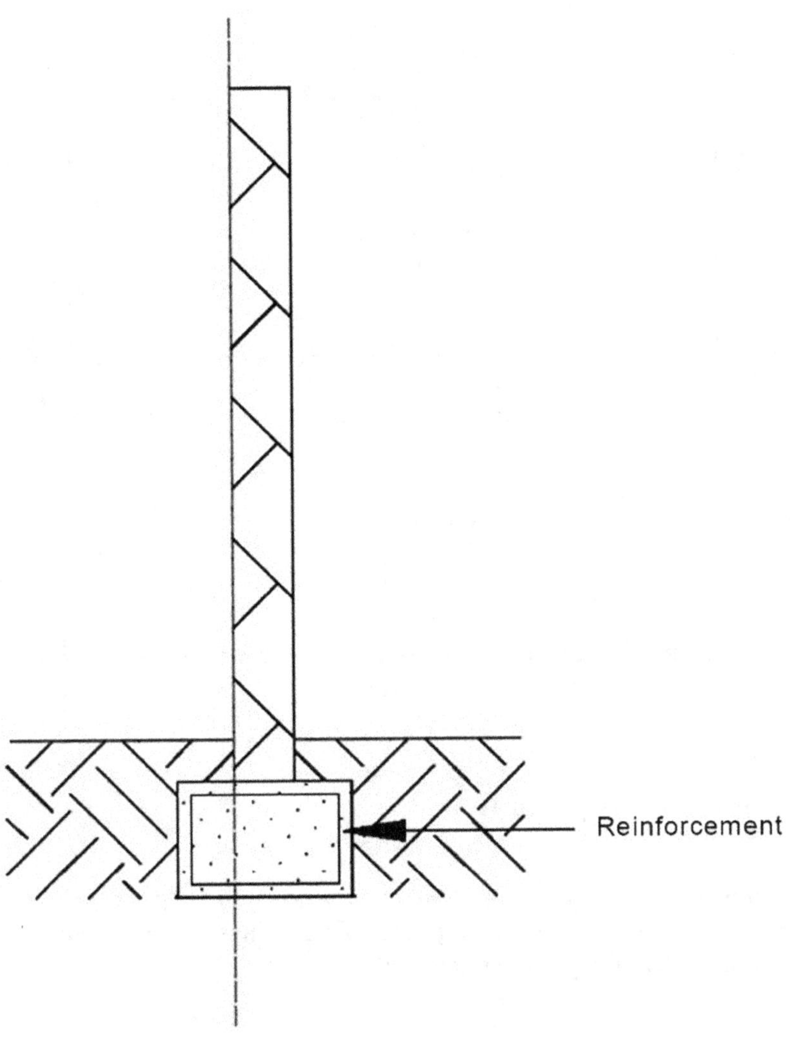

Figure 2 Wall on line of |Junction

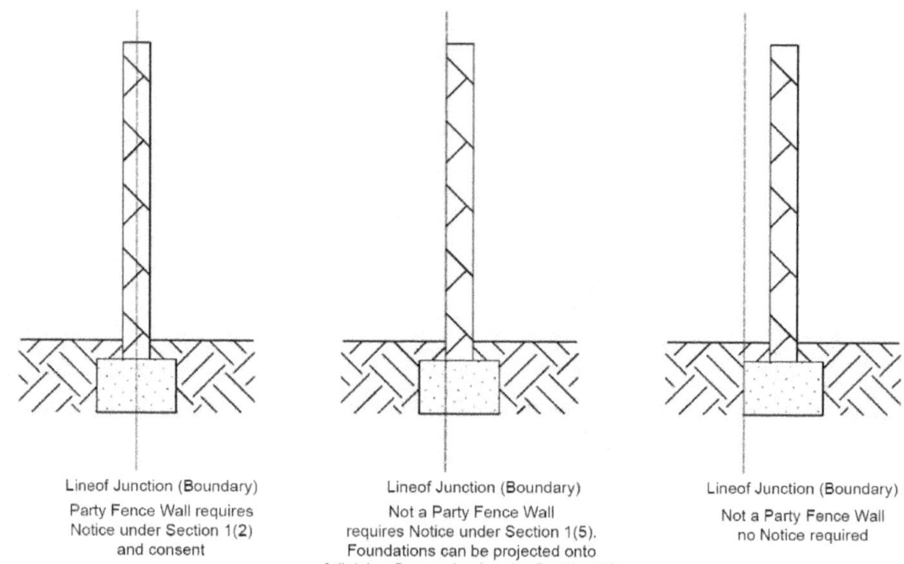

Figure 3 Examples of Walls Across, On and Away from the Line of Junction

2.7   What is a party structure

Party structure means a party wall and also a floor partition or other structure separating buildings or parts of buildings approached solely by separate staircases or separate entrances.

A party structure applies to both walls and floors (see Figure No 4) that separate structures within different legal title/ownership. However, establishing which elements of a building are a party wall or a party structure can be difficult[108] and requires a detailed understanding of construction technology. Insofar as it is reasonably foreseeable to do so, the surveyor should be able to determine correctly which adjoining owner is entitled to notice, but where there is doubt extensive enquiries will be necessary, and if these do not yield the information, the advice to a building owner should always be to serve notice as a precautionary step to avoid an injunction.

---

108 Flying freehold.

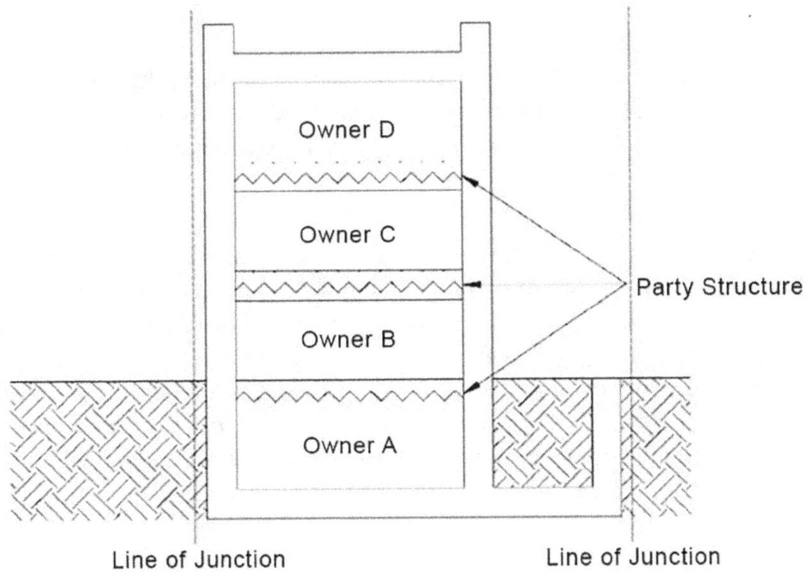

Figure 4 Example of a Party Structure

2.8   What is a party wall

The Act provides a party wall as being either a type (a) or (b). The former is when the wall is astride (see Figure No 5) the line of junction (irrespective of whether it is or is not enclosed upon by another structure) and are tenants in common over the whole width of the wall.[109] This relationship was clarified in a planning appeal decision[110] and in a case where the circumstances of how the wall was built were unknown. If the location of the line of junction[111] is disputed, the surveyor's jurisdiction entitles them to determine the position of the line of junction[112] (but not the boundary) in order to determine the status of the wall for the purpose of bringing the statutory procedures to a natural conclusion.[113] If either of the owners wish to challenge the surveyor's determination of the line of junction, they do so by appealing the Award[114] to seek the Courts assistance at common law for a boundary determination.[115]

---

109 Watson v Gray (1880) 14 Ch. D 192.
110 Planning appeal Ref: APP/Q5300/X01/1062324.
111 Antino, P. (2014) "A Practitioner's Approach and Interpretation of Neighbourly Matters" Xlibris.
112 See Chapter 4, subsection 4.6.
113 See Chapter 4, subsection 4.6.
114 See Chapter 10, subsection 10.14.2.
115 Loost v Kremer [1997] West London County Court.

2.8.1   Type (a) party wall

Party wall means: - a wall which forms part of a building and stands on lands of different owners to a greater extent than the projection of any artificially formed support on which the wall rests; and

For a wall to be defined as a type (a) party wall, the wall must have been built across the line of junction (boundary) but not specifically enclosed upon by adjacent structures (see Figure Nos 5 & 6). If the adjoining owners' structure encloses upon only part of the wall, as long as the unenclosed areas of the wall are built across the line of junction (boundary) then it is a type (a) party wall for the full length and height. This creates legal rights for both owners as 'tenants in common' and therefore one owner cannot interfere with the wall without the owners' consent or participation.

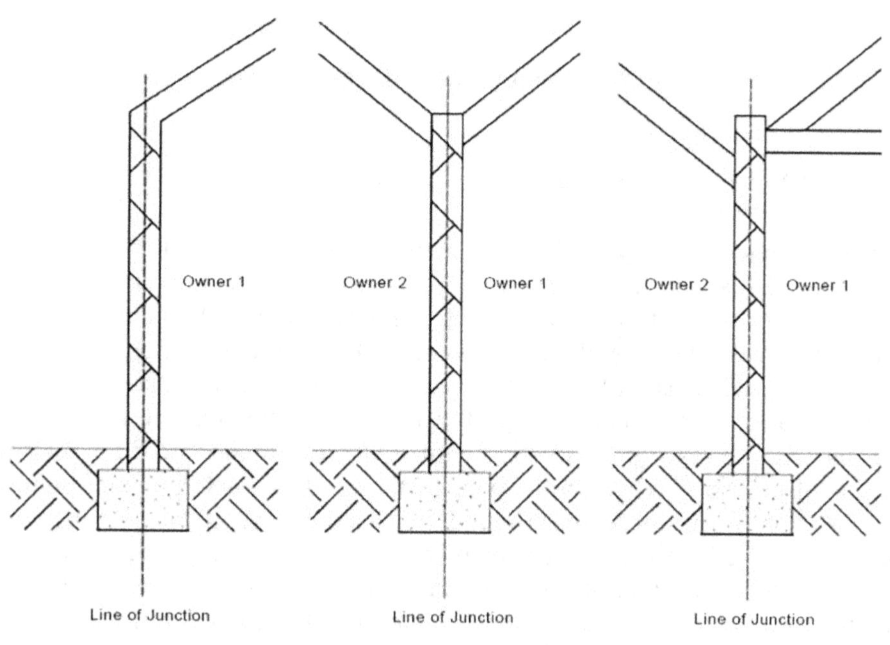

Figure 5 Section through Type A Party Wall

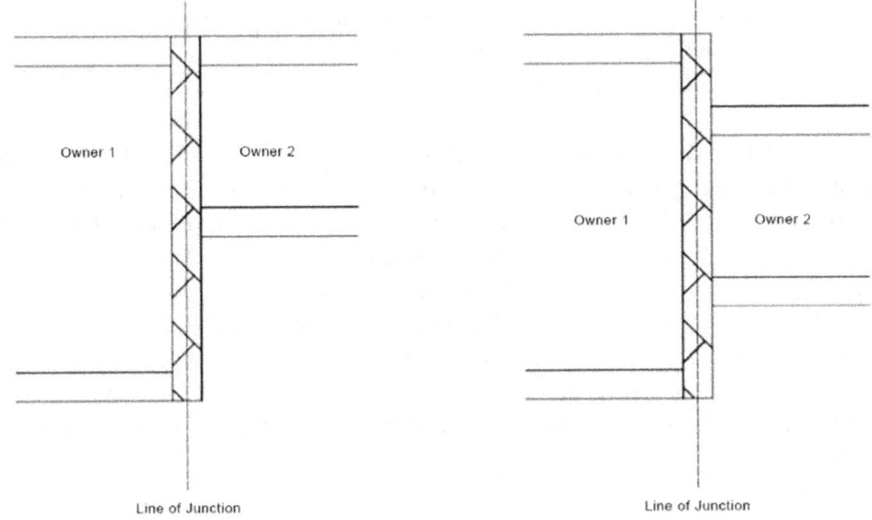

Figure 6 Plan of Type A party Wall

2.8.2 Type (b) party wall

So much of a wall not being a wall referred to in paragraph (a) above as separates buildings belonging to different owners;

For a wall to be defined as a type (b) party wall, the must have been built either on or inside the line of junction (boundary) but specifically enclosed upon by an adjoining structure (see Figure Nos 7 & 8) for any part of its height or length. It is only the part that is enclosed upon that creates a type b party wall. This creates the same legal rights for both owners as 'tenants in common' and therefore an owner cannot interfere with the enclosed area of wall without the adjoining owners' consent or participation through service of notice.

An early case[116] recognised the distinction between: -

> "The words party wall is used, not in their technical sense, but as a convenient phrase for

---

116 Dury v Army & Navy Auxiliary Cooperative Supply Ltd (1896) 2 QB 271.

dividing the wall. The walls in question here will be dividing walls up to the top of the first storey and to that extent section 75 applies to them, any point above cease to be a party wall where not enclosed upon."

Some type (b) walls have been created by stealth[117] where an owner trespasses on to another owner's structure. As soon as an owner becomes aware of the enclosure, they should forthwith request the structure is removed. Remaining silent or inactive is not advisable because it could be interpreted as acquiescence[118] to any alleged trespass and/or to create the right to enclose upon that wall by prescription.[119] Whilst obtaining property rights under the law of adverse possession[120] and demonstrating the right of adverse possession has in recent years become more difficult.[121] Nonetheless an owner should protect their land and sending a letter/email recording the trespass would record the objection.

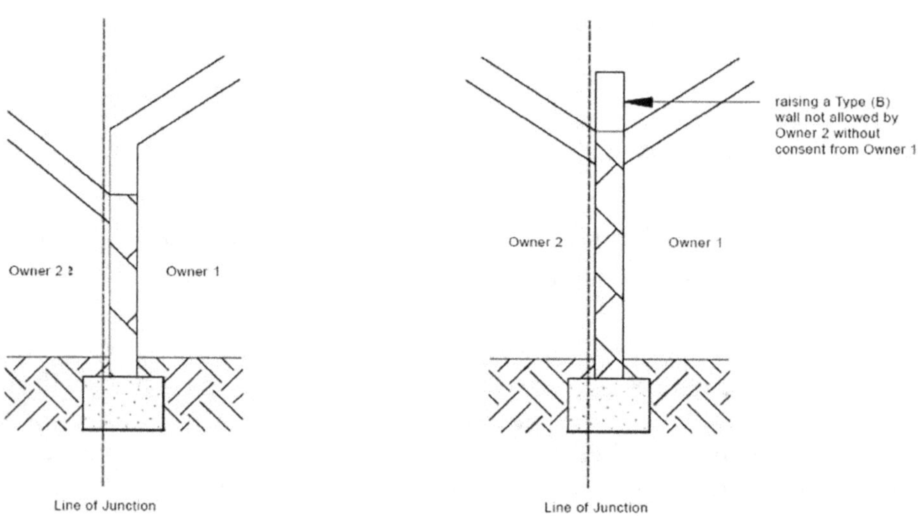

Figure 7 Section through Type B Party Wall

117 JSA Properties (UK) Ltd v Gary Harvey Waldman G20CL109.
118 Antino, P. (2014) "A Practitioner's Approach and Interpretation of Neighbourly Matters" Xilbris.
119 The Prescription Act 1832.
120 Prudential Assurance Co Ltd v Waterloo Real Estate Inc (1999) 2 EGLR 85.
121 The Land Registration Act 2002.

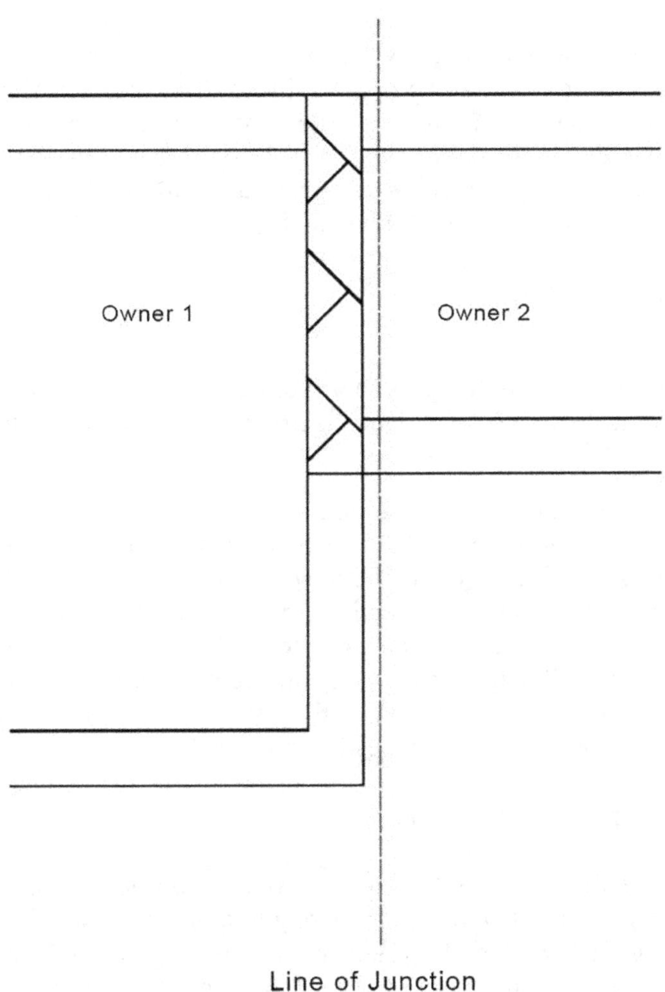

Figure 8 Plan of Type B Party Wall

2.10   Surveyor

Surveyor means any person not being a party to the matter appointed or selected under section 10 to determine disputes in accordance with the procedures set out in this Act.

Clearly, it would be wrong for an owner to represent themselves given the rules of natural justice, 'no man can be his own judge'.[122] However, this definition has created significant issues for those professionals administering the Act, where in some cases, surprisingly was not anticipated by Parliament the building owners have appointed their father/father-in-law[123] which obviously complicated matters but is not prohibited under the legislation.

2.10   Appointing Officer

Appointing officer means the person appointed under this Act by the local authority to make such appointments as are required under section 10(8);

When the surveyors cannot agree on the selection of a third surveyor, either of the surveyors can request the local authority's assistance under section 10(8) to select the third surveyor.[124] This is the appointing officers[125] only duty, he/she has no further involvement or jurisdiction. If the surveyors proceed absent of a third surveyor, the tribunal is incomplete and everything is *ultra vires*. However, in party wall matters even these apparently simple procedures can be complicated by those wanting to evade their statutory duties and liabilities [126] and/or indeed by operating in a clandestine manner.[127]

2.11   Supplemental definitions

The absence of sufficiently detailed and reasoned definitions within section 20 has undoubtedly contributed to the conflicting interpretations and is the gift that keeps on giving for barristers. Unless there is a meeting of minds, the disparity between the surveyors and certain barristers approaches the interpretation of the Act will continue to create disputes and expose owners to unnecessary litigation.   I have therefore revisited the first edition and rather boldly introduced some additional definitions based on my experience, views, and

---

122 See Chapter 4, 4.6.
123 Mills & Mills v Savage & Savage [2016] Central London County Court (Case No 1) and Mills & Mills v Sell & Sell [2016] Central London County Court (Case No 1).
124 See Chapter 11, section 11.8.
125 See Chapter 10, subsection 10.8.
126 Zaman v Zala (2020) County Court of Central London.
127 See Chapter 1, section 1.10.4.

indeed in instances the opinions of other party wall surveyors, solicitors and/or barristers to provide greater clarity to the reader. I hope these will either provide clarity or further debate.

"Structure" I define a structure as *"any part or parts of a building or structure including ancillary parts that are constructed/assembled from similar and/or different materials that contribute to and/or form a part or the sum of the parts necessary to create the complete structure, irrespective of whether they contribute to the function of a building or are ancillary elements to the building."* I have found one legal reference albeit in the context of property ratings legislation where Lord Denning[128] proffered the following definition: -

> "A structure is something which is constructed, but
> not everything which is constructed is a structure.
> A ship, for instance, is constructed, but it is not a
> structure. A structure is something of substantial
> size which is built up from component parts and
> intended to remain permanently on a permanent
> foundation; but it is still a structure even though
> some of its parts may be movable, as, for instance,
> about a pivot. Thus, a windmill or a turntable is a
> structure."

I personally do not subscribe to the premise that a ship (or indeed an aircraft) is not a structure, but given the case related to rateable valuations for properties, I can understand why Lord Denning excluded a ship from his definition.

In the same case, Jenkins J. said: -

> "Is or is in the nature of a building or structure"
> indicated certain characteristics and the general
> range of things in view consists of things built or
> constructed, I think, in addition to coming within
> this general range, the things in question must, in
> relation to the hereditament, answer the description
> of buildings or structures, or, at all events, be in the
> nature of buildings or structures. That suggests
> built or constructed things of substantial size: I
> think of such size that they either have been in fact,
> or would normally be, built or constructed on the
> hereditament as opposed to being brought on to the
> hereditament ready-made. It further suggests some
> degree of permanence in relation to the

---

128 Cardiff Rating Authority v Guest Keen Baldwin's Iron and Steel Co Ltd [1941] KB 485.

> hereditament i.e., things which once installed on
> the hereditament would normally remain in situ
> and would only be removed by a process
> amounting to pulling down or taking to pieces.[129]

In essence the case established three criteria that would define a structure; -

- Size;
- Permanence; and
- Physical attachment to ground.

Applying these criteria to the elements associated with construction, pavements, paths, patios, drains, inspection chambers, concrete bases, fences, patios, driveways, fish ponds, electric pylons, garden walls, swimming pools and any permanent hard landscaping would all fall within the definition of a structure.

"On" is extremely important in relation to determining whether section 1(5) applies. The ordinary and natural meaning of *'on'* must mean that the proposed wall is physically on or astride the line of junction, (See Figure Nos 2, 3, & 5) therefore, close to or in the vicinity of the line of junction would not qualify as on.

"Partition" I draw no distinction between a partition and the party wall definition. If any part or parts of a building are constructed/assembled from similar and/or different materials and contribute to a part or the sum of the parts necessary to create a building that separates the whole or parts thereof from distinct areas under different ownership and or occupation, they must by definition fall within either the type (a) or (b) party wall definition.

"Footings" Historically this term has been used in construction to refer to brickwork footings and/or indeed concrete (with or without reinforcement) and would in my opinion fall within the Act's definition of foundations.

"Sub-structure" Historically this term has been used within the construction industry when referring to any and/or all parts of the structure that is below damp-proof course ("DPC"). I see no reason to deviate away from this historic principle. The sub-structure's function is to support the structure that rests upon it and to safely distribute the loads from the structure above DPC safely through the sub-structure onto the ground.

---

129 His approach was endorsed by Pill LJ in the case of Skerrits of Nottingham Ltd v Secretary of State for the Environment, Transport and the Regions and Harrow LBC (No. 2) [2002] 2 PLR 102.

"Superstructure" This term is historically used to refer to any and/or all parts of the structure above DPC level.

"Compensate" means to make amends for any reasonable loss[130] or injury arising out of or incidental to[131] the cause which under the Act would include the works and/or the execution thereof. There is one qualification that surveyors must consider and that is the compensation shall be limited to returning the affected property to the same position as if the damage or loss had not arisen. Therefore, this would in my view include compensation for diminution of a property's value where such has been caused by the notifiable works.

"Dispute" includes any conflict or controversy, a conflict of claims or right; an assertion of a right, claim, or demand on a party met by counter claims and allegations from the other side. The resolution process involves litigation or ADR or where the administration of quasi-judicial functions is applicable.

"Dissent" withholding consent to the notifiable works will trigger the section 10 and can arise by silence or explicitly when appointing a surveyor.

"Drilling" Is a form of cutting and used for the purposes of penetrating soil, a structure, and or any of its numerous elements. The depth of penetration for cutting or drilling is irrelevant for the purposes of applying section 3 and specifically sections 2 (2) (f) and (j).

"Due diligence" Is the obligation/process that the appointed surveyors must adopt when assessing the potential risks of an activity or course of action that may create or impose a liability upon a third party such as their appointing owner.

"Basement Walls" are either a foundation or a special foundation because their function is four-fold

> (i)   They supplant the original foundation, thus becoming the foundation supporting the existing super-structure,
>
> (ii)   Are a retaining wall in touch with the soil to maintain the adjoining owner's natural right of support following the building owners[132] removal of land by transferring the loads to the ground;
>
> (iii)   The vertical (walls) and horizontal (floor) elements of the basement when formed in reinforced concrete create a contiguous (three dimensional) structure which is dependent

---

130 Actionable as a tort.
131 See Chapter 8.
132 Chapter 11, para 11.5.

upon the assemblage of beams and/or rods to distribute any load; and

(iv)   A reinforced basement box is in touch with the ground and its function is to distribute 'any' load safely to the ground.[133]

"Shall" the introduction/use of the word 'shall' make the process mandatory, not permissive. And is an instruction and not an option.

"Forthwith" in law means immediately; promptly; without delay; directly; within a reasonable time given the circumstances of the case.

"Shall forthwith" when these words are conjoined it is a mandatory.

"Functus Officio" The doctrine of *functus officio* (having performed his office) for example holds that once an Arbitrator/Judge renders a decision regarding the issues he/she lacks any power to re-examine that decision. This principle is well established in international arbitration, adjudication and common law.[134] Some barristers use this as a tactic to challenge a surveyor's jurisdiction by claiming there was no dispute. Indeed, once an Award has been served the surveyors jurisdiction is functus officio until a fresh dispute arises.

"Bad Faith" *Mala Fides* refers to the sustained form of deception which consists of entertaining or pretending to entertain one set of feelings while acting as if influenced by another. This would apply to a surveyor knowingly awarding access on to an adjoining owner's land whilst knowing there is no legal right to do so.[135]

"Mitigation" This is the act of lessening the force or intensity of something unpleasant, if it can be demonstrated that someone has executed 'best endeavours' to mitigate the consequences of their actions any subsequent punishment or liability to damages and/or costs may be reduced.

"Ex Parte" means 'by or for one party' or 'by one side'. ... As per the rules of natural justice, any case must be decided within the presence of all the parties who should be given proper opportunity to present their case. However, when one party refuses to engage, the right to proceed ex parte can be adopted.[136]

---

133 See Definition of foundation and special foundation.
134 Hence the need for appeal procedures.
135 Reeves v Blake [2009] EWCA C iv 611.
136 See Chapter 11, subsection 11.7.

CHAPTER 3

3.0   SECTION 15: - Service of notices etc. and Dissent

3.1   Section 15 Service of statutory documents

There is a growing tactic adopted by the recipient to claim they never received the Award or notice and that service was not affected.   Parliament clearly intended the quasi-judicial process to be effective, fair and equitable, with formal procedures that establish the surveyor's jurisdiction being distinctly[137] set out.   Therefore, they must be explicitly followed to demonstrate compliance, and trigger certain rights to move matters forward.

3.2   Formality of service of notice and content

The first and most important point that all party wall surveyors must understand is that the service of a notice has to be completed in order to trigger the Act, a failure or refusal to serve a notice renders the act inoperable. The adjoining owners only legal position is to obtain an injunction.[138] Woodhouse[139] (albeit under the previous legislation) is often cited as the authority for the general proposition that the dispute mechanisms within the Act are consequent upon a valid notice or works that are envisaged by a notice has been served. The decision in the Blake[140] case (under the 96 Act) directly determined the division between those matters in respect of which surveyors appointed under the Act had jurisdiction and those where they had no jurisdiction. Etherton LJ's characterised the purpose of the Act and its predecessors as being "to constitute a means of dispute resolution which avoids recourse to the courts." Specifically, surveyors do not have jurisdiction to determine common law matters as appointed surveyors, conversely, they do not have jurisdiction to determine party wall matters without the Act being triggered by service of a notice.

In 2021, the concept that surveyors could be appointed without service of a notice came before HHJ Parfitt and then on appeal before the Hon Mr. Justice Eyre.[141] In reaching his judgement which rejected the grounds of appeal

---

137 See Chapter 10.
138 See Chapter 19.
139 Woodhouse v Consolidated Property Corp 1993, 1 EGLR 174.
140 Blake v Reeves [2009] EWCA Civ 611 [2010] 1 WLR 1.
141 Shah v Ken Power & Lee Kyson [2022] EWHC 209 (QB) Mr Justice Eyre

advanced by Counsel[142] for the appellants, Mr. Justice Eyre considered HHJ Parfitt's reliance on HHJ Luba decision in the Schmidt[143] case that the invalidity of the notice deprived the surveyors of jurisdiction under the Act *obiter "Judge Luba gave the Act a wide scope and took the view that the surveyors had jurisdiction notwithstanding the absence of a valid notice."* The actual position flowing from the Schmidt case is that whilst the notice was invalid the adjoining owner had consented to the works, thus, waiving any invalidity. The dispute arose when Schmidt deviated away from the drawings that had been agreed to and thus, the author was appointed to resolve the dispute on the basis that jurisdiction arising under section 10(12)(c). Therefore, the Act could now be applied. Mr. Justice Eyre correctly rejected the appeal, thus the mantra of "no notice, no act" accurately summarises the true legal position. The Act cannot be applied unilaterally so as to supersede the parties' common law rights and obligations.

Any discrepancy and/or irregularity in the service of a notice (unless waived) may give rise to a challenge and if upheld the process must start *de novo*. The notice must relate to notifiable works as set out within the three distinct notifiable areas, in addition to which there are numerous subsection notices and counter notices, which may be served[144] by the building and/or adjoining owners.

As well as intending to give guidance, notices are instructions which advise the recipient of their statutory rights subject to following the formalities contained therein. The process of giving notice or instructions is not a new phenomenon. There are numerous examples of instructions and/or notice. For example; 'do not alight while the bus is in motion' is clearly both a notice and an instruction. The consequences of disregarding the instruction are obvious and can remove or limit any liability or duty of care if a person ignores the notice/instruction and suffers as a consequence. The same principle applies to the Act, the surveyors owe a duty of care to ensure that the notice is clear and free of ambiguity, ensuring that the recipient understands their rights and what they are required/entitled to do. In the event that they do not follow the instruction, i.e., fail to respond within 14-days, then under section 5 a dispute is deemed to have arisen. There are procedures that allow the surveyor to progress[145] the party wall matters through to their natural conclusion when an adjoining owner does not respond to participate.

3.2.1 Notices format and content

---

142 Mr. N. Isaac QC and Mr. Fain both of Tanfield Chambers.
143 Schmid v Hulls & Athanasou [2016] TCC County Court at Central London
144 Sections 2, 4, 5, 8, 12, and 13 of the Act.
145 See Chapter 11, subsection 11.5.

Given the importance of serving notice, it is somewhat surprising that the Act does not in itself provide a prescribed format for notices. However, the ever-ingenious surveying profession have developed recognised formats that satisfy the Act's requirements.[146] Because the notices have to be served, it is implied that all notices should be in writing, in the event that a dispute or challenge arises in regards to their validity and in particular service (and proof thereof) having written notice and a certificate of posting should establish a defence against any allegations that the Act has not been followed. Indeed, there are numerous cases which have emphasised the importance of getting things right: -

> "The steps laid down by the Act should be scrupulously followed throughout and short cuts are not desirable".[147]

Applying the Act is like building a house, if the foundations are defective, the whole house will eventually come tumbling down. Therefore, by ensuring the notices are correct, everything thereafter should flow smoothly. Being able to demonstrate a notice is valid will be dependent upon the correct interpretation of the relevant section under which the notice has been served. It is important to remember that the notice is a statutory requirement. The key question will always be: is the notice sufficiently detailed for the purpose of satisfying the relevant statutory provision?[148]

For example, where the works are notifiable under section 6 (1) or (2), the Act requires that the notice must be accompanied with plans under subsection 6(6)(a) that indicate the location and depth of the proposed excavations. If the drawings are not included the notice is invalid, because the recipient cannot identify how (if at all) the proposed works will impact upon them.

The Courts may overlook an obvious minor error, such as addressing the notice to Ms. when it should be Mrs. or other typographical errors, which in such instances any reasonably fair-minded person would consider do not materially change the intention or content of the notice.[149] However failing to include an owner[150] may result in an invalid notice.

---

146 The information contained therein must be accurate.
147 Gyle-Thompson v Wall Street (Properties) Ltd 1 WLR 123 [1974] 1 ALL ER 295.
148 Speedwell Estates Ltd and Covent Garden Group Ltd v Daziel [2001] EWCA Civ 1277 per Rimer J; McDonald v Fernandez [2003] 4 A11 ER 1033, CA.
149 HHJ Bailey in Bibizadeh v Dodosh.
150 Leadbetter v Marylebone Corporation [No. 1] [1904] 2 KB 893.

3.3   Rectifying an error

Understandably timing will be important for the building owner and any errors within the notices will of course delay the work. The Act makes no explicit provision for the notice to be retrospectively amended, unless of course the parties are willing to agree and rectify the error by way of an amendment to the original notice, or they or their surveyors simply waive (see section 3.4) the irregularity. The surveyors do not have jurisdiction to accept an invalid notice without their appointed owners' consent, because a letter of appointment is only valid following receipt of a valid notice. Bickford-Smith (2017) suggests *'the surveyors ought to give notices a reasonably liberal construction, so as to avoid delay and expense arising from the need to serve notice.'* That is all good and well, when all things are equal, but in the absence of any such expressed agreement between both sets of owners any such liberal interpretation could be used against an owner/surveyor at a later date as grounds to challenge the validity of the notices and/or Award if an owner is unhappy with the outcome.[151]

3.3.1   Timing of notice

Of particular importance is the explicit requirement within the relevant sections for the service of notice, being either one or two-months prior to the commencement of the works. Serving the notice (less than the prescribed time period) before starting works will not satisfy the Act's requirements and/or encourage the adjoining owners to consent. Furthermore, it is overly optimistic to assume that the adjoining owner surveyor is available to complete the procedures and serve an Award in less than the specified time frame.[152] Recording the date and time of service of notice is important when determining when the 14-day period to respond to a notice commences and expires[153] and indeed whether any subsequent notices are required.

The date of expiry of the notice period is not critical once surveyors are appointed. Whilst it is readily accepted that the timetable for service of notice is explicit, it is open to the owners and/or their appointed surveyors with the appropriate authority to vary the timing, waive their rights and the procedures and to continue with any amended time frame that has been agreed.

3.4   Irregularities, acquiescence, and estoppel

---

151 Reeves v Young & Young & Antino [2017] Central London County Court.
152 Sections 1, 3, & 6 of the Act.
153 See Chapter 7, subsection 7.5.

There may be instances[154] where minor mistakes or the actions of the parties and/or irregularities are waived. These shortcomings if overlooked through ignorance or by agreement[155] and or by the surveyor's actions can/may invoke the legal doctrine of *"estoppel"* and/or *"waiver."* In such circumstances the parties will (more accurately should) have a difficult time at a later date claiming that the irregularities can be used to challenge an Award if it goes against them. However, with the Courts there are always exceptions to the established rules such as HHJ Bailey decision on the alleged earlier selection of a third surveyor in the Reeves case.

Estoppel/waiver is a legal principle that can be relied upon as a defence to any belated challenge as expressed in HHJ Marshall judgement[156] which describes the Act's intent as: -

> "The 1996 Act is itself concerned with bringing about a resolution of differences between adjoining owners so as to enable urgent building works to be done. In that context, any points that are to be taken concerning the alleged inadequacies of a notice served by a party are expected to be taken promptly, as soon as they are apparent. It will not therefore take much for a party to be taken to have waived a right to rely upon some deficiency in the notice."

Estoppel/waiver can prevent a challenge where it is alleged that a notice is defective[157] or objecting to the appointment/selection late in the day should generally be rejected. Why? because the initial silence may be deemed as acceptance. Therefore, owners cannot keep what they consider to be an *"ace"* up their sleeve to use at a later date, if something goes against them. The Court should not encourage them to rely on the irregularity as a defence to avoid the consequences of an Award (overlooked by HHJ Bailey in Reeves) or their obligations to comply with the Act, a principle that was upheld in the Sunsaid case[158]: -

> "It seems to me it is far too late now, whether upon the authority which Mr. Ainsworth has referred to in his statement or otherwise, to argue that they can set aside the notice now, or

---

154 Reeves v Young & Young & Antino [2017] Central London County Court.
155 Partridge v Partridge [1894] 1 Ch 351.
156 Manu v Euroview Investments Ltd [2008] 1 EGLR 165.
157 Schmid v Hulls & Athanasou [2016] TCC Central London County Court.
158 Sunsaid Property Company Ltd v Omenaka and Omenaka.

that Mr. Ainsworth is not entitled to his fees because the whole process is invalid. That cannot be done. You cannot blow hot and cold. Where a party is willing to overlook deficiencies in the other party's application, it is to that other party's advantage that they do so, that other party cannot then say when the going gets a bit rough, "Well, that's all right, it's not valid, all the assumptions you have been working under do not apply." That cannot be right and the party asserting that would be estopped from saying that the notice is of no effect whatsoever. It is of effect. It was intended to be and treated as a valid notice and is in law, therefore, a valid notice. Had the point been taken by the other side then it would not have been a valid notice. It is as simple as that. I am not persuaded that there is any invalidity in the award subsequently made".

Providing the surveyors appointment/selection is valid and they have initiated/followed the procedures correctly, their actions should protect the owners from any future allegation of non-compliance. Therefore, attention to detail should be at the forefront of every party wall surveyor's mind, as held in the Rusciani case[159] where HHJ Murfitt held: -

> "During the course of this hearing I struggled to discern any cogent reason why in response to the repeated requests made on behalf of the Claimant[160], the Defendants[161] should have instructed their surveyor not to serve any party wall act notices at all over two and half years, especially in circumstances where they had undertaken work which gave rise to this obligation. I concluded that at least part of the reason is likely to be close to the suggestion advanced by Mr. Antino: namely that the defendants hoped that any work which was undertaken retrospectively to the service of notices would fall out with the power of the surveyors to make Awards, thus leaving only a

---

159 Rusciani v Kumar & Sharma (2013) Chelmsford County Court.
160 Adjoining owner.
161 Building owner.

common law remedy available to any aggrieved
party, who might then be expected to be less
able or inclined to take action or redress, which
in many instances may prove both prohibitively
expensive and slow".

As can be seen from this small selection of cases, Judges will generally follow and apply estoppel. However, there are always exceptions to the case as evidenced by the decision in Reeves where contrary to this established legal principal HHJ Bailey rejected the legal doctrine of waiver/estoppel as a defence.[162] This was despite Counsel[163] for the respondents[164] submission regarding the Part 8 claim brought by Reeves (the Claimant) to determine two discrete points of law. There was very little dispute about the primary facts. Reeves the building owner, appointed Mr. John Westray of Vincent-Brown Associates Ltd, as her surveyor. The adjoining owners being both the First and Second Defendants had appointed Mr. James Gold, also of Vincent-Brown Associates Ltd[165] as their surveyor. Mr. Westray and Mr. Gold subsequently made an Award with the recitals therein recording Mr. Philip Antino as the selected Third Surveyor.

The Parent Award had correctly authorised excavations wholly within the building owner's land. The building owner did not appeal the Award, and excavated and completed their foundations, thus, bringing the notifiable works and the surveyor's jurisdiction to an end. The structure to be built upon the foundations were located approximately 350 mm away from the boundary. It became clear to the building owner that they would not be able to build their extension without access on to the adjoining owner's land. Mr. Westray demanded access[166] onto the adjoining owners land to erect scaffolding and warning that refusal to permit access was a criminal offence.[167] Mr. & Mrs. Young sought guidance from Mr. Gold, although a Mr. Jason Evans, an employee of Vincent-Brown Associates Ltd responded saying that he had spoken with the surveyors and they were satisfied that access was allowable under the Act.

Mr. & Mrs. Young were not content with the response from Mr. Evans and approached Mr. Antino named as the Third Surveyor in the Parent Award. Mr. Antino made an Award the effect that the notices pursuant to section 8 were invalid, therefore Reeves had no right under the Award dated 25/2/16 for access for the purpose of erecting scaffolding.

---

162 Reeves v Young & Young & Antino [2017] Central London County Court.
163 Mr. Richard Power of Lamb Chmabers.
164 Mr. & Mrs Young and Mr. Antino.
165 See Chapter 1, subsection 1.10.
166 See Chapter 9.
167 See Chapter 15.

Astonishingly, Mr. Gold, invited the 1st and 2nd defendants to ignore correspondence from Mr. Antino, and that they should contend that Mr. Antino had no jurisdiction. Reeves was also encouraged by Mr. Gold to contend that Mr. Antino had no jurisdiction, since, according to an email from Mr. Jason Evans dated 15/6/16 (four months after the date of the Parent Award) the surveyors had allegedly discussed selecting Mr. Redler as the third surveyor.

It is to be noted that, having initially encouraged Reeves to ignore Mr. Antino, Mr. Gold eventually agreed with Mr. Antino's Award and later conceded that Reeves could not obtain access for the scaffold. Reeves did not call Mr. Westray, Mr. Gold, Mr. Evans or Mr. Redler, to give evidence and did not seek to rely on any written documents to support the assertion that Mr. Redler was selected in writing. The only evidence was a letter dated 5/8/16 and an email from Mr. Evans dated 15/6/16, which simply referred to a conversation and all dated after the parent Award.

The only selection of a third surveyor in writing is the un-appealed Parent Award naming Mr. Antino as the Third Surveyor. It was submitted that the two surveyors each have been acting as their appointing owner's agent are both **estopped** from denying that Mr. Antino is not the properly selected Third Surveyor. No evidence had been provided to show that Mr. Redler was selected in writing or indeed knew anything about the matter.

Mr Power for the defendants referred HHJ Bailey to Volume 47, paragraph 307 of *Halsbury's Laws of England*: -

> ### *307. Common law estoppel by representation.*
>
> *Where a person has by words or conduct made a clear and unequivocal representation of fact to another, either knowing of its falsehood or with the intention that it should be acted upon, or having conducted himself so that another would, as a reasonable person, understand that a certain representation of fact was intended to be acted upon, and the other person has acted upon such representation and thereby altered his position, an estoppel arises against the party who made the representation, and he is not allowed to state that the fact is otherwise than he represented it to be.*

HHJ Bailey rejected the glaringly obvious facts and established legal principles preferring to accept an alleged and uncorroborated conversation between both Mr. Gold and Mr. Westray was a valid selection under section 10(2) sufficient to confirm Mr. Redler was the selected third surveyor. HHJ Bailey seemed oblivious to the explicit intent of section 10(2) and or indeed what would constitute a valid selection in writing. Further HHJ Bailey ignored the principles of waiver and estoppel, where the Parent Award naming Mr. Antino as the third surveyor had not been appealed, and used to facilitate the notifiable works.

3.5   Promissory estoppel

Promissory estoppel is a legal principle that a promise is enforceable by law when the promisor (person making the promise) makes a promise to the promisee (person being promised) who relies on it but to their detriment. For example, a person promises to pay 'x' £100.00 if 'x' lets them put scaffolding on 'x' land, but does not pay. The detriment is the nuisance caused by the scaffold. A promissory estoppel is intended to stop the promisor from denying that the statements, words or even conduct did not happen or were not agreed. Therefore, promissory estoppel will allow a party to recover their loss arising out of the promise where a party acts in bad faith.[168] It prevents, or estops, a person from arguing that the promise should not be upheld. In order to invoke a promissory estoppel, three elements must be present: the promisor, the promisee and a substantial detriment – i.e., an economic loss that occurs to the promisee if the promisor declines to honour the promise.

So where does this legal doctrine intercede with the application of the Act? It would apply where the adjoining owners have consented to the works. The consent having been given on the basis that it is implied that there will be no deviation away from the works described in the notices and/or drawings. In a recent case[169] the building owners (Rupra & Sohanpal) caused damage and indeed carried out further notifiable works without service of additional notices and in doing so trespassed onto the defendant's property which caused further damage. The damage and deviation away from the agreed notices were not a condition of the consent and therefore created a dispute. The Humbles' appointed a surveyor[170] and the building owners refused to engage with the Act, a surveyor was appointed on their behalf.[171] An Award was served, and subsequently an appeal was filed by the building owners Counsel[172] on the grounds that there was no dispute between the building owners. In their indecent haste solicitors acting for the building owners failed to include the surveyors within the section 10(17) appeal procedures[173] and therefore the appeal was technically out of time. Following a CMC[174] the appeal was

---

168 See Chapter 2, section 2.11.
169 Rupra & Sohanpal v Humble & Humble (2020) TCC unreported.
170 Mr. P. Antino.
171 See Chapter 11 subsection 11.5
172 Mr. N Isaac Q.C.
173 See Chapter 11, subsection 11,17.
174 Case Management Conference before HH J Parfitt TCC.

compromised[175] and the parties resulted to common law remedies. Notwithstanding the fact that the claimants had clearly breached their promise not to cause damage, the defendants were entitled to rely upon that promise and to revert to the Act.[176]

3.6   Method of Service

It is somewhat surprising, given the importance of service of notice that the Act refers to this process in section 15- miscellaneous (service of notices etc). The process of validly serving the notice cannot or should not be defined as a miscellaneous activity because it triggers the statutory procedures. Putting aside for one moment the fact that the notices themselves may be valid, if the notice has not been served in accordance with section 15, it is invalid. Section 15 is therefore an important element of the process.

The method of service extends to two subsections and appears relatively free of ambiguity. Regrettably, following these methods to the letter of the law has not always been recognised by the Courts.[177]   In one case it was alleged that the service of the Award at the last and/only known address of the building owners was not in compliance with section 15(1)(b) and they appealed the Award claiming they had not received the Award. The adjoining owner was clearly intimidated by the prospect of an appeal and the parties agreed to mediate which failed and ultimately brought the parties full circle to litigation several years later.[178]

Not all properties are in single ownership, it is therefore important that the owner and/or their surveyor ensures that all of the building owners are named in the notice.[179] However, it is not always possible to obtain the name of the owner or indeed their current place of residence. The property may be let to tenants and managed through an agent. The Agent may refuse to give out information under GDPR. If the notices are served at the premises, tenants being tenants will not necessarily rush to forward any post to the landlord and/or in most instances the tenants will not know the landlord. The property may be owned by a large organisation such as a Housing Association, or Local Authority and identifying the correct person and address on whom the notice should be served upon can be a frustrating and time-consuming process. Parliament recognised this predicament and specifically incorporated

---

175 Onigbanjo, A. v Mr. & Mrs Pearson [2008].
176 HHJ Parfitt indicated that the failure to serve the surveyors with the appeal was of no relevance.
177 Mohamed & Mohamed v Takhar, Takhar, & Takhar [2016] Central London County Court.
178 Mohamed & Lahrie v Takhar & Takhar & Takhar (2021) in the County Court of Central London TCC G20CL122
179 Lehmann v Herman [1993] 1 EGLR 172.

alternatives within the section 15 process to prevent delays and obstacles when all of the information is not readily available. Service on an adjoining property can be addressed to the owners. However, if their identity is known, it would be a sensible precaution to include all their names in the notices.

3.6.1   Section 15(1) (a) (b) & (c)

A notice or other document required or authorised to be served under this Act may be served on a person-

    (a)   by delivering it to him in person;

    (b)   by sending it by post to him at his usual or last known residence or place of business in the United Kingdom; or

    (c)   in the case of a body corporate, by delivering it to the secretary or clerk of that body corporate at that office.

3.6.2   Section 15(2) (a) & (b)

In the case of a notice or other document required or authorised to be served under this Act on a person as owner of premises, it may alternatively be served by-

    (a)   addressing it "the owner" of the premises (naming them), and

    (b)   delivering it to a person on the premises or, if no person to whom it can be delivered is found there, fixing it to a conspicuous part of the premises.

The three criteria set out in subsection (1) (a) – (c) are explicit and readily understandable, although compliance with subsection (1) (a) and 2(b) will only be achieved if the notice is physically passed to the person named therein. When adopting (2) (b) fixing the notice in an obvious location on part of the premises[180] is advisable and taking photographic evidence with the date and time stamp printed will assist in demonstrating service has been affected.

Compliance with subsection (1) (b) & (c) in the course of normal post is deemed to have been delivered 48-hours after posting.[181] It is recommended that certificates of posting ("COP") are obtained, although it does not necessarily follow that all Judges[182] will recognise the validity of a COP. In the alternative, compliance can be achieved if there is a written authority from an

---

180 as adopted in Rupra & Sohanpal v Humble & Humble.
181 CPR Part 6 R.6.26.
182 HHJ Bailey in Mohamed v Takhar and Mills v Sell and Mills & Mills v Sell & Sell [2016] Central London County Court.

owner that allows an agent to accept service.[183] It is now common practice for surveyor's letters of appointment[184] to include a statement that allows them to receive and serve notices by electronic means.[185] This will expedite the process especially where for example appointing owners are out of the country.

Section 7 of the Interpretation Act 1978, helpfully sets out the basis on which a party can rely upon service of documents once consigned to the post: -

> "Where an Act authorises or requires any document to be service by post. Served by post (whether the expression "serve" or the expression "give" or "send" or any other expression is used) then, unless the contrary intention appears, the service is deemed to be affected by properly addressing, pre-paying and posting a letter containing the document and, unless the contrary is proved, to have been affected at the time at which the letter would be delivered in the ordinary course of post."

Notwithstanding, compliance with subsection 1 (b) has proved to be difficult.[186] In one case the last letter on the postcode[187] was incorrect, surprisingly, HHJ Bailey held the notice to have been validly served. In Mohammed v Takhar, an Award was served at the last known and importantly the only address given for the Mohammed's. and stated clearly on the Mohammed's surveyors' letter of appointment. The Mohammed's on their counsel's advice applied for a declaration of invalidity, a similar tactic as adopted in the Mill's case[188] where surprisingly these unrelated owners also claimed they had never received the Award[189] to overcome the 14-day appeal period[190]

3.7   Electronic service

When the Act received Royal Assent, the use of electronic mail as a form of communication was in its infancy, but has now transformed the way in which industry, commerce, professional and personal environments operate. The use of electronic mail for service of documents is not unsurprisingly absent, but has

---

183 Montgomery, Jones & Co v Liebenthal & Co [1898] QB 487.
184 See Appendix I.
185 Appendix II and Chapter 3, subsection 3.7.
186 Mills & Mills v Sell & Sell [2016] Central London County Court and Mohamed & Mohamed v Antino & Stevens [2019] Central London County Court.
187 Dodosh v Bibizadeh & Bibizadeh [2015] Central London County Court.
188 Mr. Stuart Frame.
189 Mr. Nicholas Isaac Q.C.
190 See Chapter 10, subsection 10.14.2.

recently been adjusted[191] to reflect current practice, subject to specific criteria being satisfied. The benefits of electronic communications facilitate the transfer of large documents efficiently, and with the introduction of iPhones, tablets etc providing instant access, allows the downloading of data anywhere within the world at any time the day. Where email has been adopted by the surveyors and their appointing owners, (absent of any explicit agreement to use electronic communications as a means of service and/or exchange of documentation) it would reasonably follow that the use of electronic communications was by implication agreed. However, as with all matters securing an agreement in writing is the most appropriate way forward to avoid any later challenges.

---

191 See Appendix II, The Party Wall etc. Act 1996 (Electronic Communications) Order 2016.

CHAPTER 4

4.0   SECTION 1: - Construction and Repairs of a Wall on the Line of Junction

4.1   Introduction

This is the first of the three areas of notifiable works that establishes the surveyor's jurisdiction and relates to the construction, maintenance and/or repair of a wall on or astride the line of junction, where in some instances there is a need to have access onto the adjoining owner's land. Historically, these types of works have created difficulties when a neighbour refused access on to their land. These difficulties were rectified with the introduction of The Access to Neighbouring Lands Act 1992 ("ANLA") albeit, the right of access being limited to works of repair and maintenance with access for new works excluded provided some assistance and indeed still does, when the ANAL is properly adhered to.[192] Section 1 removes this last obstacle with the introduction of the substantive provisions under section 1(5), subject to one condition in that the new wall must be built on the line of junction.[193]

Etherton, L. J.[194] described the Act as rational: -

> "The Act provides procedures...... for authorising property owners to carry out works to an existing party structure or otherwise on or near to the boundary of the adjoining property, but which at the same time protect the legitimate interests of the adjoining owner."

The majority of neighbours live in relative peace until a notice is served and then a dispute arises. If a dispute arises over the precise location of the line of junction, it is in the interest of the building owner to resolve any boundary (line of junction) dispute as soon as practically possible. Few disputes will raise passions as strongly as line of junction disputes and the surveyor's ability to establish the position of the line of junction is predicated upon being able to determine whether in the first instance there is an obligation to serve notice

---

192 Bennett v Rowlins and Rowlins [2021] County Court at Brighton (G00BN668)
193 Line of junction can also be the boundary.
194 Blake v Reeves [2009] EWCA Civ 611.

under section 1(5). Therefore, the intent of section 1 must on the literal reading include an implied right for the surveyors to determine the boundary/line of junction to establish the formal procedures that the building owner 'must' adopt, if they intend to either construct a new wall on or across the line of junction or when intending to execute repairs to an existing wall. However, party wall surveyors do not have jurisdiction to determine a boundary under the act.[195]

4.2   Section 1(1)

This section shall have effect where lands of different owners adjoin and –

> *a)   are not built on at the line of junction; or*
> *b)   are built on at the line of junction only to the extent of a boundary wall (not being a party fence wall or to the external wall of a building),*

and either owner is about to build on any part of the line of junction.

The configuration of both the building and adjoining owners land and/or buildings must satisfy the explicit qualifications (a) and (b) to trigger any rights under section 1. If the surveyors and/or indeed the building owner deviate from the procedures (which are fundamental to establishing the building owners' rights) the adjoining owner will be entitled to initiate a common law action for trespass, nuisance and seek damages.

4.3   Section 1(2)

If a building owner desires to build a party wall or party fence wall on the line of junction he shall, at least one month before he intends the building work to start, serve on any adjoining owner a notice which indicates his desire to build and describes the intended wall.

Transparency and early notice are an important element of obtaining the adjoining owner's consent. Therefore, the notice shall[196] include a detailed description of the proposed wall, the type of brick, the proposed height, and accompanied with drawings showing its proposed location will increase the chance of obtaining consent.

---

195 See Chapter 4, subsection 4.6.
196 See Chapter 2, subsection 2.11.

4.4 Section 1(3)

If, having been served with notice described in subsection (2), an adjoining owner serves on the building owner a notice indicating his consent to the building of a party wall or party fence wall-

> *(a)   the wall shall be built half on the land or each of the two owners or in such other position as may be agreed between the two owners; and*
>
> *(b)   the expense of building the wall shall be from time to time defrayed by the two owners in such proportion as has regard to the use made or to be made of the wall by each of them and to the cost of labour and materials prevailing at the time when that use is made by each owner respectively.*

If consent is given for the construction of a wall across the line of junction (See Figure No 2) it does not necessarily follow that a line of junction dispute will not arise. This will be dependent upon the accuracy of the information within the notice and the owners' respective positions. Furthermore, the initial cost of constructing the wall[197] falls upon the building owners. If the adjoining owner's want to use the wall at some time in the future, the building owner is entitled (when the use is made) to request a contribution towards the cost of having built the wall. Future maintenance costs would remain with the building owner unless there is a shared use.

4.5 Section 1(4)

If, having been served with notice described in subsection (2), an adjoining owner does not consent under this subsection to the building of a party wall or party fence wall, the building owner may only build the wall -

> *(a)   at his own expense; and*
> *(b)   as an external wall or a fence wall, as the case may be, placed wholly on his own land, and consent under this subsection is consent by a notice served within the period of fourteen days*

---

197 Including professional fees.

The adjoining owner can withhold consent without being required to provide an explanation and thus, the wall must be built wholly within the building owners' land. The building owner has to respect that decision. Inevitably the construction of a wall on the line of junction will require access on to an adjoining owner's land, even if it is just to point the brickwork to create a neat and tidy finish. In some instances, the degree of access increases substantively when for example scaffolding is required. Unless the building owners can demonstrate that the access is both necessary and related to notifiable work, the adjoining owners can legitimately refuse access. This can create significant difficulties for the building owners and in some instances may prevent the works from proceeding.

4.6   Section 1(5)

If the building owner desires to build on the line of junction a wall placed wholly on his own land he shall, at least one month before he intends the building work to start, serve on any adjoining owner a notice which indicates his desire to build and describes the intended wall.

The determination of the line of junction is a critical element of the section 1(5) process. Before the right to build on the line of junction can proceed the surveyors must either be given clear instructions on the agreed position of the line of junction and/or make a determination where they believe the line of junction exists in order to be satisfied that the proposed (See Figure No 2) wall will be positioned on the line of junction. Ultimately it is for the owners to decide whether they accept the surveyor's decision when interpreting whether or not section 1(5) applies. Common sense would dictate that if the surveyor's jurisdiction did not entitle them to make this determination, then section 1 would become unworkable, since the rights under section 1(4), (5) and (6) depends upon establishing the line of junction. Accordingly, it must follow that the surveyors have jurisdiction to determine limited points of law when they are fundamental to the proper execution of their statutory duty as recognised by HHJ Cowell: -

> "It seems to me that those two points were absolutely fundamental to the matter going ahead at all. It seems to me that an arbitrator, a third surveyor, does have the jurisdiction to decide a matter, even if it is a matter of law, which is fundamental to the question whether

he makes an Award or not. It is possible for an arbitrator to say: "This is a matter of law, it ought to be decided by a Court first, then bring it back to me", but I can see nothing wrong in the arbitrator saying: "I must decide this point because it is fundamental. I will decide it and I will say what my Award should be on one basis or another", and then leave it to the party aggrieved to appeal to determine the point of law".[198]

The unreported decisions of HHJ Michael Rich QC in two cases[199] concerning the statutory jurisdiction of the Leasehold Valuation Tribunal ("LVT") assist with this approach wherein, HHJ Rich QC said: -

"I can see no basis, however, for saying that the LVT lacks jurisdiction to determine any issue not expressly the subject of some other tribunal's exclusive jurisdiction, if determination of that issue is essential to determining whether "a service charge is payable". That is the issue which s.27A gives the LVT jurisdiction to determine. That must include any issue **necessary for or incidental to such determination**." (Emphasis added).

In a 2019 case[200] a third surveyors Award was appealed before HHJ Bailey, on reading the judgement, HHJ Bailey correctly accepted that the third surveyor had jurisdiction to determine the boundary for the purposes of concluding the party wall procedures.

Therefore, the general principle is that surveyors do have jurisdiction to determine secondary issues if they are essential to the primary issue. Interestingly, no criticism as to the surveyor's jurisdiction was raised in the grounds of appeal. In relation to section 1(5) a determination of the line of junction even if it falls within the traditional definition of common legal remedies must be a secondary issue. Indeed, this approach is reinforced by the inclusion of the very board jurisdiction given to surveyors to deal with 'any

198 Loost v Kremer [1997] West London County Court.
199 Canary Riverside PTE Ltd v Dr & Mrs Schilling LTL 8/6/2006 and Continental Property Ventures Inc -v- Mr. & Mrs White, LTL 21/3/2006.
200 Lacy v Baker (2019) County Court Central London D20CL111 & E20CL228.

matter that is incidental to' 'or arising out of the notifiable works'[201] ergo if the line of junction is in dispute the surveyors also have jurisdiction to make a determination.

Notwithstanding, the owners do not have to agree with the surveyor's determination and before an Award is served, any dispute could be referred to the third surveyor[202] or after the Award is served, through the appeals procedure.[203] The surveyors are not required to wait for a legal determination (unless legal proceedings have been commenced) because they have a statutory duty to bring the party wall procedures to the natural conclusion as soon as is reasonably possible.

4.6.1   What does 'on' mean

Surveyors have to be live to the fact that the inclusion of certain words are intended to have specific meanings and intentions. In the context of section 1 (5), Parliament's inclusion of the word 'on' was intended to have an explicit meaning (See Figure No 9). In order to interpret any statutory instrument, there has to be an understanding of the ordinary meaning and application of the English language.

---

201 See Chapter 11, subsection 11.12.
202 Chapter 11, subsection 11.11.
203 Chapter 11, subsection 11.17.

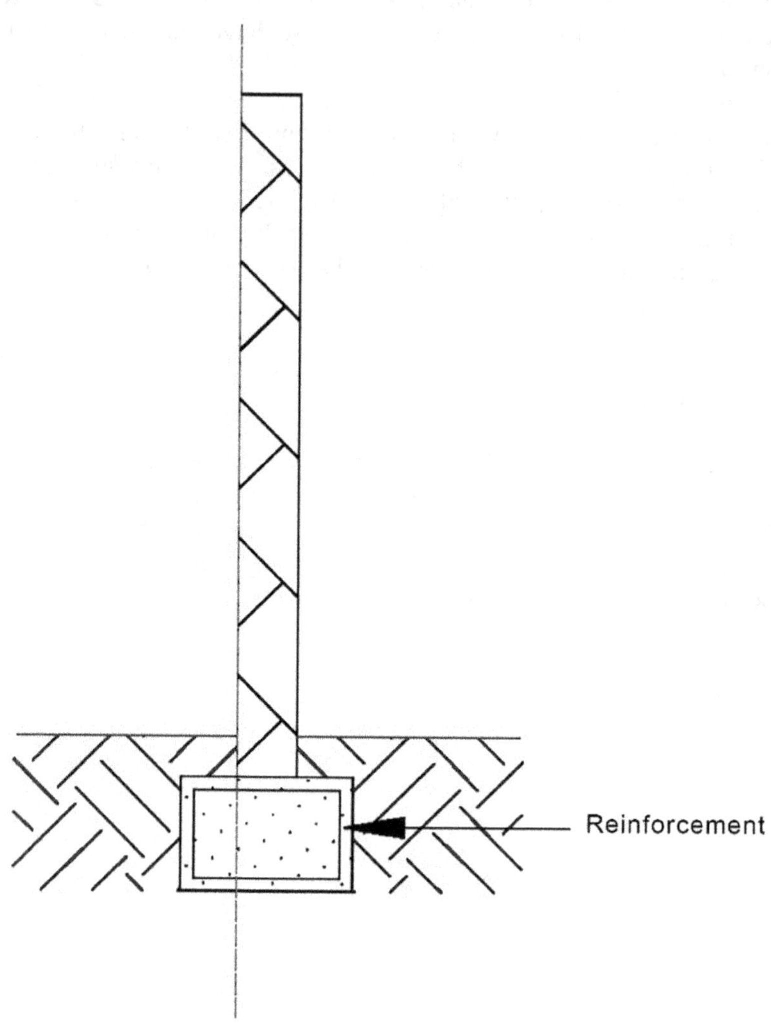

Figure 9 Example of a Wall on a line of Junction

Surveyors cannot (although they often do) introduce their own definitions, which ironically is exactly what I have done[204] although I again emphasise these are my opinions, it is for you the reader to decide to accept or reject them. Any

---

204 See Chapter 2, subsection 2.11.

dispute over the intent and/or meaning of a specific word or phrase will create conflict and fundamental to section 1(5) is the explicit qualification that the proposed wall must be 'on' the line of junction. To make matters a little more complicated section 1(1) defines the line of junction as 'where lands of different owners adjoin' which is not per se necessarily the boundary. Bickford-Smith recognised the contradiction:

> "The application of section 1 has given rise to some difficulty; it contains the self-contradictory concept of a wall which is built **on** the boundary and yet is also placed on the land of one owner".[205]

Hence the importance behind the surveyor's jurisdiction to determine the line of junction. The wording does not include 'near to' or 'in the vicinity of' therefore what does 'on' really mean? If the proposed wall is away from the line of junction for any distance it is clearly not 'on' the line of junction and section 1(5) cannot apply.[206] This can be frustrating for building owners because any rights of access simply fall away. Accordingly, the surveyors must have a clear understanding that 'on' means 'on' before determining whether the proposed works trigger the section 1(5) rights to avoid third surveyor referrals and appeals. Robin Ainsworth attempted to clarify the interpretation of 'on' as follows: -

> "I would suggest that if the courts were asked to define "on" they would apply one of a number of plain and natural meaning (sic) such as "in contact or connection with", "attached to" or "in the immediate vicinity of" These definitions would sit comfortably within both section 1(2) and 1(5) of the Act without causing confusion or absurdity".[207]

The suggestion that 'in contact or connection with' or 'attached to' has limited value and will only satisfy the definition[208] of 'on' at the location of the wall and at the point of contact. If Mr. Ainsworth's definition was adopted, it could /would be extended to include the whole of the wall, which is plainly wrong. Therefore, Mr. Ainsworth's suggestion 'in the immediate vicinity of' does not sit easily within the ordinary meaning of 'on'. If this interpretation was

205 Bickford-Smith, S. and Sydenham, C. 3rd Ed, (2009) "Party Walls Law and Practice", Jordan Publishing Ltd.
206 Davies & Sleep v Wise [2006] Barnet County Court.
207 Ainsworth, R., Differences of Opinion Interpreting Section 1, Structural Survey Vol. 18 No 5 2000 pp. 213-217.
208 Antino, P. 'Using the Party Wall etc. Act 1996 to gain access to a neighbouring property' Emerald Group Publishing Limited, Structural Survey, Journal of Building Pathology and Refurbishment, Vol. 29 issue No 3 2011 pp. 210-220.

applied, it would open the flood gates for surveyors to wrongly determine that a wall any distance away from the line of junction satisfied section 1(5) and created a right of access.[209] In such circumstances the Court could apply the mischief rule, because any reasonably informed independent observer would recognise that if the wall is away from the line of junction for any distance, it will be wholly on the building owners' land and cannot by definition be 'on' the line of junction.

A good example of the confusion flowing from the interpretation of section 1(5) was demonstrated in an appeal[210] where the case turned on whether the third surveyor had properly interpreted the definition of 'on'. Having served notice under section 6 (1) the building owners mistakenly expected to achieve a right of access to build their extension that was close to, but not 'on' the line of junction. A dispute was referred to the third surveyor, who wrongly determined that the proposed works satisfied section 1(5) and awarded the building owner's access. The adjoining owner's appeal was upheld, with HHJ Pearl stating: -

> *A surveyor only has jurisdiction to allow access under section 8(1) of the Act "for the purposes of executing **any work in pursuance of the Act**" 'I emphasise I heard no argument that the respondents[211] require access to the appellants[212] land for any purposes which would fall within any of the limited categories of section 1, 2 or section 6 of the Act'.* (Emphasis added).

This case clearly establishes that the right of access will turn on whether or not the wall is or is not 'on' the line of junction. The Act helpfully sets out limitations and control measures for access within section 8. In Grey v Pearson[213] the Judge demonstrated that the Courts' will where possible, adopt the ordinary meaning to explain the rationale behind the judgment as follows: -

> "The grammatical and ordinary sense of the words is to be adhered to unless that would lead to some absurdity, or some repugnance or inconsistency with the rest of the instrument, in which case the grammatical and ordinary sense of the words may be modified so as to avoid that absurdity or inconsistency, but no further."

---

209 Reeves v Young, Young & Antino [2017] Central London County Court.
210 Davies & Sleep v Wise [2006] Barnet County Court.
211 The building owners.
212 The adjoining owners.
213 Grey v Pearson [1857] 6 HL.C. 61.

Any absurd manipulation of the meaning of 'on' to achieve an unlawful objective would or should be subject to the Court's scrutiny. The Court is unlikely to be driven by semantic niceties to avoid improbable and un-business-like interpretations, when the sensible and business-like one is readily available. But there are always exceptions to the rule.[214]

4.6.2   Getting it right

A third surveyor's Award[215] was appealed, interestingly the grounds did not challenge whether the tribunal's jurisdiction included making a determination on the line of junction, but whether on the historical and factual background/evidence the third surveyor had properly determined the position of the line of junction. In such circumstances the surveyors should be live to the fact that there is a significantly greater chance that an Award determining the line of junction will be appealed. HHJ Bailey[216] renowned for providing lengthy and detailed judgements, does not disappoint with the Lacy v Baker Judgement providing an exceptionally detailed narrative of the factual/historical background within all of the documents to ensure a full investigation, analysis, diagnosis and prognosis of the facts before reaching a decision on the line of junction.

4.6.3 There's a wall on the line of junction?

This is not an unusual scenario, if there is a wall on the line of junction then section 1(5) does not apply. If that wall is being extended laterally then section 1(5) would apply to the extended section of the wall[217]. However, if the existing wall is not suitable for the building owners intended use, for example, it will not comply with current building regulations. The building owner can demolish the whole wall for its full length and width along the line of junction, and then adopt section 1(5) because a new wall is now being built. The whole of the existing wall must be removed, you cannot leave any of the wall in-situ otherwise that is just raising an existing wall and section 1(5) does not apply. Demolish the whole wall, serve a section 1(5) notice and you build a new wall. it really is as straightforward and as simple as that.

4.7   Section 1(6)

---

214 HHJ Bailey in Reeves v Young & Young & Antino County Court in Central London.
215 Lacy v Baker (2019) County Court Central London D20CL111 & E20CL228.
216 Now retired.
217 Not the whole wall.

As with section 1(5) above, there has to be an understanding relating to the ordinary meaning of the English language because the inclusion of the word 'necessary' has a specific meaning and application. The surveyors must determine whether the projecting foundations are necessary for the construction of the wall.   This is fundamental to the jurisdiction to Award section 1(6). If it can be demonstrated that the projecting foundations are not necessary i.e., an alternative design is available the surveyors have no jurisdiction to Award any projecting foundation.

Figure 9 is an alternative foundation design that avoids projecting onto the neighbour's foundation. This alternative design to 'off set' the foundation to the wall requires an increased foundation width allowing the foundation to be positioned on the line of junction and thus avoiding any trespass. The foundations' increased width will counter the eccentric loading and remove any potential rotational movement. This is the correct design which maintains (i) the building owners' right to build on the line of junction, and (ii) the right for limited access. More importantly it removes any projecting foundation and any potential dispute or future issues should the adjoining owner want to build on the line of junction, whereby they do not have to overcome any projecting foundations. Accordingly, the only logical and reasonable conclusion that any party wall surveyor can reach is that it is never 'necessary' to project the foundations of a new wall on to another owner's land and thus in my opinion renders section 1 (6) impotent.

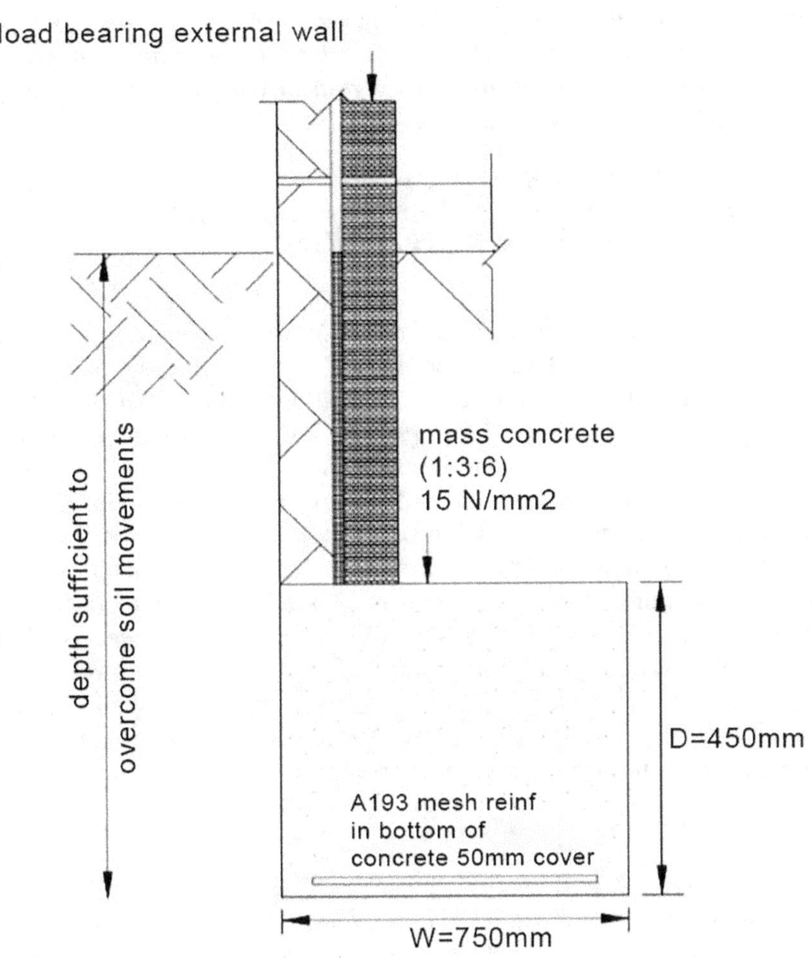

Figure 10 Offset foundation with reinforcing mesh

4.8   Section 1 (7)

Where the building owner builds a wall wholly on his own land in accordance with subsection (4) or (5) he shall do so at his own expense and shall compensate any adjoining owner and any adjoining occupier for any damage to his property occasioned by-

> *(a)   the building of the wall;*
>
> *(b)   the placing of any footings or foundations placed in accordance with subsection (6).*

The broad liability created by section 1 (7) is a continuation of Parliaments recognition that the building owner 'shall'[218] compensate the adjoining owner 'for any damage' if foundations are projected under section 1(6). Let's assume the surveyors have not adopted Figure No 9 and at some time in the future the adjoining owner wanted to build up to the line of junction the projecting foundation will have to be removed. Any cost incurred in removing the projecting foundation and/or additional underpinning of the existing walls foundation would/should fall upon the building owner who projected the foundations because they are costs arising out of the first notifiable works. Therefore, further demonstrating the difficulties created by section 1 (6). The surveyors have jurisdiction to determine (i) the legitimacy of any claim and (ii) the quantum.[219]   The inclusion of the words 'any' and 'shall' have explicit meanings emphasising the importance Parliament place upon the surveyors to ensure the adjoining owners do not suffer any loss.

4.9   Section 1 (8)

Where any dispute arises under this section between the building owner and any adjoining owner or occupier it is to be determined in accordance with section 10.

An adjoining owner cannot object to the building of a wall on the line of junction; however, they can reject a notice under section 1 (2), (3) and (6) to protect their property rights. A common mistake by owners and surveyors is to assume that where the section 1(5) wall requires scaffolding for the construction of that wall, that the scaffolding can also be used for the construction of the roof it cannot. If the scaffolding is to be used for rendering the wall or applying a paint finish or pointing the brickwork that would be captured under section 1(5) and access would be allowable. As soon as the

---

218 See Chapter 2, Section 2.
219 See Chapter 11, subsection 11.12.

wall is finished in accordance with the drawings, any rights of access are extinct and the scaffolding must be removed.

If the building owner requires the scaffolding to facilitate the building of the roof, they would have to enter into a separate licence agreement[220] to retain the scaffolding on the adjoining owners land until the works are completed. The surveyor's jurisdiction is *functus officio* and in such cases, the adjoining owner can (i) refuse and/or (ii) demand compensation for the time scaffold is in place, at a level that they consider reasonable. In these situations, the building owner is vulnerable to a 'ransom strip' approach and substantial costs in order to build his extension.

---

220 See Appendix V.

CHAPTER 5

5.0 SECTIONS 2 & 3: - Repair etc. of party wall: rights of owner

5.1 Introduction - works to the Party Wall

Before an owner is entitled to execute the works as set out within section 2, they must first serve notice in compliance with the Act under section 3(1) and (2). The provisions within sections 3 (1) and (2) are subject to the limitations set out within the 13 subsections under section 2 (2). These define the various elements of works that are subject to notice. However, there is one exception to the rule that avoids the need to serve notice which is set out in section 3(3)(b), which relates to a structure where a dangerous structures notice has been issued.[221]

5.2 Section 3 (1) (a) (b)&(c)

Before exercising any right conferred on him by section 2 a building owner shall serve on any adjoining owner a notice (in this Act referred to as a "party structure notice") stating-

> *(a)   the name and address of the building owner;*
>
> *(b)   the nature and particulars of the proposed work including, in cases where the building owner proposed to construct special foundations, plans, sections and details of construction of the special foundations together with reasonable particulars of the loads to be carried thereby; and*
>
> *(c)   the date on which the proposed work will begin.*

The notice should include such particulars of the proposed works as are known and/or reasonably necessary at the time of preparing the notice. The purpose of a notice is to inform the adjoining owner; therefore, the must include as a minimum the information to satisfy subsections (a)-(c) above.[222] The notice must include the building owner's name, current address, whilst the adjoining owners' can simply be referred to as the owners.[223] Nonetheless, this is the

---

221 See Chapter 5, subsection 5.4.
222 Lehman v Herman [1923] 1 EGLR 172,
223 See Chapter 2, subsection 2.4.

opportunity for the building owners to be transparent and thus hopefully obtain consent, anything less than full disclosure is likely to encourage dissent.

5.3   Section 3 (2) (a)&(b)

A party structure notice shall-

> *(a)   be served at least two months before the date on which the proposed work will begin;*
>
> *(b)   cease to have effect if the work to which it relates-*
>
>> *(i)   has not begun within the period of twelve months beginning with the day on which the notice is served; and*
>>
>> *(ii)   is not prosecuted with due diligence.*

Giving two months' notice prior to the intended commencement date should provide the adjoining owners with sufficient time to allow the party wall surveyors to agree an Award. Section 3(2)(b) is intended to eradicate uncertainty, minimise inconvenience and nuisance caused by the building works or specifically non-performance with finality to the statutory proceedings. However, construction works are not always straightforward, for example, if after commencement of the works, unstable ground conditions are identified requiring redesigning of the foundations, this would suspend the works without creating a failure to prosecute the works with due diligence. The adjoining owners may not be so sympathetic, especially if their property has been laid open. The surveyors would have to make a decision based on the circumstances of each situation and the inconvenience caused when determining any further measures to minimise inconvenience arising from any delay and that would include compensation.[224]

5.4   Section 3(3)(a) &(b)

Nothing in this section shall-

> **(a)   prevent a building owner from exercising with the consent in writing of the adjoining owner's and of the adjoining occupiers any right conferred on him by section 2; or**

---

224 See Chapter 8.

<blockquote>

(b)   **require a building owner to serve any party structure notice before complying with any notice served under statutory provisions relating to dangerous or neglected structures.**

</blockquote>

Section 3(3)(a) is self-explanatory and intended to prevent the adjoining owner's from changing their mind at the last minute and withdrawing consent, once given it cannot be rescinded.[225] However, the consent is limited to the works stated within the notices.[226] If significant deviations[227] to the original notifiable works arise a fresh notice must be served, because an owner cannot have consented to something that was not disclosed.

Section 3(3)(b) removes the obligation to serve notice if the works are to stabilise or remove a dangerous structure. Independent surveyors or engineers can express an opinion that a structure is in a dangerous condition, but they must refer it to the Local Authority Building Control who will investigate and issue the dangerous structure notice ("DSN"). The building owners can then execute emergency works necessary to render the structure safe. This could include erecting temporary supports or partial demolition. It is the responsibility of the Local Authority Building Control Service to issue a DSN and to take the necessary and reasonable enforcement proceedings to ensure the safety of any occupants or passers-by. The process is relatively straightforward, a senior building control inspector will inspect on all reported cases and assess the merits when assessing the degree of danger on the following basis: -

- If the property/structure is considered to be in danger of collapse, DSN will be served, giving the building owner reasonable time to respond with their proposed remedial works;
- Where minor defects are reported the council will carry out an inspection and offer informal advice on the best way of rectifying the problem to avoid a DSN;
- Before issuing a DSN the Council they will make every effort to contact the building owners, if this is not possible, a card will be left at the premises indicating what action has/or will have to be taken and who should be contacted for further advice; and
- Where necessary the danger will be removed immediately by the Council's appointed specialist contractor under the close supervision of an experienced senior building control officer.

---

225 See Chapter 11, subsection 11.3.
226 See Chapter 5, subsection 5.2.
227 Schmid v Hulls & Athanasou [2016] TCC Central London County Court.

A DSN can be issued on any element of a building or structure that may be considered to be a threat to safety to avoid danger to occupants and/or members of the public such as: -

- Loose or falling roof tiles;
- Failed roofs, distorted walls and/or fences that are in danger of collapse; and
- Unstable chimneys.

Once the danger is abated or stabilised, the works to rebuild or repair the dangerous structure would still require notice.

5.5   Section 2(1)   Party Fence wall, Party Wall, External wall of a building

This section applies where lands of different owners adjoin and at the line of junction the said lands are built on or a boundary wall, being a party fence wall or the external wall of a building, has been erected.

Section 2(1) introduces the elements of a building that are captured by the Act. Accordingly, it falls upon the surveyor to properly advise upon the correct subsections within the notice. The building owners notice must set out[228] which of the 13 subsections[229] are applicable. It is not acceptable to state all "works pursuant to section 2(2) as a 'catch all' approach.[230] Not only is this likely to encourage dissent, it is a failure to be transparent. It is important to remember that the purpose of the notice is to ensure the adjoining owners are able to make an informed decision on whether they will consent or dissent.

5.6   Section 2(2) subsections

The Act recognises two types of party wall, and introducing 13 subsections 2(2)(a)(b)(c)(d)(e)(f)(g)(h)(j) which apply to a type a or b party wall.

5.6.1   (a) Underpin, thicken or raise -

---

228 Hobbs, Hart & Co v Grover [1899] No. 1 Ch 11.
229 subsections 2(2)(a)(b)(c)(d)(e)(f)(g)(h)(j)(k)(l)(m)(n).
230 Unless they actually do arise within the project.

to underpin, thicken or raise a party structure, a party fence wall, or an external wall which belongs to the building owner and is built against a party structure fence wall;

Underpinning a party wall/structure or an external wall on the line of junction is a common occurrence for various reasons. The most common cause is a failed foundation (caused by subsidence). Whilst the right to undertake excavations for new builds are subject to notice under section 6(1), section 2(2)(a) triggers the right to underpin and therefore removes the obligation to serve a separate section 6(1) notice.

The right to underpin is also permitted under the Access to Neighbouring Lands Act 1992 ("ANAL") if the underpinning is a method of repair/maintenance of the foundations. However, to avoid any subsequent challenges, it is advisable to also serve a section 6(1) notice, because there are certain barristers/surveyors who would argue that not to do so would invalidate the right to do the works. If the underpinning incorporates reinforcement, it creates a special foundation and written consent[231] is required.

However, given that underpinning is a failed foundation beneath a party wall and benefits both owners, the section 7(4) veto should not become an issue. The cost of underpinning a failed party wall foundation shall be determined[232] by the surveyors and generally apportioned equally between the owners or their respective insurers because of the shared liabilities and benefits as tenants in common arising out of their respective use and ownership of the wall.

If the underpinning is required because of the building owner's intention to increase the structural capacity of the party wall[233] any costs associated with underpinning or rebuilding the party wall in part or full will most certainly remain with the building owner, irrespective of the fact that both owners continue to use the original full width and height of the existing wall.[234]

The adjoining owner cannot limit the right to raise the wall to the centre of the wall, because the owners are 'tenants in common'.[235] However, there is no obligation to raise the party structure wall for its full width, as long as the raised section of wall complies with the relevant statutory provisions and building regulations the raised section of wall can be less than its full width. This is often the case when constructing dormer windows that are positioned on the party wall. If the proposed raised section of wall has to be wider than the existing party walls width, then the increased width can only project into the building owner's side to avoid a trespass. When raising the party structure wall downwards for a basement, the same principles of preventing a projecting wall

---

231 See Chapter 8, subsection 8.5.
232 See Chapter 11, subsection 11.12 and 11.13.
233 Maddows-v-Fernandez (2020) TCC.
234 Bennett v Harrod's Stores Ltd (1907) The Builder, Dec 7 P.624.
235 Cubitt v Porter (1828) 8BC 256.

or foundation apply, but whether the basement walls only function is as a wall or also a foundation is a complex argument that was substantively researched by the Author.[236]

5.6.2   (b) Various work to the party wall

> **(b)**   *to make good, repair, or demolish and rebuild, a party structure or party fence wall in a case where such work is necessary on account of defect or want of repair of the structure or wall;*

There are no reasonable grounds for an owner to dispute the need to make good, repair, or demolish, and rebuild (if that is the only economical means of repairing the wall) because it will be for the benefit of all the owners. Notwithstanding, if an owner can establish for example that a right of support[237] exists for the enclosed parts of the wall is dependent upon the structural stability of the unenclosed sections of wall, then the scope of works can be extended beyond those limited to the party wall under.[238] However, it does not necessarily follow those costs are payable by an adjoining owner. In Sachs v Jones[239] one house suffered subsidence dragging the other over, the adjoining owners claim for damages failed because there was no obligation on Jones to keep his house in good repair and had done nothing to cause the damage. For example, if it had been proven that the subsidence had been caused by Jones tree roots then a claim would/may have been upheld as the roots created a trespass and a nuisance which is actionable as a tort.

5.6.3   (c) Partitions

To demolish a partition which separates buildings belonging to different owners but does not conform with statutory requirements and to build instead a party wall which does so conform;

This is one of the many frustrating nuances within the Act, because the introduction of the term "partition"[240] is unnecessary. Why? Any wall that separates parts of a building belonging to different owners must by definition be either be a type (a) or (b) party wall. The suggestion that it should be re-built as a party wall is erroneous because it is already by definition a party wall. Furthermore, the materials used to construct the wall or partition do not dictate

---

236 See Chapter 18.
237 Selby v Whitbread & Co [1917] 1 KB 736 and Chapter 11.
238 See Chapter 10, section 10(12).
239 Sachs v Jones [1925] AER 514.
240 See Chapter 2 Definitions.

the status of the wall. The inclusion of "does not confirm with statutory requirements" would cover virtually every partition and indeed party wall because of the continually changing Building Regulations cannot be applied retrospectively, so any works to upgrade the existing partition/party wall unless covered under (2)(b) must be a direct result of new works being executed by the building owner to other parts of his property and therefore, would remain responsible for all of the costs associated with the works.[241]

5.6.4   (d) Connections

In the case of buildings connected by arches or structures over public ways or over passages belonging to other persons, to demolish the whole or part of such buildings, arches or structures which do not conform with statutory requirements and to rebuild them so that they do so conform;

Before the building owner can demolish the whole or part of any building, arch and/or structure of another owner, they will have to demonstrate that they do not comply with building regulations and that creates a significant difficulty. Because they would have to identify which Building Regulations were applicable at the time of construction to be able to demonstrate non-compliance at the time it was constructed. If the building owners desire to demolish the party wall, is a direct result of new works and not repair the building owner remains responsible for all of the costs associated with the works.[242]

5.6.5   (e) Reconstruction

To demolish a party structure which is of insufficient strength or height for the purposes of any intended building of the building owner and to rebuild it of sufficient strength or height for the said purposes (including rebuilding to a lesser height or thickness where the rebuilt structure is of sufficient strength and height for the purposes of any adjoining owner).

The surveyor's must be aware of the explicit obligations created under section 2(4)[243] and would have to provide structural calculations to demonstrate that the party wall is structurally unsound for the purposes of any intended reconstruction/alteration or improvement. Demonstrating non-compliance with building regulations will not be sufficient, because a wall can be structurally sound whilst not complying with current building regulations. This section was

---

241 Maddows-v-Fernandez (2020) TCC.
242 Maddows-v-Fernandez (2020) TCC.
243 See Chapter 5, subsection 5.7.2.

wrongly relied upon in a recent case[244] where the notice described the works as follows: -

> "Removal of existing party wall due to poor foundations and structural strength preventing extension of the property, the erection of a new party wall and propping to the adjoining owners' property whilst the wall is removed."

In this case the building owner wanted to build on top of his existing single storey extension, which shared a party wall with the neighbour. The party wall had been used by both owners without any problems for decades and therefore was fit for purpose. However, the foundations and party wall were insufficient to support the increased loads created by the proposed extension. The building owner believed the adjoining owner should share the cost of new foundations and a new party wall and served a demand for a contribution towards the cost. Not unsurprisingly the adjoining owner rejected this request and rightly so. The dispute was referred to the third surveyor who correctly determined that the adjoining owner was not liable to 50% of the costs.

The appeal was before HHJ Parfitt whose judgment summarised that the third surveyor is required to focus on the present state of the disputed wall and whether its condition is satisfactory for its present purpose. Accordingly, if the answer to that question was in the positive then the appellants case that the cost of those works when carried out should be divided under section 2(2)(b) falls away. The appellants[245] submitted that their intention to build an extension on the wall at first floor was irrelevant to the issue of shared costs.

Mr. Isaac argued that the third surveyor's assessment was simply wrong and that the costs should be divided between the owners. On any logical basis or from any aspect of the Act Mr. Isaac's submission is not a rational concept because the need to rebuild was purely to accommodate the building owners desire to increase the height of the party wall and build above the original extension. The party wall was not in disrepair and there was no benefit being gained by the adjoining owners. There was no evidence of disrepair or any historical issues of maintenance and repair raised by the appellants or the fact that the wall was so weak that it required above normal maintenance and repair. The party wall had been and would continue performing its function as originally designed. It was only because the building owner intended to change the dynamics of the wall by increasing its loadings and more importantly (often overlooked by party wall surveyors) changing its 'function' that the party wall and foundations required reconstruction.

---

244 Maddows-v-Fernandez (2020) TCC.
245 Building owner.

If at some time in the future the adjoining owners wanted to construct a similar first floor extension and enclose upon the proposed raised new wall, they would be required to contribute to the cost of the demolition of the original party wall, the new foundations and the construction of the wall as is required under section 2(2)(e).

5.6.6   (f) Penetrating the Wall

To cut into a party structure for any purpose (which may be or include the purpose of inserting a damp proof course);

The surveyor's must be aware of the explicit obligations attached to this section under section 2(5)[246] which provides a very broad remit for the surveyors to authorise any work that involves cutting into the party wall. Notwithstanding, some surveyors consider that certain activities are exempt from notice because the works are *de minimis*.[247] This is misconceived because the Act of cutting into the wall can cause problems irrespective of the purpose and/or depth of the cutting into the wall. For example; cutting into the wall to insert a conduit or cable is a small (in construction terms) activity but it can still cause substantial damage to the other side of the wall and/or interfere with the materials that create the walls' function.   This argument is often adopted where for example an owner wants to cut away the plaster.

HHJ Forbes QC[248] held: -

> "Plaster has often been considered a separate
> entity from the physical masonry/block work
> that forms the party wall/structure and therefore
> not subject to notice under this section"

I cannot accept this very broad definition of the function of plaster, the surveyor must satisfy themselves that they fully understand the existing construction and materials used to create the party wall, before advising their owners whether they should or should not to serve notice. Why? because it does not follow that the plaster's function is limited to be being a decorative finish. It can and indeed often is an integral element of the party wall's function for example contributing to the walls u-value calculations. Another example, is where the plaster or plasterboard[249] contributes to the acoustic or fire resistance capabilities, it is therefore a building regulation requirement, and thus makes it an integral part of the structure and not just a decorative finish.   One case

---

246 See Chapter 5, subsection 5.7.3.
247 See Chapter 1, subsection 1.8.
248 Irvine -v- Moran [1991] 1 EGLR 261.
249 15 mm Gyproc fire and/or 15 mm Gyproc sound bloc plaster board.

although related to a Landlord and Tenant matter assists in clarifying the issue, Rimmer LJ held: -

> "Plaster work is generally as being ordinarily in the nature of a smooth construction finish, to which decorations can then be applied rather than a decorative finish itself".[250]

Rimmer L.J. in reaching his decision considered that the function of plaster went beyond HHJ Forbes definition, and this should also be at the forefront of the surveyor's assessment when considering whether notice should be served for certain works.

The following is a sample of various incorrect surveyors' advice to owners on whether to serve notice: -

(i)   "Drilling into the party wall/structure is exempt because "to **cut** into a party structure" is not the same as drilling"

(ii)   "Chasing into the party wall/structure to insert cables or conduits is de minimus works which does not require notice"

(iii)   "Inserting a chemical DPC into the wall is achieved by drilling and therefore does not require notice".

In relation to (i) a 'drill bit' cuts, in a circular motion and therefore would satisfy the literal and natural language 'to cut into…' used within the provisions of the Act. The surveyors must consider the explicit inclusion of 'for any purpose'. The example provided within the Act's narrative 'the purpose of inserting a damp-proof course' is not a limitation, therefore cutting into a party structure for inserting 'Helifix' reinforcing bars, or 'beams and pad stones' are all subject to service of notice. Any penetration into the wall in my opinion requires notice, the absence of which renders the works unlawful, especially where the plaster falls within the freeholder's title under a lease.

As for point (ii) there is an ex-council housing estate built in the 1950's in Witham, Essex. The party walls are in some instances single skin brickwork (102.5 mm thickness). It is reasonably foreseeable that cutting into the wall to form a chasing or to remove plaster could affect the adjoining owner's side of the wall more so than if it was a cavity wall or a double skin (225 mm thick wall).

---

250 Grand v Gill [2011] EWHC Civ 554.

Therefore, resolving the obligation of de minimis works is not as clear cut as HHJ Forbes QC would suggest. The consequences of not serving notice under section 2(2)(f) should never be underestimated. In one matter, the adjoining owners served section 6(1) notice for excavations upon the adjoining owner's art gallery in the famous Portobello Road, North London. The adjoining owner arrived one morning to find a large number of their pieces of high value Art having fallen off the party wall had been damaged. On inspection of the building owner's property, it was discovered that they had cut 20 – 30 mm deep 'chasings' into the 225 mm wide party wall. These chasings had been considered de minimis, by the building owners' surveyor who advised that notice was not required. The building owner was subsequently held liable under common for the damage which ran into many thousands of pounds.[251] had they served notice, the surveyors would have recommended that the Art could have been temporarily removed whilst the works were undertaken.

Furthermore, some older buildings may not have a damp-proof course and whilst inserting a DPC may be deemed an improvement, the Act is unclear if the adjoining owners have to contribute towards the costs of improving the wall. In my view if the adjoining owners can demonstrate that their property is not suffering from dampness, they could avoid any liability to pay towards the costs by adopting the same principle held in Maddow's.[252] However, if damp is present, they will obtain a benefit from the new DPC and the surveyors should award the costs equally.

5.6.7 (g) Cutting away from the party wall

To cut away from a party wall, party fence wall, external wall or boundary wall any footing or any projecting chimney breast, jamb or flue, or other projection on or over the land of the building owner in order to erect, raise or underpin any such wall or for any other purpose;

The surveyor's must be aware of the explicit obligations attached to this section under section 2(5).[253] Before exercising any rights under this section, careful consideration must be given to avoid an interference with the walls structural integrity and whether section 9 bites.[254] If the works involve cutting away a projecting footing, it will alter the structural integrity of the existing foundation and interfere with the easement that was created when the projection was created. The building owner will have to consider the cost of alternative works, such as underpinning to ensure 'the right of support' is maintained. Removing

---

251 Six figures in 1998.
252 Maddows-v-Fernandez (2020) TCC.
253 See 5.7.3.
254 See Chapter 9, section 9.2.

chimney breasts, requires an alternative means of support to any remaining breast and/or stack and to prevent rotational movement are required.

5.6.8   (h) Cutting away overhanging projections

To cut away or demolish parts of any wall or building of an adjoining owner over hanging the land of the building owner or overhanging a party wall, to the extent that it is necessary to cut away or demolish parts to enable a vertical wall to be erected or raised against the wall or building of the adjoining owner;

The surveyor's must be aware of and consider the explicit criteria attached to this section under section 2(5)[255] and the implications of section 9 before authorising the cutting away of any part of the adjoining owner's property where it is overhanging the building owner's land. The surveyors must be live to the possibility that they will be authorising an interference with an easement that is prohibited under section 9.[256]   A common issue (see figure 11) arises where an owner's gutters and/or eaves overhangs the boundary, preventing the building owner from building on the line of junction. It would be perverse if the Act prevented an owner from fully exploring and developing the use of their property and a compromise must be achievable. This would flow from the premise that an interference of an easement is allowable, if an alternative design can ensure that there is no detrimental effect upon the adjoining owners property rights' (See Figure No 12) will demonstrate how a building owner can contrary to section 9 alter a projecting gutter facia to allow them to build up to their line.

---

255 Chapter 5, subsection 5.7.3.
256 See Chapter 10.

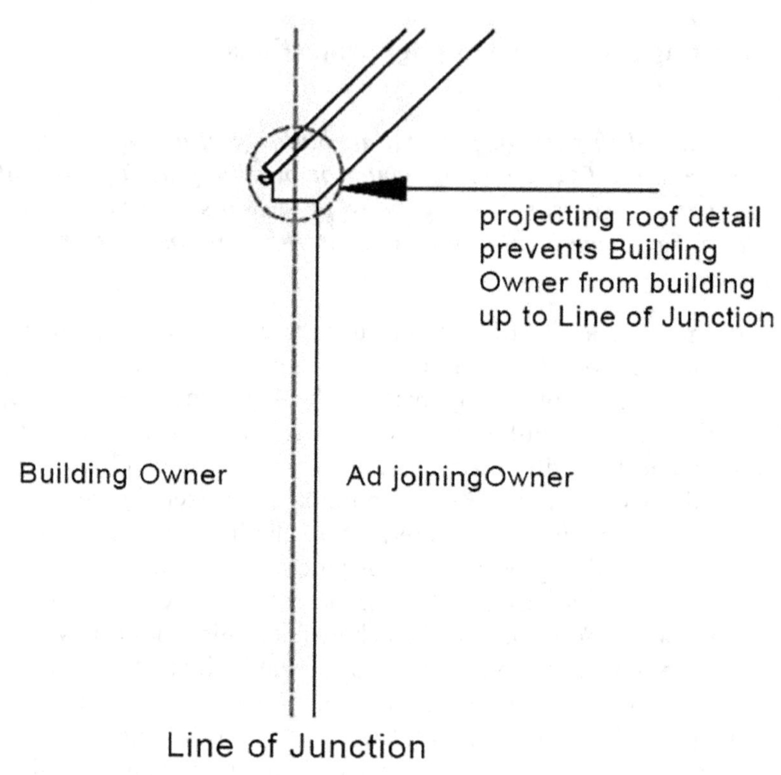

Figure 11 Overhanging projections

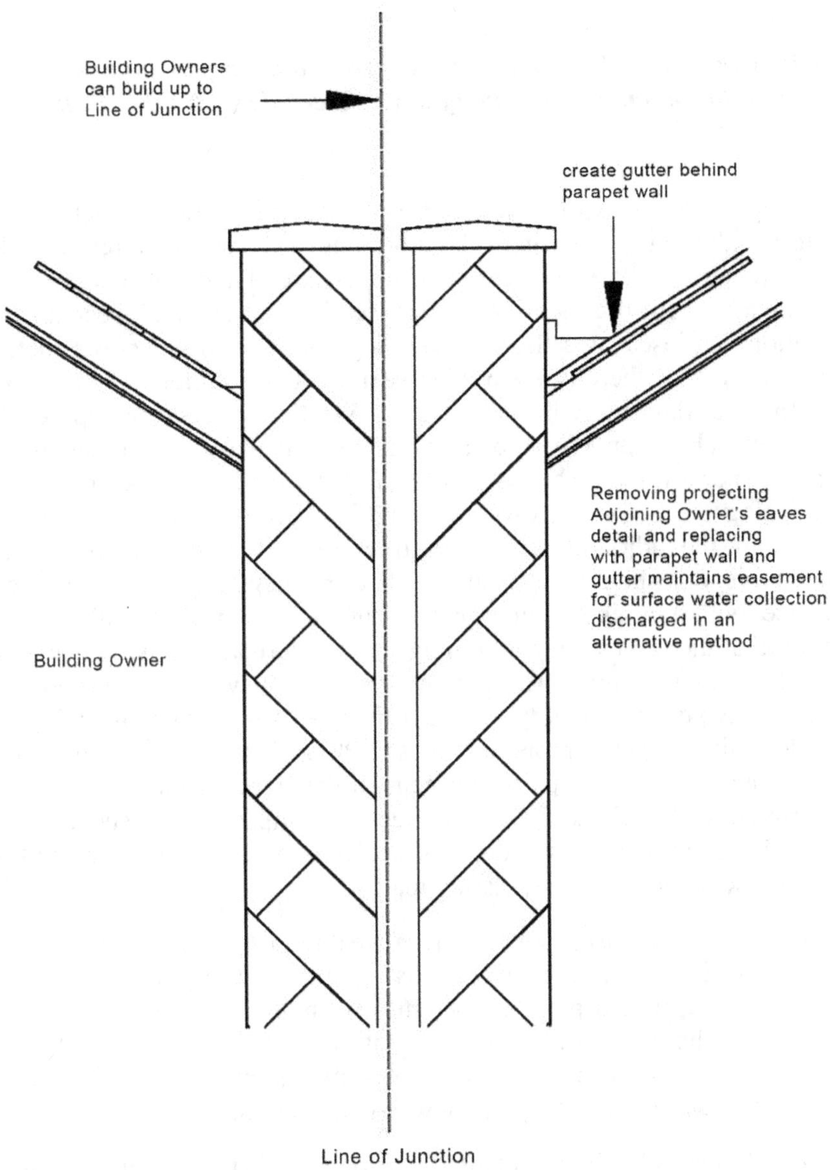

Figure 12 Allowable Alteration to Remove Projecting Eaves/Gutter (Figure 10) Without Breaching Section 9

5.6.9 (j) Weathering between abutting structures

To cut into the wall of an adjoining owner's building in order to insert a flashing or other weather-proofing of a wall erected against that wall;

Building up to the line of junction can create difficulties in achieving an adequate weathering detail where the adjoining owners have already built on the line of junction.   The surveyor's must be aware of and consider the explicit criteria attached to this section under section 2(6)[257] and recognise the qualification that inserting a flashing can only apply where the new structure is 'against the wall. If there is a gap[258] between the two structures the right to cut in and form a flashing will fall away.   Whilst the sensible approach as suggested in subsection (j) is to allow the building owners to cut into the adjoining owner's wall and to insert a flashing subsection (j) does not allow or include lifting the adjoining owners roof tiles, it does not create a right of support from the adjoining owner's structure.   Accordingly, the building owners' surveyors should be ensuring that the new wall is constructed in compliance with building regulations as an external wall to allow for the possibility that the pre-existing adjoining owners' structure may be demolished at some time in the future leaving the proposed new wall exposed to the elements to avoid any liability.   This principle was argued in 1964, when Pears[259] demolition of their property exposed Phipps' flank wall. Phipps sought to recover the cost of the repairs and general damages on the basis that Pears had interfered with Phipps right of protection, Phipps was unsuccessful and appealed, Denning L.J.[260], set out his decision based on the principles of positive and negative easements stating that: -

> "a right to protection from weather, (if it exists)
> is entirely negative. It is a right to stop your
> neighbour pulling down his own house. Seeing
> that it is a negative easement, it must be looked
> at with caution, because the law has been very
> wary of creating any new negative easements".

Denning L.J. was clearly reluctant to recognise that a negative easement had/could be established, simply on the basis that two owners had built independent structures adjacent to each other.   Denning held that any such

---

257 Chapter 5, subsection 5.7.4.
258 Therefore, not on the line of junction.
259 Phipps v Pears [1964] 2 WLR 996.
260 Lord Denning, Master of the Rolls is the most celebrated English judge of the 20th century, for 38 years, and was known as "the people's judge" for his willingness to override precedent to do what he saw as justice and for his simply-worded judgments delivered in a Hampshire burr, Lord Denning's legacy was to leave an unprecedented mark on the development of English law.

precedent would prevent property owners from exercising their right to improve, alter, and/or adjust their property at some time in the future contrary to common law. However, the narrative above should not be confused with the obligation to maintain or provide adequate weathering and/or support to a type 'a' or 'b' party wall, whereby easements and legal precedents also arise.[261]

5.6.10 (k) Additional/supplemental works

To execute any other necessary works incidental to the connection of a party structure with the premises adjoining it;

It is not always possible to identify the full extent of the notifiable works when the notices are prepared. Parliament's inclusion of subsection (k) within the originating notice allows the surveyors to address unforeseen additional works without exposing building owners to delays, although section 10(12) also provides for this eventuality.[262] However, the surveyors must be satisfied that the ancillary works are *"necessary and incidental to"* the originating notifiable works. For example, if notice has been given under (j) additional works under section 2(2)(b) may not be *"incidental to"* the works. If there is no direct link then a fresh notice must be served, which should be relatively straightforward given that surveyors will have already be appointed and a simple exchange of a notice will suffice, with an addendum Award served thereafter.

5.6.11 (l) Change of use

To raise a party fence wall, or to raise such a wall for use as a party wall, and to demolish a party fence wall and rebuild it as a party fence wall or as a party wall;

An owners intended use of their property may change and/or evolve requiring extensive remodelling and the adjoining owners would have limited grounds (if any at all) to challenge those works. However, just because one owner wants to alter/modify it does not follow that they can apportion any of the cost on to the adjoining owner unless they can demonstrate that it is due to disrepair. In a recent case, the building owners[263] attempted to recover half the costs of the proposed works from the adjoining owner. This approach was doomed to

---

261 Selby v Whitbread & Co [1917] 1 KB 736.
262 See Chapter 11, subsection 11.12.
263 Maddow v Fernandez (2020) TCC.

failure because the wall was not in disrepair or unable to perform the very function that it had been performing for decades. The proposed change of use was solely for the building owners' benefit; therefore, costs follow the event.

5.6.12 (m) Demolition and Reconstruction

Subject to the provisions of section 11(7), to reduce, or to demolish and rebuild, a party wall or party fence wall to-

> (i)   *a height of not less than two metres where the wall is not used by an adjoining owner to any greater extent than a boundary wall; or*

> (ii)   *a height currently enclosed upon by the building of an adjoining owner;*

If the adjoining owner has enclosed upon the wall to a height greater than the proposed reduction, the minimum height restriction allowable under (i) is superseded by (ii) because the adjoining owners have established an easement granting a right to the use of the wall for the height of the enclosure which cannot be removed. This is also reinforced by section 9.[264] However, the adjoining owner now becomes liable for the cost of maintaining the section of wall above the 2 m, but only if the building owner is not using or enclosed upon that section of wall.

5.6.13 (n) Exposure

To expose a party wall or party structure hitherto enclosed subject to providing adequate weathering.

If the building owners proposed works expose either temporarily or permanently any part of the party wall, and/or the adjoining owner's property they are at risk of damage and inconvenience. This principle was addressed in Selby[265] following the building owner's demolition of their structure and construction of a new building with the front façade located behind the original position which left an element of the party wall exposed. On completion of the works the adjoining owners raised concerns over (i) the interference with the

---

264 See Chapter 9, subsection 9.2.
265 Selby v Whitbread & Co [1917] 1 KB 736.

right of support enjoyed by both properties and (ii) the exposure of part of the party wall. Whilst the Courts will recognise that an interference of an easement in some instance may be unavoidable, they are allowable contrary to section 9[266] so long as alternative proposals maintain and/or reinstate the adjoining owners' rights, albeit in another manner. The costs of executing these additional works would quite reasonably fall upon the building owners who created the interference with the easement.

5.7   Compensation

5.7.1   Section 2(3) Chimneys and flues

Parliament's intent behind the following sections 2(3), (4), (5), (6), & (7) is to establish the surveyor's jurisdiction to determine the adjoining owner's compensation. The Act's jurisdiction incorporates a very broad spectrum of circumstances but limited to ensuring that the adjoining owner's property is returned to the same condition that existed prior to the commencement of the notifiable works. The adjoining owner is not entitled to obtain a material benefit and cannot unreasonably demand additional or enhanced specification works unless it can be demonstrated that the upgraded works are necessary for compliance with current Building Regulations.

Where work mentioned in paragraph (a) of subsection (2) is not necessary on account of defect or want of repair of the structure or wall concerned, the right falling within that paragraph is exercisable.
(a)   subject to making good all damage occasioned by the work to the adjoining premises or to their internal furnishings and decorations; and
(b)   where the work is to a party structure or external wall, subject to carrying any relevant flues and chimney stacks up to such a height and in such materials as may be agreed between the building owner and the adjoining owner concerned, or in the event of a dispute, determined in accordance with section 10;
and relevant flues and chimney stacks are those which belong to an adjoining owner and either form part of or rest on or against the party structure or external wall.

Unless the building owners proposed works are necessary to rectify a defect or disrepair, the building owner has an explicit obligation to compensate the adjoining owner for any damage occasioned by the works. The inclusion of the word 'furnishings' is important because that will include for example carpets, furniture and/or tiled finishes. This broad definition places a substantial liability

---

266 See Chapter 9.

upon the building owner and more so on the surveyors to ensure the adjoining owners' property is protected.

5.7.2   Section 2(4) Liabilities and obligations

The right falling within subsection (2) (e) is exercisable subject to-
> *(a)   making good all damage occasioned by the work to the adjoining premises or to their internal furnishings and decorations; and*
> *(b)   carrying any relevant flues and chimney stacks up to such a height and in such materials as may be agreed between the building owner and the adjoining owner concerned or, in any event of dispute, determined in accordance with section 10;*
> *and relevant flues and chimney stacks are those which belong to an adjoining owner and either form part of or rest on or against the party structure.*

5.7.3   Section 2(5) Damage (2) (f), (g) or (h)

Any right falling within subsection is exercisable subject to making good all damage occasioned by the work to the adjoining owners' premises or to their internal furnishings and decorations.

5.7.4   Section 2(6) Damage under (2) (j)

The right falling within subsection (2) (j) is exercisable subject to making good all damage occasioned by the work to the wall of the adjoining owner's building.

5.7.5   Section 2(7) (a)&(b) reinstatement/replacement

The right falling within subsection (2)(m) is exercisable subject to-
(a)   Reconstructing any parapet or replacing an existing parapet with another one; or
(b)   Constructing a parapet where one is needed but did not exist before.

This further reinforces the obligation to repair/reinstate any disturbed elements of the adjoining owner's property.

5.8   Section 2 (8) Deemed statutory compliance

For the purposes of this section a building or structure which was erected before the day on which this Act was passed shall be deemed to conform with statutory requirements if it conforms with the statutes regulating buildings or structures on the date on which it was erected.

This section creates an impossible barrier to demonstrating non-compliance with Building Regulations because the surveyors are left with no option but to accept compliance. In any event demonstrating non-compliance with the regulations of a building that is possibly 70 or 80 years (if not more) of age is a difficult if not impossible task, but nonetheless this reinforces the position that as long as the structure is not in disrepair, there is no obligation on the adjoining owner to contribute to the cost of meeting current Building Regulations. This is helpfully reinforced in a recent case.[267]

---

267 Maddows-v-Fernandez (2020) TCC.

CHAPTER 6

6.0   SECTION 6: - Adjacent excavations and construction

6.1   Introduction – Excavations

The reason for notification flows from the common law easement that provides a right of support for owners of adjacent land. Excavations may interfere with existing soil foundations and/or structures when undertaken within specific distances and depths. The Act also recognises that as the depth and distance between the proposed excavation and the adjoining/adjacent land and structures[268] increase, the risk of damage or interference decreases. The Act therefore introduces clear criteria (two triggers) being depth and distance that must be satisfied before requiring the building owner to serve notice. However, the use of the word *"excavation"* is not limited to foundations. It includes excavations for drains, a swimming pool, ponds, patios and/or the reduction of the ground level.[269] Bickford-Smith suggests *"The installation of utilities are carried out by statutory undertakers, since statutory undertakers are not owners they are covered by other legislation."*[270] Whilst this theory has yet to be tested in Court, and may be applicable if the utilities are being positioned within the public highway. What happens if the utility company is installing a new service through private property under a way leave agreement, thus requiring an excavation that satisfies both triggers. It remains an excavation, which the building owner or his agents[271] undertakes and that would require notice.

6.2   Notice of excavations

6.2.1   Section 6(1) (a) & (b) & Section 6(2) (a) & (b)

The section applies where-

---

268 Refer to definitions on structures.
269 Crowley v Rushmore Borough Council [2010] EWHC 2237.
270 Bickford-Smith, S. and Sydenham, C. 3rd Ed, (2009) "Party Walls Law and Practice", Jordan Publishing Ltd, Page 47.
271 Utility companies.

(a)   *a building owner proposes to excavate, or excavate for and erect a building or structure, within a distance of three metres measured horizontally from any part of a building or structure of an adjoining owner; and*

(b)   *any part of the proposed excavation, building or structure will within those three metres extend to a lower level than the level of the bottom of the foundations of the building or structure of the adjoining owner.*

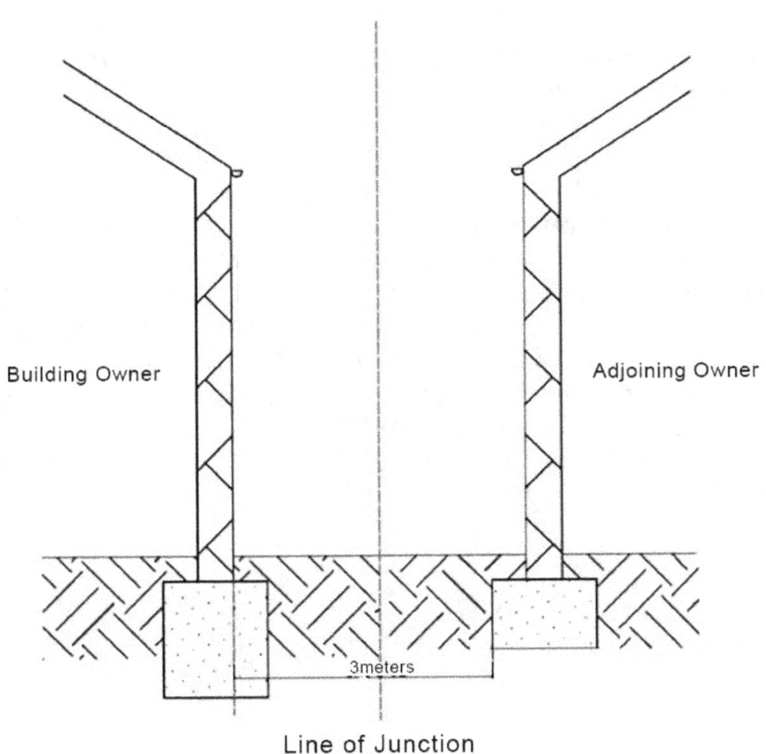

Figure 13 Establishing whether Section 6 (1) applies

Section 6(2)(a) &(b)

This section also applies where-

(a)   a building owner proposes to excavate, or excavate for and erect a building or structure, within a distance of six metres measured horizontally from any part of a building or structure of an adjoining owner; and

(b)   any part of the proposed excavation, building or structure will within those six metres meet a plane drawn downwards in the direction of the excavation, building or structure of the building owner at an angle of forty-five degrees to the horizontal from the line formed by the intersection of the plane of the level of the bottom of the foundations of the building or structure of the adjoining owner with the plane of the external face of the external wall of the building or structure of the adjoining owner.

The obligation to serve notice is defined by two mandatory triggers distance and depth as set out under sections 6 (1) & (2). However, many have tried to avoid their statutory obligations and as recently as 2020[272] a building owner Mr. Patel[273] intended large scale works to convert several family homes into unlicensed houses in multiple occupancy and ignored section 6(1) and (2). It is clear that the Act does not draw any distinction between the intended use of the excavation i.e., to create a foundation or indeed the method of excavating for a specific foundation design. Irrespective of whether the excavation is for a raft foundation, mass trench, or indeed piled foundation, if the two triggers (a) distance and (b) depth are satisfied the obligation to serve notice must be complied with.

---

272 Zaher & Zaher v Patel, [2020] Central London County Court & MacLachlan v Patel, [2020] Central London County Court. (unreported).
273 A residential landlord.

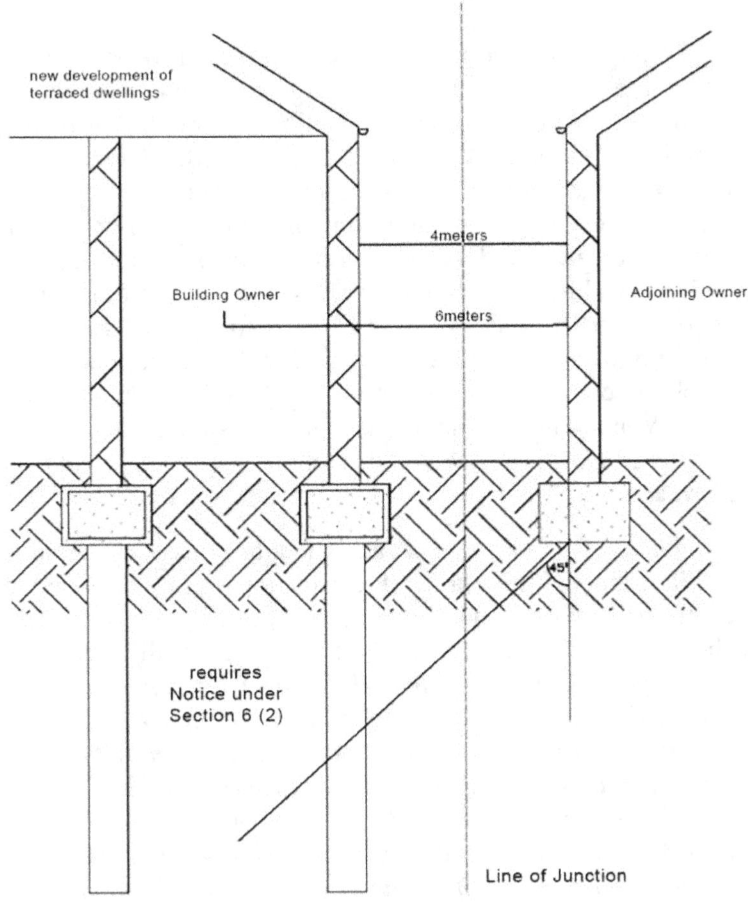

Figure 14 Establishing whether Section 6 (2) applies

Whilst both section 6 (1) & (2) are silent (See Figure Nos 13 & 14) on the method of excavation. It matters not that the excavation hollow is formed by shovel, JCB excavator or indeed by a piling method[274] none of these methods remove the obligation to serve notice.

---

274 Mr. David Mayall of Lamb Chambers.

6.2.3 What qualifies as an excavation?

This is a very important question that clearly needed to be examined in two cases[275] where the use of driven steel lined piled foundations was claimed by Counsel[276] not to be an excavation. The adjoining owners on their surveyor's advice[277] obtained two separate injunctions against Mr. Patel.[278] At the return date hearing Mr. Isaac argued that steel lined driven piles did not create an excavation, because compacting the soil through the driving motion of the piling rig did not create a hollow and therefore was not a notifiable excavation. Mr. Isaac clearly did not understand or recognise that the function of the steel lining was to support the sides of the hollow before it was subsequently filled with the steel reinforcement and concrete. Mr. Mayall argued to the contrary and HHJ Roberts comment in respect of Mr. Isaac's position was "this is all very Alice in Wonderland." The learned Judge rose to consider judgment and during the recess Mr. Isaac settled his client's case in favour of the two adjoining owners.

For the avoidance of doubt an excavation is any process that removes and/or displaces soil. The Latin source of excavation is 'a hollowing out,' from 'excavare', 'to hollow out' and 'cavare', 'to hollow.' A driven pile therefore satisfies the meaning of 'excavation'. This has helpfully been addressed in other publications. *"Thus, it is clear that the section applies even where the **void formed by the excavation is designed to be occupied by a structure**. It is considered that the digging of trenches in connection with repairs to, or installation of, services, is an example of excavation within the first part of the provision"* and continues *"an example of the second part would be the digging of deep excavations in which several levels of basement are intended to be installed as part of a new building"* (Emphasis added).[279]

To assist the reader the following construction methods are used to form piled foundations: -

Solid driven concrete piles: The concrete piles are prefabricated and transported to site and then driven into the ground by displacing the soil without forming a hollow or excavation. Accordingly, in these circumstances an excavation (hollow) is not formed. The act of **driving solid piles or sheet piles** into the ground would be unlikely to be held to constitute an excavation.

---

275 Zaher & Zaher v Patel, [2020] Central London County Court & MacLachlan v Patel, [2020] Central London County Court. (unreported).

276 Mr. N. Isaac Q.C.

277 Mr. Philip Antino BSc (Hons), MSc, MRes, ICIOB, FCABE, MCIArb.

278 See Chapter 19.

279 Bickford-Smith & Sydenham "Party Walls Law and Practice 3rd Edition".

Even though the soil is displaced it is replaced immediately with a solid object without any hollowing of the soil (emphasis added). [280]

Cast in-situ piles: There are two methods for forming a cast in-situ pile.

The first method involves a probe being inserted into and driven through a steel lining to displace the soil through compaction. Thus, creating a hollow[281] which is filled with reinforcement and concrete at a later date. It is important to note that whilst the casing will remain buried it is not part of the structural integrity of the pile, its only function is to form a permanent shuttering to prevent the hollow from collapsing before being filled with concrete and reinforcing.

The second method are 'auger' piles, which drill into the ground whilst simultaneously removing the soil to create a self-supporting hollow and filled with reinforcement and concrete. Ultimately the soil conditions will dictate which method of piling is specified by the structural engineer/piling contractor.

6.2.4   Leasehold Interest & blocks of flats

There is considerable conflict between surveyors on whether notice should be served on individual adjoining owners/occupiers leaseholders and/or just the freeholder of blocks of apartments. In my opinion, if the lease places a liability on the lessee to contribute proportionally towards the maintenance and repair of the external fabric or building as a whole, then they are by definition 'tenants in common' and are adjoining owners. Irrespective of whether their apartment is outside the 3 m or 6 m notifiable distances, their liability is to maintain the whole of the building and are therefore entitled to notice and the protection the Act provides. However, it is not unusual for leaseholders to also own part of the freehold in which case service on the freeholders would satisfy the leasehold interest.

To explain the point further, because the leaseholders are tenants in common and have a liability, they must therefore have common law and statutory rights to protect themselves from being exposed to any third-party interference and/or costs. This approach increases costs for the building owners but they could attempt to limit their exposure by giving certain assurances, security of expenses, bonds to reassure the leaseholders that they are protected from any likely costs or indeed obtain the appropriate insurance to cover any damage caused and subsequent failure by the building owners to meet those liabilities, but this in itself is a complicated and costly process, and requires their consent.

---

280 Bickford-Smith & Sydenham "Party Walls Law and Practice 3rd Edition".
281 adopted in both Zaher and McLaughlan cases.

If the building owner is unable to or simply refuses to pay any compensation the freeholder will turn to all the leaseholders[282] to recover their costs.[283]

6.3 Section 6(3) Preventative measures

The building owner may, and if required by the adjoining owner shall, at his expense underpin or otherwise strengthen or safeguard the foundations of the building or structure of the adjoining owner so far as may be necessary.

The inclusion of the word "may" would indicate that this is optional (not mandatory) and provides the building owners with discretion to decide whether to undertake works to safe guard the adjoining owner's property or not. The adjoining owners' surveyors should consider if it is reasonably foreseeable that damage may arise and suggest reasonable preventative works at the building owner's expense. However, if the adjoining owners insist then it becomes mandatory. The issue is whether the adjoining owners is advised of his right to insist on underpinning works. The cost of these works *'shall'* be borne by the building owner and that is not be open to debate.

6.4 Section 6(4) Definition

Where the buildings or structures of different owners are within the respective distances mentioned in subsections (1) and (2) the owners of those buildings or structures shall be deemed to be adjoining owners for the purposes of this section.

This helpfully establishes who is entitled to receive notice, and self-explanatory.

6.5 Section 6(5) Reasonable notice

In any case where this section applies the building owner shall, at least one month before beginning to excavate, or excavate for and erect a building or structure, serve on the adjoining owner a notice indicating his proposals and

---

282 Block 6 Ashley Gardens Ltd v David Franses, Simon Franses, S Franses Ltd, James Ramsay and the Receiver of Basement Flat, Block 6 Ashley Gardens, Thirleby Road, London, SW1P 1HG (2021) in the First-Tier Tribunal Property Chamber, Residential Property Case No. LON/00BK/LDC/2021/0143.
283 See Chapter 13, subsection 13.2.

stating whether he proposes to underpin or otherwise strengthen or safeguard the foundations of the building or structure of the adjoining owner.

It is not clear why one-months' notice is sufficient when section 3(2)(a) requires two months especially if there is an intention to undertake works to safeguard or strengthen the adjoining owner's property. These will be intrusive and create an inconvenience that could require significant time to assess and determine. The surveyors must be particularly sensitive towards creating any unnecessary nuisance and/or inconvenience.[284] The adjoining owners' concerns should not be dismissed as obstructive, or seeking to delay or frustrate the building owner's works[285], it is simply part of the process to avoid unnecessary inconvenience and protect their property rights. In some circumstances the adjoining owner's may be required to relocate whilst the notifiable works are undertaken and this creates additional logistical as well as financial issues. The surveyors are of course statutorily obliged to resolve these issues within an Award[286] including determining compensation for nuisance and inconvenience. However, if damage arises because the preventative works were refused by the adjoining owners, it would be unreasonable to place any greater burden upon the building owner where they had attempted to mitigate their liability but were prevented from doing so.

6.6 Section 6(6) Drawings, plans and sections

The notice referred to in subsection (5) shall be accompanied by plans and sections showing-

> *(a) the site and depth of any excavation the building owner proposes to make;*
>
> *(b) if he proposes to erect a building or structure, its site.*

This section is often overlooked especially if the notice is prepared by the building owners who do not understand the legal importance of shall[287] creating a mandatory obligation. If drawings are not included, the notices are invalid because the adjoining owners are statutorily entitled to sufficient information to identify the depth and location triggers before making an informed decision.

---

284 See Chapter 8, subsection 8.2.
285 Unless they are blatantly being unreasonable.
286 See Chapter 11, subsection 11.12.
287 See Chapter 2, subsection 2.11.

Transparency will facilitate consent. Non-disclosure will encourage dissent[288]. It would be extremely embarrassing for the party wall surveyor *"Professionals cannot afford to relax their standards"[289]* not to include drawings. In two recent cases[290] an injunction was obtained because, the building owner's surveyor served notices and plans, which showed a proposed mass filled concrete foundation, when in fact the building owner had already commenced (but not completed) driven piled foundations. The surveyor's explanation was to claim the notices were only intended 'to show an intent to do something' and were 'kept intentionally vague'.[291] This approach did not satisfy section 6(6), in fact the surveyors[292] reluctance to be open about the nature of the works was undoubtedly the catalyst for the injunctions.

In a more recent case[293] Dr Antino was the Southwell's' appointed surveyor following an agreement on the Award. Ms Burrows surveyor[294] introduced two additional plans (not seen by Dr Antino) in the Award bundle. The Award was appealed[295] seeking the Courts assistance to remove the two plans and to amend the Award. Burrows conceded the Appeal and a consent order was agreed and costs paid by Burrows. The plans had not been agreed between the surveyors and they should never have been added to the Award.

6.7   Section 6(7) Dissent

If an owner on whom a notice referred to in subsection (5) has been served does not serve a notice indicating his consent to it within the period of fourteen days beginning with the day on which the notice referred to in subsection (5) was served, he shall be deemed to have dissented from the notice and a dispute shall be deemed to have arisen between the parties.

The 14-day period is mandatory and begins on the date of receipt of the notices, (an allowance of two days for postage should be added) before deemed dissent arises.[296] The adjoining owners can reply earlier, but this 14-day period should be built into the building owners time frame for completing party wall procedures. If there is no reply then the building owners must adopt section

---

288 See Chapter 1, subsection 1.10.4

289 Manu v Euroview Investments Ltd [2008] 1 EGLR 165.

290 Zaher & Zaher v Patel (2019) - Central London County Court HHJ Luba QC and MacLachlan v Patel (2019) - Central London County Court HHJ Luba QC.

291 MacLachlan v Patel (2019) - County Court at Central London HHJ Luba (injunction), Zaher & Zaher v Patel (2019) - County Court at Central London HHJ Luba

292 Mr. S Dove MRICS.

293 Southwell & Southwell v Burrows [2021] H20CL102.

294 Mr. Mike Harry.

295 See Chapter 11, subsection 11.17.

296 The Interpretation Act 1978.

10(4)[297] and cannot assume silence is consent, which is exactly what Mr. & Mrs Seekings-Denham did in 2020[298] and were subject to an injunction.

6.8   Section 6(8) (a) & (b) Statutory notice and due diligence

The notice referred to in subsection (5) shall cease to have effect if the work to which the notice relates-

> *(a)   has not begun within the period of twelve months beginning with the day on which the notice was served; and*

> *(b)   is not prosecuted with due diligence.*

The life expectancy of a party wall notice was considered in a 1905[299] case which established the principle that a notice must have a life expectancy. Helpfully, the 1996 Act recognises the importance of finality and addresses this issue by requiring the works to be commenced within 12 months of the date of notice and thereafter to be prosecuted with due diligence.   If it can be demonstrated that the building owner's works have not progressed in accordance with section 6(8)(a) and (b) the notice will be invalid by the passing of time.   However, construction is not always straightforward and if the building owners can provide legitimate reasons for suspending or slow progress of the works the time frame falls away.

6.9   Section 6(9) Amended drawings, plans, and sections

On completion of any work executed in pursuance of this section the building owner shall if so, requested by the adjoining owner supply him with particulars including plans and sections of the work.

This section is often overlooked by surveyors who simply do not advise the adjoining owners of their right to request updated drawings when the notifiable works have changed (limited to drawings relating to the notifiable works), and of course should be drawn to the correct scale, legible and contain accurate information of the completed notifiable works.

---

297 See Chapter 11, section 11.5.
298 Peter J Edmond v Nicholas Bartholomew Denham & Helen Julie Seekings-Denham (2021) H00PE335
299 Leadbetter v Marylebone Corporation [No. 2] [1904] 2 KB 893.

6.10   Section 6(10) Injury and Loss

Nothing in this section shall relieve the building owner from any liability to which he would otherwise be subject for injury to any adjoining owner or any adjoining occupier by reason of work executed by him.

The term 'injury' has broad implications and would include damage to property, financial loss[300] and/or physical injury. The liability created by this section is potentially very wide in its context and reinforces the surveyor's jurisdiction[301] which will include compensation for the injured[302] owner without having to pursue a claim for damages through the Courts.

---

300 Diminution in value.
301 Chapter 11, subsection 11.12 & 11.13.
302 Jones & Lovegrove v Ruth & Ruth [2012] EWHC 1538.

CHAPTER 7

7.0 Sections 4 & 5: - Counter notices and response to notices

7.1   Introduction – Serving a counter notice and responding to a notice

Section 4 entitles the adjoining owners to participate in the design and specification of the party fence wall and/ or a party structure works to protect their rights but only so long as the appointed surveyors advise the adjoining owners of their statutory rights to serve a counter notice. The obligation to advise the adjoining owner's always falls upon the appointed surveyors. The Act anticipates that some adjoining owner's may not be receptive to the works and/or understand what they are required to do upon receipt of notices. In some instances, the adjoining owner may be out of the country and not aware that notices have been served. Whatever the reason it would be plainly unfair to leave the building owner waiting indefinitely for a response. Parliament's inclusion of section 5 is to assist the building owner to move matters forward whilst simultaneously ensuring the adjoining owners' property rights are not overlooked even if they refuse or fail to engage with the procedures.

7.2   Section 4(1)(a) &(b)

An adjoining owner may, having been served with a party structure notice serve on the building owner a notice (in this Act referred to as a "counter notice") setting out-

(a)   in respect of a party fence wall or party structure, a requirement that the building owner build in or on the wall or structure to which the notice relates such chimney copings, breasts, jambs or flues, or such piers or recesses or other like works, as may reasonably be required for the convenience of the adjoining owner.

(b)   in respect of special foundations to which the adjoining owner consents under section 7(4) below, a requirement that the special foundations-

(i)   be placed at a specified greater depth than that proposed by the building owner; or

(ii)   **be constructed of sufficient strength to bear the load to be carried by columns of any intended building of the adjoining owner, or both.**

The adjoining owner's counter notice may specify works that they consider are reasonably required to maintain the structure and integrity of the party structure[303] or party fence wall and/or change the function of the wall to include flues, copings etc. Whilst special foundations remain subject to the adjoining owner's written consent, the adjoining owners can influence their design and specification, in anticipation of any intended future use. Unfortunately, the Act is silent on liability for the additional costs incurred when the building owner's accommodate changes to the specified works. The surveyors would have jurisdiction to determine liability for the reasonable costs[304] under section 10(12)(c). However, the adjoining owners could award liability for the costs a condition of granting the permission to project special foundations. Furthermore, this potential liability for incurring additional costs may persuade the building owners to reconsider projecting foundations.

7.3   Section 4(2)(a) &(b)

A counter notice shall-

(a)   **specify the works required by the notice to be executed and shall be accompanied by plans, sections and particulars of such works; and**

(b)   **be served within the period of one month beginning with the day on which the party structure notice is served.**

Timing is key, miss the one-month period and/or fail to provide adequate information plans[305] etc and the right falls away. An effective counter notice ought to be sufficiently clear and intelligible to allow the building owner's and/or their surveyor to make an informed decision. Therefore, transparency and full disclosure is required.[306] The emphasis is upon the adjoining owners to produce the specification and design for their proposed additional works or

---

303 Selby v Whitbread & Co [1917] 1 KB 736
304 Chapter 12, subsections 12.12, 12.14 and 12.15.
305 Should include specifications and method statements etc.
306 See Chapter 1, subsection 1.10.4.

changes, and it follows that the adjoining owners would be responsible for the additional costs.

7.4   Section 4(3)(a)(b) &(c)

A building owner on whom a counter notice has been served shall comply with the requirements of the counter notice unless the execution of the works required by the counter notice would-

(a)   be injurious to him;
(b)   cause unnecessary inconvenience to him; or
(c)   cause unnecessary delay in the execution of the works pursuant to the party structure notice.

This prevents the adjoining owners from requesting unreasonable and unnecessary works. Deciding whether the counter notice is unreasonable will be a matter for the appointed surveyors to determine, and of course the building owners are entitled to compensation for any additional costs and inconvenience arising out of the counter notice, including delays in completing the works, increased professional fees etc.

7.5   Section 5: - Deemed dispute

If an owner on whom a party structure notice or a counter notice has been served does not serve a notice indicating his consent to it within the period of fourteen days beginning with the day on which the party structure notice or counter notice was served, he shall be deemed to have dissented from the notice and a dispute shall be deemed to have arisen between the parties.

There are many examples where the Courts[307] have determined that the right to do certain works did not arise or a surveyor's jurisdiction was invalid[308] because the procedures were either ignored or incorrectly applied, and thereafter deemed invalid. The Gyle Thompson and subsequent case[309] demonstrates how the Court will forensically examine the surveyor's approach and all relevant documents to determine if they have acted within their statutory jurisdiction. If any deviation from the correct process is identified the Court will uphold an appeal.

---

307 Manu v Euroview Investments Ltd [2008] 1 EGLR 165.
308 Gyle-Thompson v Wall Street (Properties) Ltd 1 WLR 123 [1974] 1 ALL ER 295.
309 Lacy v Baker [2019] TCC

The important point being that the building owner must in order to move forward in the absence of any response to the notice[310] demonstrate that the notices have been validly served before proceeding with any other options.

If an adjoining owner fails to respond within the statutory time limit of 14-days, dissent is deemed to have arisen. In such circumstance the building owners only statutory option is to adopt section 10(4). There is nothing within the Act that prevents the adjoining owners from consenting after the 14-day period even when surveyors have been appointed. The statutory procedures simply cease, the only issue that remains within the surveyor's jurisdiction is the reasonable costs for any work which they have undertaken up to the date of consent. However, there have been some very bizarre attempts by certain counsel to prevent the surveyors from obtaining their fees/costs under the Act, in my opinion regrettably and wrongly assisted by HHJ Bailey[311] but the reader might feel differently.

---

310 See Chapter 3.
311 Mohamed & Mohamed v Antino & Stevens [2017] County Court at Central London.

CHAPTER 8

8.0   Section 7: - Compensation etc

8.1   Introduction

Section 7(1) introduces a mandatory obligation that the building owners work and or conduct[312] shall not cause unnecessary inconvenience. Section 7(2) provides the surveyor's jurisdiction to include awarding compensation to an adjoining owner if such arises[313] and the remedy.[314] However understanding what will constitute unnecessary inconvenience is subjective, it is an unfortunate consequence that construction works will to differing levels create noise, dust and general disruption. Some adjoining owners will view all such activities as a nuisance and inconvenience. However, not all construction activities create an actionable inconvenience and whilst section 7 allows the surveyors to compensate for the potential consequences of the works, they must be able to conclude that some inconvenience is either inevitable or unnecessary before doing so[315].

8.2   Section 7(1) Unnecessary inconvenience

A building owner shall not exercise any right conferred on him by this Act in such a manner or at such time as to cause unnecessary inconvenience to any adjoining owner or to any adjoining occupier.

The adjoining owner or occupiers' personal circumstances will form an integral part of the concept of what can be considered an unnecessary inconvenience. For example, whilst writing the first edition of my book I could hear a cement mixer and pneumatic drills operating within a building site adjacent to my office. The noise made it difficult for me to attend at the telephone, but is that sufficient to deem the works are creating an unnecessary inconvenience. These were normal building activities[316] being undertaken between 10.30 am until approximately 3.30 pm. Adopting a pragmatic approach[317] these activities were

---

312 Jones & Lovegrove v Ruth & Ruth [2011] EWHC Civ 804.

313 Chynoweth, P. (2000) "Unnecessary Inconvenience and compensation within the party wall Legislation" Structural Survey Volume 18 No. 2.

314 Morrow, N.S (1998), "Party Walls Workbook" RIBA Publications, London.

315 Dr Chynoweth's paper is an excellent piece that should be read in conjunction with this chapter.

316 Section 6(1) & (2).

317 Emms v Polya [1973] 227 EG 1659.

not unnecessary and therefore could not create an unnecessary inconvenience. I accept that this is a relatively simple example, but it sets out the core principle that surveyors must consider the activity and its timing when faced with a claim for compensation. The surveyors should be live to the fact that exercising notifiable works does not automatically create an unnecessary inconvenience or an automatic right for compensation. The circumstances surrounding each project and the conduct of the parties will be fact-sensitive. In some instances, where the adjoining owner's may be conducting commercial operations and would prefer that noisy works are undertaken outside of their business hours or at weekends. Conversely, residential owners may prefer that noisy works are undertaken during the week when they are at work and not on a Saturday morning. However, noise is not the only activity that must be considered, working hours, access, vibration, dust, traffic movement,[318] radios, contractors, anti-social behaviour have all been viewed by the Courts as an unnecessary nuisance[319] and indeed the Act includes section 10(12) giving jurisdiction to deal with such issues.

8.2.1   What is an unnecessary inconvenience?

Whilst the law has developed various tests[320] in the absence of any explicit guidance on what is an unnecessary inconvenience the surveyors can find themselves in a difficult situation. Especially where the appointing owner is particularly aggressive, abusive and threatens the appointed surveyor with complaints to their professional body or with physical violence[321] because the surveyor will not succumb to their bidding or they do not agree with the surveyor's opinion and/or determination. However, the surveyors must remain steadfast in their opinion and not waiver or collapse when threatened. A failure to comply with the statutory obligations can inconvenience an adjoining owner and give rise to a claim for compensation[322] which HHJ Parfitt addressed in his judgment awarding a modest amount of £4000.00.

> At para 59;
>
> "I accept the Claimant's evidence in his witness statement and oral evidence supported by his schedules and by the evidence of Mr. Innis and Mr. Koukoulis that the noise nuisance was a regular and disturbing feature of the Claimant's

---

318 Deliveries and parking implications.
319 Jones & Lovegrove v Ruth & Ruth [2012] EWHC 1538 and in the Court of Appeal [2011].
320 Lord Philips test for 'Bias'.
321 Mr Bibizadeh.
322 Nutt v Veda Road Ltd & Podger [2021] County Court at Central London.

Saturday afternoons from June 2020 until October 2020."

And at para 61;
"On the basis of the type of disturbance that the Claimant describes, its nature and frequency over the period and the lack of any justification for those works taking place on Saturday afternoon rather than during normal working hours, I will award £2,000 damages."

8.2.2   Appropriate test

I suggest the following is an appropriate test that surveyors should apply when considering whether an unnecessary inconvenience arises.

"Is there an alternative activity or timing of such activities that can be adopted to ensure the notifiable works can be properly and safely executed whilst removing and/or mitigating any inconvenience caused to the adjoining owner without causing significant cost increases and/or delaying the execution of the works"

The ordinarily reasonably competent surveyor operating with impartiality is required to investigate all claims, assess the works and their execution, and where possible recommend an alternative method of working before proceeding with a compensation claim.[323]   If the building owner rejects the alternative activity, they are not mitigating their liability and become liable to pay compensation to the adjoining owner under section 7(2).

8.3   Section 7(2) Loss and Damage

The building owner shall compensate any adjoining owner and any adjoining occupier for any loss or damage which may result to any of them by reason of any work executed in pursuance of this Act.

Managing the adjoining owners' expectations of what is 'reasonable compensation' is an important aspect of the surveyor's personal and professional skills. Any assessment should be quantifiable, for example, the physical cost of rebuilding a wall. It is suggested by some that any the loss or damage must be directly related to the notifiable works.[324]   In my opinion that

---

323 See Chapter 11, subsection 11.12.
324 See Chapters 4, 5 and 6.

is the starting point, but section 7(2) goes substantively further with the with the words 'any loss or damage'. Section 7(2) together with section 10(12)(c) and 10(13)(c) extends the surveyors jurisdiction beyond the cost of physical rebuilding/repairing of notifiable works. When assessing any loss, the surveyors should apply the common law principal that damages should return the adjoining owner and their property[325] (so far as they are able to) to the same condition/standard as recorded in the schedule of condition.

One approach adopted by myself and another surveyor related to an adjoining owner's commercial activities of manufacturing and servicing laser equipment. The building owner's demolition of their building (outside of the Act) interfered with the adjoining owner's very sensitive laser calibrating equipment. Thus, creating an inconvenience resulting in a threatened common law action of nuisance and interference to their business activities. Given the proposed notifiable piled foundations, there were justified concerns of further interference and nuisance. To avoid litigation, the building and adjoining owners sensibly agreed to be bound by the appointed surveyor's recommendations for removing, limiting and compensating for any loss and damage caused during the initial demolition and assessing the potential compensation for the anticipated inconvenience when the piling foundations etc. began.

This was addressed in the following way: -

(i) The piling vibration would interfere with the adjoining owners' ordinary commercial activities entitling compensation under section 7(2) for 'any loss';

(ii) In determining (i) compensation the surveyors were mindful of the earlier decision[326] where "an adjoining owner had no general right to compensation for loss of trade for work lawfully carried out." Given that piling activities were lawful (albeit noisy) and created vibration, they would not amount to an "unnecessary inconvenience" and was not covered under section 7(1);

(iii) It was recognised that the piling would materially affect the adjoining owner's business if conducted without respite and would trigger both section 7(1) & (2) which would create an unnecessary nuisance.

---

325 Murdoch, J. and Hughes, W. (1993) "Construction contracts: law and Management" E & FN Spon P.333.
326 Adams v Marylebone Borough Council [1907] 2 KB 822.

The development site was within an industrial estate and therefore weekend working did not create any additional issues. As a compromise, the adjoining owners were prepared not to undertake any laser calibrating works on a Friday or Monday, allowing the piled foundations to be undertaken within a 4-day window over a long weekend.

Alternatively, the surveyors are entitled to suggest alternative methods to mitigate inconvenience and liability, (see 8.2 above) by suggesting the building considers alternative designs to minimise or remove the interference/nuisance. Whilst it is imperative, that the party wall surveyors maintain their impartiality and distance themselves from the role of designer, they can make reasonable suggestions for the owners to consider. Unreasonable suggestions will be rejected as considered by HHJ Bailey in paragraphs 64 – 67 [327]: -

> "I share Mr. Winser's concerns. They were, if anything, understated. I would expect the surveyor's profession to be aghast if the Court imposed a duty such as this suggested by Mr. Isaac."

In the Gray v Elite, Mr. Isaac was proposing a bizarre alternative that clearly did not impress HHJ Bailey. Accordingly, alternative schemes should be left to the surveyors/engineers to suggest options but they should be careful not to step into the Architect's role as the designer.

The Gray case should not be confused with situations where there is a complete disregard for the statutory legislation[328] and where the Court will most certainly impose severe sanctions on the building owner. In Jones & Lovegrove, the judgement demonstrated that the claimant only had to prove that the consequence of any harassment was reasonably foreseeable rather than demonstrating a direct causal link. The building owner's failure to serve notice, and subsequent unacceptable behaviour such as deliberately playing radios in the garden at high volume, verbal abuse, failing to keep the adjoining owner's informed of their actions and then building an additional floor annexed onto the adjoining owner's property without consent caused the adjoining owners to suffer psychological injury[329] and financial loss. At the first hearing the building owners counsel successfully argued that they should not be liable for the injury or the consequential loss of the adjoining owner's earnings.

The judgment was appealed and the Court of Appeal clarified the test for damages and held that the conduct of the builders[330] and the defective building

---

327 Gray v Elite Town Management Ltd (2015) TCC Central London County Court.
328 Jones & Lovegrove v Ruth & Ruth [2012] EWHC 1538.
329 From the abuse relating to their sexual orientation.
330 Also the building owners.

works did amount to harassment.[331] This judgment sends a clear warning to all those building owners that do not serve notice and then consequently compound the non-compliance by carrying out the works in such a way to deliberately cause injury. Thankfully, some Judges will not sit idly by when there is such a blatant disregard for the law as can be seen from the value of damages circa £250,000 plus costs awarded against the Ruth & Ruth.

8.4   Section 7(3) Maintaining security and structural stability

Where a building owner in exercising any right conferred on him by this Act lays open any part of the adjoining land or building, he shall at his own expense make and maintain so long as may be necessary a proper hoarding, shoring or fans or temporary construction for the protection of the adjoining land or building and the security of any adjoining occupier.

The specific nature of the works will determine the necessary degree of protection that should be provided. Laying open will include such works as the removal of roof coverings, demolition of a structure exposing the party wall[332] or part thereof, removing fence panels or other parts of the adjoining owner's property for access to execute the works. In such circumstances there can be no doubt the building owners are responsible for the costs of maintaining adequate security (hoardings), temporary coverings, shoring (temporary supports) to protect the adjoining owners' property and land.

Unfortunately, numerous properties have suffered damage as a consequence of building owners works, where the means of support was not insufficient. In some instances, such as the Mohamed v Takhar case the damages caused by additional excavations of a trench circa 60 feet in length and to a depth of 2 – 2.5 m outside of the agreed section 6(1)excavations.[333] This trench had not been included within the original plans and therefore did not comply with section 6(6) of the Act.[334] The surveyors knew nothing about this trench when they made the Award, and these excavations started some 12 months after the Award had been served and works were underway. Therefore, on any simple analysis of the facts, it is correct to conclude that these excavations albeit notifiable were not covered by the original notices or Award and required new notice.

The Mohamed's were asked to serve notice, they refused and pressed ahead. An injunction was sought and it went before HHJ Bailey. At the hearing HHJ Bailey rejected outright any obligation to serve a notice for these additional excavations on the basis that it was covered under the original Award. That

---

331 Protection from Harassment Act 1997.
332 Selby v Whitbread & Co [1917] 1 KB 736.
333 See Chapter 1, sub-section 1.10.4.
334 See Chapter 6, section 6.6.

was simply wrong, because the surveyor's jurisdiction flows from those works stated within the notices, which under the original section 6 (6) plans did not include these excavations. HHJ Bailey gave no consideration to the damage and ongoing potential consequences of this additional excavation within 1 m of the adjoining owners property and refused the injunction. Security of expenses had been agreed at £150,000.00 and the damages exceeded that sum.

A more recent collapse of a multimillion-pound property in Chelsea, West London following substantial internal alterations, remodelling of the property and excavating for a basement[335] is a clear example of how projects can go horribly wrong. The collapse also caused substantial structural damage to two adjoining properties. There had clearly been a failure under section 7(3) to ensure that appropriate methods were in place to maintain the two adjoining properties structural integrity.

There were a number of ways in which this collapse could have been eliminated or mitigated by the party wall surveyors ensuring the works were executed in a sequential programme, The full facts at the time of publication are not fully known.[336] I would suggest as a minimum the works should have been staggered i.e., basement completed before any internal structural alterations were commenced. Retaining as much of the original structural integrity of the building would have minimised any potential movement and collapse, not only to the subject property but the adjoining properties.

8.5   Section 7(4) Special Foundations

Nothing in this Act shall authorise the building owner to place special foundations on land of an adjoining owner without his previous consent in writing.

The obligation to avoid an unnecessary inconvenience under section 7(1) is reinforced by the section 7(4) veto which explicitly prevents special foundations being projected on to the adjoining owner's land without their written consent. Indeed, the case of a reinforced concrete basement box was identified as the singular most common area of conflict amongst the party wall community and the focus of the authors Ph.D. research.[337]

In essence, the issue regarding whether or not a foundation is or is not a special foundation should be relatively straightforward for the ordinarily reasonably competent party wall surveyor, engineer, architect or contractor because the Act is clear and places only one qualification on the definition and that is that if it

---

335 See Chapter 6, subsection 6.6.
336 Because of the ongoing litigation and potential negligence claim against the surveyors, engineers, architects etc.
337 Antino, P. (2021) Interpreting the Party Wall etc. Act 1996 and the Implications of building below ground.

includes an assemblage of beams and/or rods it is a special foundation. However, there has been considerable concern with the interpretation and application of the term "special foundations" when a basement construction is intended. This is addressed fully in chapter 18.

8.6   Section 7(5) Statutory Approvals

Any works executed in pursuance of this Act shall-

(a)   comply with the provisions of statutory requirements; and
(b)   be executed in accordance with such plans, sections and particulars as may be agreed between the owners or in the event of dispute determined in accordance with section 10;

and no deviation shall be made from those plans, sections, and particulars except such as may be agreed between the owners (or surveyors acting on their behalf) or in the event of a dispute determined in accordance with section 10.

Another misconception amongst party wall surveyors is that they do not supervise the works, however the purpose of this section ensures that the surveyors can and in fact should supervise the progress of the notifiable works to ensure the building owner complies with the drawings appended to the Award and where necessary to agree any variations. Whilst the Award includes a clause that requires the works to be carried out in accordance with various statutory legislation such as Building Regulations. It is certainly within the surveyor's jurisdiction[338] to undertake the necessary enquires with the local authority,[339] it is not a case of stepping into the inspectors or contractors' shoes but ensuring that whatever interference with the adjoining owner's proprietary rights arise are in accordance with the Award.

8.6.1   Permitted development

Permitted development rights allow certain works to proceed without requiring planning permission under the Town & Country Planning General Permitted Development Order 1995 (GDPO). There have been conflicting interpretations on whether the GDPO would entitle section 2(2)(a) works. In a recent case,[340] the adjoining owners objected to the raising of the full width of the party wall claiming GDPO rights only applied where the works were wholly within the curtilage of the applicant's property, and where half of the party wall is on the adjoining owners land the works did not fall within the GDPO criteria.

---

338 See Chapter 11, subsection 11.12.
339 Or approved inspectors.
340 Planning Appeal Ref. APP/Q5300/X01/1062324.

Unfortunately, there is no statutory definition for the term *'curtilage'* but it was held[341] "that for one piece of land or building to fall within the curtilage of another, the former must be so intimately associated with the latter as to lead to the conclusion that the former in truth formed part and parcel of the latter."
Therefore, the party wall does by definition have an intimate relationship with both owners and therefore clearly falls within the curtilage of both properties as tenants in common. It was therefore determined that where a type 'a' party wall extends across the boundary, it can for the purposes of the GPDO be considered to have satisfied the permitted development criteria.

8.6.2   Presumed ownership

In the absence of an explicit declaration within the title deed or other legal document that sets out who owns a wall, or circumstances where the wall as built is unknown, the Courts will adopt the legal presumption that the wall is in joint ownership. This presumption flows from the principle that both owners have a common right to the use and enjoyment of the wall. The law will recognise (unless title documents state something to the contrary) that upon the transfer of title each owner has an equal share of the wall. Quite sensible the LPA states that the wall is divided vertically for its full height and length with each owner having reciprocal easements of support and use over the wall.

---

341 Planning Appeal Ref. APP/Q5300/X01/1062324.

CHAPTER 9

9.0   Section 8: - Rights of entry

9.1   Introduction

Certain building works require access on/or through the adjoining owners' property, historically rights of access would have to be negotiated unless the works satisfied the Access to Neighbouring Lands Act 1992 ("ANLA"). This legislation creates limited rights of access for maintenance and repair. However, the Act goes beyond the ANLA, allowing access to execute notifiable works. Any access will inevitably cause inconvenience to the adjoining owners,[342] therefore, the intent of section 8 is to provide a mechanism allowing a building owner that requires access onto the adjoining owners' property without unnecessary inconvenience being caused to the adjoining owner.

9.2   Section 8(1) Lawful access

A building owner, his servants, agents and workmen may during usual working hours enter and remain on any land or premises for the purpose of executing any work in pursuance of this Act and may remove any furniture or fittings or take any other action necessary for that purpose.

The surveyors must remain sensitive to the adjoining owner's concerns and personal circumstances when assessing if the access onto or through an adjoining owner's property will be disruptive and inconvenient and very importantly whether the access is necessary and/or justified and in pursuance of the Act.

Clearly the right of access cannot be used to carry out ancillary works.[343] For example, building a new wall on the line of junction[344] may require scaffolding being placed on the adjoining owner's land. This is allowable but the scaffolding cannot be used to facilitate the roof construction, because the right of access only applies to the notifiable works being the new wall. As soon as the wall is completed, the scaffolding, and all other materials, plant etc. must be removed.

Surveyors should be mindful that where the *foundations* project onto an adjoining owner's property will obviously require access but are they necessary

---

342 Chapter 8, subsection 8.2.
343 non-notifiable works.
344 Chapter 3, subsection 3.5.

works?   If an alternative foundation design can remove the projecting foundations, firstly removing access and secondly any inconvenience.   The surveyors[345] owe a duty of care and should seek clarification to establish if the proposed design is reasonable and necessary. If an alternative design removes the projection, then it is clearly unnecessary. It is irrelevant that the alternative design may be more expensive or difficult to construct. The surveyor's primary duty is to minimise unnecessary inconvenience and nuisance to the adjoining owners. If the building owner requires access for works of repair and maintenance, they can initiate the procedures available under the ANLA, outside of this legislation they would have to negotiate a license.

The Reeves case[346] is a clear example of surveyors incorrectly using the statutory powers to award access. The building owner had served a request for access to build the wall, erect scaffolding and construct the roof to her extension.   The adjoining owners refused and referred the matter to the third surveyor[347] under section 10(8).[348]   The third surveyors Award rejected the request for access on the grounds that (i) the notifiable works were limited to section 6(1), (ii), there were no section 1(5) works. Accordingly, there was no jurisdiction to award access for the construction of the wall and/or the roof to the extension.

9.3   Section 8(2) Forced access

If the premises are closed, the building owner, his agents and workmen may, if accompanied by a constable or other police officer, break open any fences or doors in order to enter the premises.

The appointed surveyors must be satisfied they are acting lawfully if this approach is adopted. Where access is forced, it must naturally follow that the building owners are responsible for (i) reinstating any damage and (ii) maintaining the security of the adjoining owners' property until such time as the access is no longer required. Furthermore, there is an implied obligation that the building owner's use reasonable force simply battering the door down is not reasonable. In Dodosh v Bibizadeh[349] numerous requests for access to inspect notifiable works that had begun unlawfully were rejected.   The adjoining owner had to obtain a Court Order for access under section 8(2) because of the Bibizadeh's having been abusive and aggressive, Mr Antino insisted the police attend to avoid any further abuse and threats.

---

345 Chapter 9.
346 Reeves v Young, Young & Antino [2017] County Court at Central London.
347 Mr. Philip Antino.
348 Chapter 12 subsection 12.10.
349 Dodosh v Bibizadeh & Bibizadeh [2015] Central London County Court.

9.4 Section 8(3)(a) &(b) Access without notice

No land or premises may be entered by any person under subsection (1) unless the building owner serves on the owner and the occupier of the land or premises-

(a)   in case of emergency, such notice of the intention to enter as may be reasonably practicable;
(b)   in any other case, such notice of the intention to enter as complies with subsection (4).

The building owner and/or their surveyors should make absolutely sure that they can demonstrate (i) having served a notice, (ii) the urgency and therefore the reasonableness of such actions otherwise the principles of common law, trespass and injury will apply[350] potentially exposing the building owner to a criminal/common law action.

9.5 Section 8(4) Reasonable notice

Notice complies with this subsection if it is served in a period of not less than fourteen days ending with the day of the proposed entry.

The purpose of serving notice 14 days before the date of access is to forewarn the adjoining owners of the intention to enter onto their land. However, the notice does not guarantee entry, if the adjoining owners can demonstrate that the date of entry is inconvenient, they can prevent access until a more convenient time. There is a view that the 14-day period is unreasonable because it may unnecessarily delay the works but I do not accept that position. All building projects require planning and the works requiring access should be scheduled into the construction programme. The 14-day notice period could easily be identified and therefore is not restrictive if the project managers have performed their duties correctly. It is not unreasonable to expect the building owner's and or his agents to actively communicate the works programme to the appointed surveyors to be able to give appropriate notice and to arrange reasonable access.

9.6 Section 8(5) Surveyors access

A surveyor appointed or selected under section 10 may during usual working hours enter and remain on any land or premises for the purpose of carrying out the object for which he is appointed or selected.

---

350 Jones & Lovegrove v Ruth & Ruth [2012} EWHC 1538 and in the Court of Appeal [2011].

This section is self-explanatory however the obligation to give notice under section 8(4) would apply before attempting access.

9.7   Section 8(6)(a) &(b) Emergency access

No land or premises may be entered by a surveyor under subsection (5) unless the building owner who is a party to the dispute concerned serves on the owner and the occupier of the land or premises-

(a)   in case of emergency, such notice of the intention to enter as may be reasonably practicable;
(b)   in any other case, such notice of the intention to enter as complies with subsection (4).

If the building owners have not served notice of their intent to enter the adjoining owners land, access can be refused. There is no obligation placed upon the adjoining owner's surveyor to serve a notice before requiring access onto the building owner's property. Although the purpose must be reasonable and related to the notifiable works. This allows the adjoining owners' surveyor to inspect[351] certain aspects of the building owner's works and obviously, he/she can only do that if access is afforded. Furthermore, all Awards will/should contain a sub-clause that grants the adjoining owners surveyor access.

9.8   Right to repair

The right to repair is not restricted to access rights under section 8, alternative legislation can assist with access onto the neighbouring owner's land[352] to undertake works of preservation and maintenance such as repairing water courses, property or indeed drainage.[353] These may or may not be notifiable works. The adjoining owner cannot lawfully obstruct or physically prevent access. The Courts will order the removal of any obstruction[354] to facilitate and maintain access. Any access is of course always subject to the principles of reasonable notice and behaviour unless an emergency arises. It is important to note that the dominant owners are not under a duty to repair their property, but if they fail to do so, any escape of water onto the neighbouring owner's land, becomes an actionable tort of trespass and nuisance for any damage and/or loss caused.

---

351 See subsection 8.6.
352 The Access to Neighbouring Lands Act 1992.
353 Duke of Westminster v Guild [1985] 1 Q.B. 688 at 700E   Thurrock Grays & Tilbury Joint Sewage Board v E.J. & W. Goldsmith (1914) 79 J.P.17.
354 Goodhart v Hyett (1884) 25 Ch.D. 182.

CHAPTER 10

10.0   Section 9: - Easements
10.1   Introduction

This section is invariably overlooked either because it contains only one section and is therefore wrongly considered irrelevant and/or the party wall surveyors do not understand the law surrounding easements. Therefore, it is in fact an important area of property law and in the absence of any legal clarification within the Act was correctly raised by Counsel.[355]

> "The relationship between existing easements
> and the operation of the statutes leading up to
> and including the 1996 Act has never been
> comprehensively analysed and understood and
> cannot operate without qualification."

It is impossible to comprehensively address the legal doctrine of easements within a single chapter, suffice to say that those who wish to extend their understanding of this fascinating area of law are referred to the leading authority on easements.[356] However, it is important that party wall surveyors are able to determine (i) whether there are any easements, (ii) whether the proposed works will create an easement, and (iii) whether the proposed works will interfere with an easement. Where the surveyors are unsure, they should take independent legal advice to obtain a full and proper understanding of any potential issues that may arise before serving the Award. This could save time and money and avoid an appeal.

10.2   Section 9 (a)&(b) Interference of easements

Nothing in this Act shall-
(a)   authorise any interference with an easement of light or other easements in or relating to a party wall; or
(b)   prejudicially affect any right of any person to preserve or restore any right of other thing in or connected with a party wall in case of the party wall being pulled down or rebuilt.

On the literal reading of section 9 the narrative plainly removes the surveyor's ability to create an interference with an easement. Although, that clearly cannot

---

355 Christopher Cant, Barrister.
356 Gaunt, J.Q.C. and Morgan, P.C.C. (2002) "Gale on Easements" 7th Edition Sweet & Maxwell Ltd.

have been Parliament's intention, because an excavation[357] interferes with an adjoining owner's natural right of support. Accordingly, it follows that in certain circumstances the Act will authorise the surveyors to award a limited interference with an easement.[358] This entitles an owner to perform a *"positive"* act on another owner's property subject to maintaining albeit in an adjusted manner as demonstrated in: -

> "Easements as may be necessary to carry out
> what was the common intention of the parties
> with regard to the user of the wall."[359]

And;

> "An easement is a right enjoyed by the owner of
> one piece of land over a piece of land owned by
> someone else."[360]

The Ellenborough[361] case identified various elements that are necessary to demonstrate that an easement exists: -

i)   A dominant and a servient owner;
ii)   An easement must accommodate the dominant owner;
iii)   The dominant and servient owners must be different;
iv)   Right over land cannot create an easement, unless it is capable of forming the subject matter of a grant.

Understanding and applying this criterion will enable the surveyors to establish when section 9 applies or to the implications in the context of determining what additional and independent professional legal advice their owners should take.

10.3   Rights of light

A right of light arises irrespective of whether it is claimed by prescription, under statute, or by implied and/or lost grant[362] with one unique quality that sets it aside from other easements. The use of the right of light can be acquired under section 3[363] which provides a mechanism that is distinguishable between either perpendicular and/or lateral light to establish a right of light. One

---

357 Chapter 8 subsections 8.2 and 8.3.
358 Selby v Whitbread & Co [1917] 1 KB 736.
359 Jones v Pritchard [1908] 1 Ch. 630.
360 Wood, D. Chynoweth, P. Adshead, A. and Mason, J. (2011) 'Law and the Built Environment' Wiley-Blackwell P.196.
361 Ellenborough Park [1956] Ch. 131.
362 Chapter 1 subsection 1.3.
363 The Prescription Act 1832.

qualification is that the strict rights of light only entitle the owners to so much light only as falls perpendicular on his land[364] whilst acquiring the right to lateral light without obstruction; which is the *"easement"*.

An owner may build up to their land without fear of an actionable claim for interfering with the right of light.[365] However, if the owners whose light is affected can demonstrate that they have enjoyed an uninterrupted enjoyment of light[366] for twenty or more years, they will have legally adopted the right by prescription. Although, this entitlement does not apply to vacant and /or undeveloped land.[367] The important point to note is that the dominant owner is not required to demonstrate that his enjoyment of the light has been obtained 'as of right'. Furthermore, where any works which involve raising a structure could potentially interfere with a right of light, it is incumbent upon the surveyors to advise the owners to consider this particular aspect very carefully.

There are surveyors that specialise in rights of light and assessing the loss of light involves a complicated series of measurements and calculations. The level of damages will vary and are dependent upon the loss suffered by the dominant owner. However, when considering an actionable interference, the surveyors must also be live to the fact that an interference does not automatically create a cause of action and will be relative to any actionable recovery for damages or loss arising from the interference. The House of Lords[368] decision was reinforced in a later case[369] that established the basic principles that the measure of the light has to be seen to demonstrate the interference as a nuisance. If the amount of light that remains after the interference is sufficient for the comfortable enjoyment of the property according to the ordinary notions of mankind, there is no actionable interference because there is no loss.

One significant difference between a right of light easement and other easements under section 3[370] is that there is no restriction on who can acquire the right. A tenant can acquire a right of light over an adjacent property owned by their landlord irrespective of whether as a lease has been granted to another person,[371] and a right to light can be acquired by the tenants use from his landlord.[372]

---

364 Jones v Pritchard [1908] 1 Ch. 63.
365 Chandler v Thompson (1811) 3 Camp. 80.
366 The Prescription Act 1832.
367 Garritt v Sharp (1835) 3.A & E.
368 Colls v Holmes and Colonial Stores (1894) 3 Ch. 659.
369 Car-Saunder v Dick McNeil Associates Ltd) [1986] 1 WLR 922.
370 The Prescription Act 1832.
371 Morgan v Fear [1907] AC 429.
372 Simper v Foley (1862) 2 J&H 555.

10.4   Right of way

A Right of way is a positive easement that grants the neighbouring owner or specified parties the right to move onto, over and/or across an adjoining owner's land. The easement may be created by agreement or by prescription.[373] Section 8(1) of the Act entitles the surveyors to award a temporary easement for access insofar as it is limited to 'works in pursuance' of the Act.[374] When determining a right of access, it is critical that the surveyors set out the terms of the temporary right of access the building owners will enjoy over the adjoining owner's land. Conversely, there may be situations where the adjoining owners also enjoy a right of way over the building owner's property. In Rusciani[375] the building owners blocked the adjoining owners' right of way through a pedestrian passageway between their respective properties that was critical to the operation of the adjoining owner's business activities and then submitted a revised planning application to permanently remove the adjoining owner's easement. If the building owner's works, (as in the Rusciani case) attempts to create a permanent interference with the right of access an actionable claim arises in the same way that a temporary interference is claimable.

Rusciani's legal right of way was recorded within the Land Registry's Charges Register title numbered EX 606922 and a conveyance dated 4 March 1975. The entry in the charges register recorded on the 19 November 1998 that: -

> "The land has the benefit of the following rights granted by a conveyance of the land in this title and other land dated 4 March 1975 made between (1) Emily Lillian Thompson Reginald Edward Washington Thompson (the vendors) and (2) Murray James Wood and others (the partners): Together with the right of way over and along the passageway coloured green on the plan annexed hereto and Together also with the right to use the pipes and cables wires and other installations installed in the said passageway coloured green. Note: the passageway-coloured green referred (to) is shown tinted brown on the filed plan."

> "The conveyancing document dated 4th of March 1975 recited that Emily Thompson (as vendor) agreed to sell the property to the named

---

373 The Prescription Act 1832.
374 See Chapter 9.
375 Rusciani v Kumar & Sharma (2013) Chelmsford County Court.

members of the Woods family (as partners) for
£27,500 and conveyed the shop and bakery to
them at 8 Broomfield Rd together with certain
rights of way. The part of that document upon
which the adjoining owner relied upon:

"TOGETHER ALSO WITH the right of way
over and along the passage way coloured green
on the plan annexed hereto.   TOGETHER
ALSO WITH the right to use the pipes cables
wires and other installations in the said
passageway coloured green".

The adjoining owner's surveyor correctly concluded that an explicit right of
way existed and attempted to explain this to the building owners and their
surveyor whose response was to continue to block the access. The building
owner's surveyor's response encapsulated a rather laissez faire approach to the
statutory Party Wall legislation: -

"Regrettably the only thing that you can hang
onto (sic) is words of the Party Wall Act as
being some form of gospel. Unlike you, I have
always adopted the approach of dealing with
things as expediently as possible in a
professional manner without having to hang on
every word of any particular piece of legislation
where it bears no specific difference to the task
in hand"

It was accepted that a temporary interruption to the adjoining owner's access
was reasonable whilst notifiable works were undertaken, but on the basis that
the interference could not be undertaken before service of an Award, and could
not permanently remove the right of access.

In contrast the building owner's surveyor
expressed the rather dismissive view that: -

"The right of way had next to no use to
anybody, and if there have been short periods
when access was not possible, I don't think it
was necessary for anyone to use it".

Although, the building owner's surveyor also
conceded that "whilst work was going on, the

need to use it might resurrect as being very important."

It is not for a surveyor to express such views and indeed the party wall surveyor must be objective and above all impartial. Rusciani's right of way was an important means of escape from their restaurant which if removed would force closure for non-compliance with building regulations, planning conditions and health and safety. The important point to take from this case is that the surveyors do not have the right to prevent and/or permanently remove a right of access. As HHJ Murfitt correctly determined, the Courts will always ensure that property rights are protected even if they are used on an infrequent basis.

10.5   Right of Support

There are two types of right of support: -

The first is a natural right to support such as adjacent land, any potential disturbance which is the premise for serving notice under sections 6(1) & (2). It is reasonably foreseeable that an excavation close to and/or below the depth of an adjoining owner's foundations and/or structure could disturb the soils natural equilibrium having dire consequences.[376] However, the natural right of support is only in relation to the land and not the building thereon.[377]

The second is created either by grant or prescription, as Lord Selbourne held: -

> "Support to that which is artificially imposed
> upon land cannot exists '*Ex jure natur*'
> because the thing supported does not itself
> exist."

However, it is restricted to the land upon which it rests which if affected due to changes caused by the excavation, (thereby removing/altering the natural support) damages may be recoverable for anything built thereon. An example of the adjoining owner's continuing right of support was illustrated[378] when the removal of the adjoining structure had exposed 13 feet of the type (a) party wall to the elements. This required both temporary protection[379] during the works and permanent protection and support after the replacement building was set back from the original building line. It was held that the right to protection and support had to be reinstated albeit in a different manner. This flows from the

376 Louis v Sadiq [1997] 1 EGLR 136; (1998) 59 Con LR 127 and Mohamed & Mohamed v Takhar, Takhar, & Takhar [2016] Central London County Court.
377 Dalton v Argus (1881) 6 APP.CAS 740 at 792.
378 Selby v Whitbread & Co [1917] 1 KB 736.
379 Chapter 9, subsection 9.4 and Chapter 11 para 11.8.

adjoining owners[380] having enjoyed the positive easement of a right of support from the adjoining building and that the exposed section of wall was now unsafe due to the absence of the missing building. Consequently, the building owners were required to reinstate the support by constructing a buttress pier on the front corner of the building. This demonstrates the principle, that as long as an alternative means of maintaining the support (easement) can be implemented, the surveyors can award an interference can be authorised under the Act.

In another case[381] the Court had cause to consider an interference with the right of support following the reduction of ground levels for new paving works which resulted in the partial collapse of the adjoining owner's property. Notice had not been served under section 6(1) whether through ignorance or because the proposed reduction of the ground level and depth of the excavation did not give rise to notice.[382] However, the onus was on the building owner's to properly assess the adjoining owner's property and therefore the mantra is that if in doubt to serve notice.

10.5.1 Transferring the obligation to support

A right of support is two dimensional applying to both vertically and lateral forces/loads. In the Rees[383] case, structural cracking was not caused by the weight of the structure but by the effect of wind suction. It was held that it was not appropriate to distinguish between *"wind support"* and the more commonly accepted principle of *"weight support."* It was held that an owner cannot transfer an obligation to provide or maintain a right of support to another person, which is important when dealing with works where a mid-terrace house is removed and temporary supports introduced to support adjacent properties.

Figures 15, 16 and 17 demonstrates the situation where property (a) shares a mutual right of support with property (b). Property (b) shares a mutual right of support with property (a) & (c). Property (c) shares a right of support with property (b). If property (b) was demolished (see Figure 16) the surveyors will have to ensure that properties (a) and (c) right of support from property (b) is maintained. Figures 16 and 17 show how that support was achieved.

Property (b) has an obligation to maintain the support with property (a) and (c), but this methodology has created a temporary right of support between property (a) and (c), which on the Rees judgment can be achieved without the adjoining

---

380 Selby v Whitbread & Co [1917] 1 KB 736.
381 Crowley v Rushmore Borough Council [2010] EWHC 2237.
382 Chapter 8, subsections 8.2 & 8.3.
383 Rees v Skerrett [2001] 1 WLR 1541.

owner's permission.   This is outside the appointed surveyor's jurisdiction unless the owners of property (a) and (c) have agreed to be reliant on each other for support. The surveyor's jurisdiction is therefore limited to the scheme in Figure 17 which maintains the original right of support independently between (a) & (b) & (b) & (c).

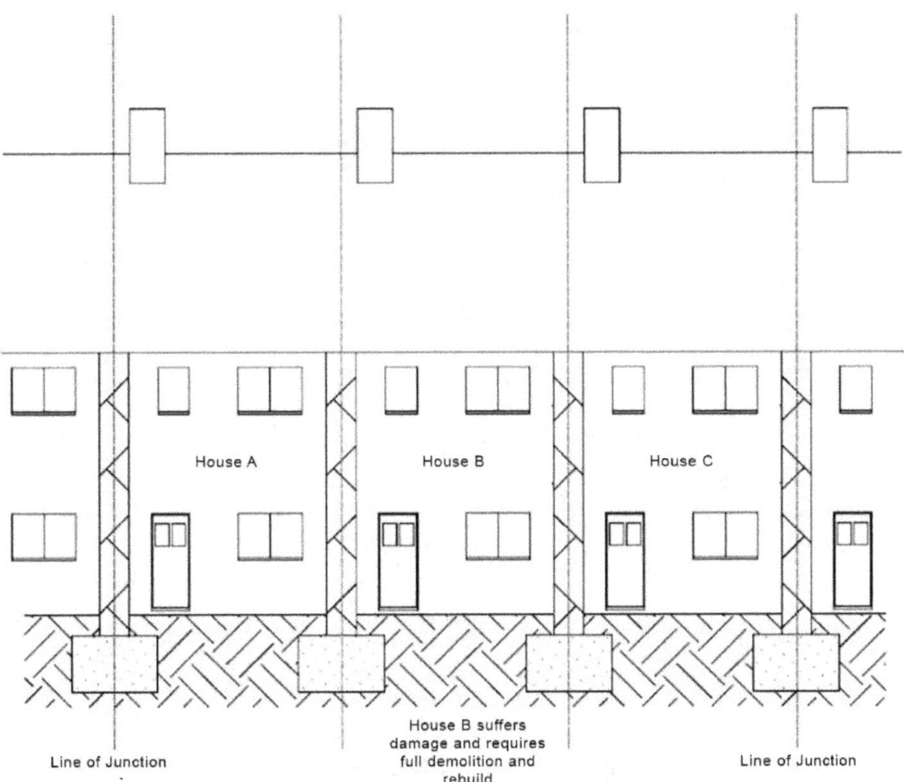

Figure 15 Mid-Terraced House Suffers Catastrophic failure

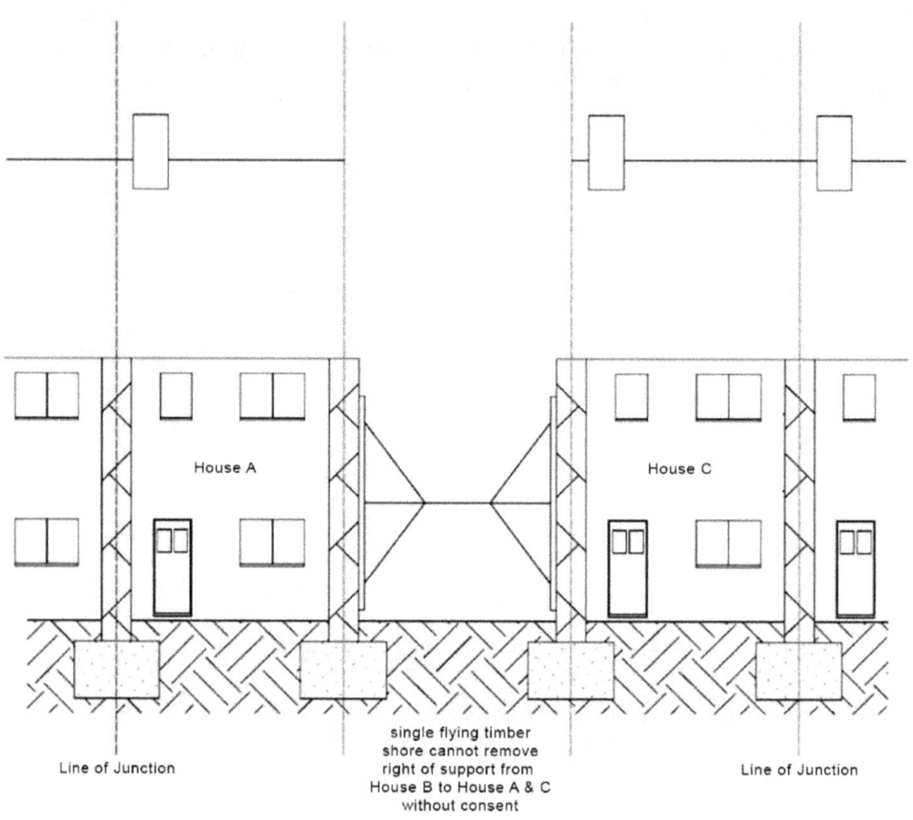

Figure 16 Single Flying Timber Shoring to Adjoining Properties

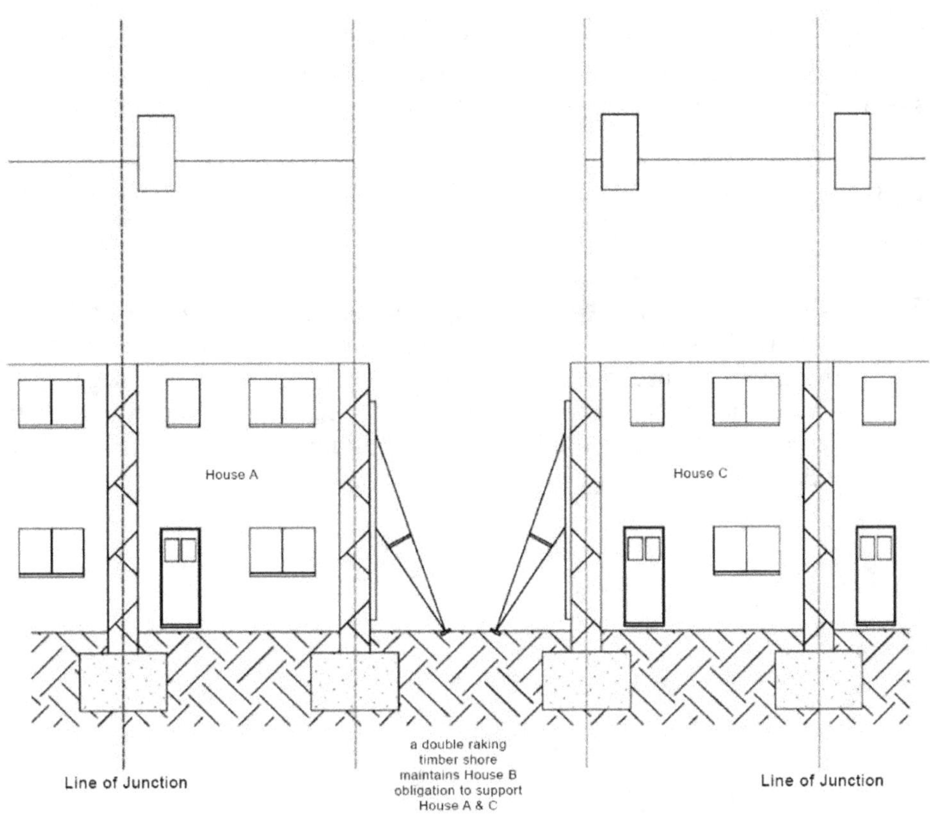

Figure 17 Double Raking Shore

10.6   Drainage rights

Easements also apply to drainage and whilst independent from the wall or excavations for foundations may have to be taken into account when considering the proposed excavations. For example, a gutter fixed along the flank wall of a building and overhanging the boundary line (see Figure 11) created an easement by prescription. Applying the principles established in the Selby case[384] the surveyors would be entitled to award an alteration to the easement so long as the alternative construction is compliant with the appropriate statutory requirements (see Figure 12) to maintain an adequate water collection and drainage system.

---

384 Selby v Whitbread & Co [1917] 1 KB 736.

10.7   Weather protection

Applying section 7(3) there is an explicit obligation for the building owner to provide and maintain adequate weathering when the adjoining owner's property is laid open either temporarily or permanently.[385]

s.7(3)

(3)   Where a building owner in exercising any right conferred on him by this Act lays open any part of the adjoining land or building, he shall at his own expense make and maintain so long as may be necessary a proper hoarding, shoring or fans or temporary construction for the protection of the adjoining land or building and the security of any adjoining   occupier.

---

385 Selby v Whitbread & Co [1917] 1 KB 736.

CHAPTER 11

11.0   Section 10: - Resolution of disputes

11.1   Introduction

Section 10 sets out the provisions that establish the framework that allows the surveyors to conclude matters where the owners are in a "theoretical dispute" referred to as dissent. In its broad context, the Act is a form of Alternative Dispute Resolution ("ADR") as Thomas L.J. observed[386]

> "Experience has shown in relation to disputes between neighbours, a failure to observe proper formalities is often, as it was in this case, the source of a dispute…. the professionalism of the surveyors experienced in the Party Wall Act will result in a clear agreement as to what is lawfully required. Consent on the basis of adherence to the terms of the planning permission and party wall Awards and agreements makes a certainty and thus diminution of the risk of such costly disputes between neighbours".

11.2   Section 10(1) (a) & (b) Appointment of the surveyors

Where a dispute arises or is deemed to have arisen between a building owner and an adjoining owner in respect of any matter connected with any work to which this Act relates either-

> *(a)   both parties shall concur in the appointment of one surveyor (in this section referred to as an "agreed surveyor"); or*

---

386 Seef v Ho [2011] EWCA Civ 186.

> **(b)** **each party shall appoint a surveyor and the two surveyors so appointed shall forthwith select a third surveyor (all of whom are in this section referred to as "the three surveyors").**

On receipt of a notice the adjoining owner has three options the first is to consent thereafter, section 10(1)(a) allows the appointment of a single surveyor referred to as an agreed surveyor. This is akin to the accepted practice of a single joint expert regularly adopted and encouraged within civil litigation and some adjoining owners struggle with this concept. It is an attractive option to the building owner because it minimises costs and time. The agreed surveyor's appointment places him/her outside the traditional client/surveyor relationship of agency, removing a potential claim for a perceived or actual conflict of interest requiring the surveyors to act impartially and without bias to either owner, but that is ultimately determined by the surveyor's conduct, transparency and honesty.

If the adjoining owner fails to respond to the notice within 14-days[387], the building owner's surveyor cannot appoint himself as an agreed surveyor because the literal meaning of "agreed surveyor" can only flow from an explicit agreement between the two owners. Furthermore, the owners must be advised that the agreed surveyor's role is not to do the bidding of either owner, occasionally to the frustration of some owners who try to use the surveyor to frustrate the works. This is clearly against the spirit of the Act and the surveyor should resist such pressures. Regrettably, some surveyors do not have sufficient presence to resist such blatant intimidation.

11.2.1 Section 10(1) (b) Appointments and selecting the third surveyor

The second option is section 10(1)(b) requiring the owners to each appoint a surveyor. Their first activity is to *"forthwith"* select a third surveyor. Until a third surveyor is selected the tribunal is incomplete and the absence of a third surveyor suspends the surveyor's jurisdiction[388] and removes the appointing owners' rights under section 10(11). The law applies explicit meanings to certain words, *'forthwith'*[389] means immediately. Therefore, the appointed surveyors should agree the selection before proceeding with any aspect of the Act. The Act does not define the selection process, but this is often the first

---

387 See Chapter 7 subsection 7.5.
388 See Chapter 11, subsection 11.8.1.
389 See Chapter 2, subsection 2.11.

area of dispute between the surveyors. Generally, the accepted practice is that the building owner's surveyor will provide a list of three surveyors for the adjoining owner's surveyor to consider. The adjoining owner's surveyor can reject any proposals without explanation, and propose alternative names. These can also be rejected by the building owner's surveyor without explanation. If the selection process reaches a stalemate, then section 10(8) must be adopted, which in itself can have disastrous consequences.[390]

In the context of the Act, the word *'selection'* also has an important meaning because a third surveyor is not appointed, and indeed can refuse to accept the selection. As part of the surveyor's due diligence, they should notify the third surveyor once selected and request confirmation that they are prepared to accept. Whilst this is not mandatory, it is a professional, courteous and good practice. It can avoid issues at a later date if the selection is rejected following a referral. On one occasion a surveyor was insistent on selecting a third surveyor because he always used that surveyor. He was shocked when advised that the surveyor had passed away some two years previous. Thus, reinforcing the availability of the third surveyor is practical and sensible.

Because the party wall surveying community is relatively small, it is inevitable that professional and personal relationships will exist/form. It is not uncommon for some surveyors to adopt the old boy network and propose their friends and colleagues, which surprisingly is not prohibited under the legislation.[391] In such circumstances the surveyors should be open and disclose any such relationship. There is also a tendency amongst some surveyors to continually suggest the same group of surveyors who are perceived to be knowledgeable and experienced in party wall matters. Therefore, the selection of the third surveyor should be made with transparency and caution. Any concerns regarding the surveyors perceived or actual bias should be raised immediately, otherwise the right to challenge their selection at a late date could be prohibited.[392]

11.2.2 Conditional appointments

It has been held that a surveyor can be appointed prior to service of a notice.[393]

---

390 See Chapter 1, subsection 1.10.3.
391 See Chapter 2, subsection 2.10.
392 See Chapter 1, subsection 1.10.
393 Loost v Kremer [1997] West London County Court 12 May (Unreported).

> "An appointment under section 10(1)(b) can be made before the service of a party wall notice in respect of the proposals to which it relates"[394] and "the appointment.... is put in that conditional way 'I would appoint'...." The matter is quite sensibly put in terms of it being a conditional appointment".

As soon as the adjoining owners become aware of the proposed works, they can appoint a surveyor in anticipation of and conditional upon a notice being served. Once appointed in writing the surveyor should make the building owner aware of his/her appointment. The letter of appointment has no specific format[395] but a standard format commonly used is available and to allow the appointing owner to authorise the surveyor to serve the notices and awards. The surveyor should also advise their appointing owners that costs/fees incurred prior to service of notice are not necessarily payable by the building owner.

11.2.3 Surveyor's impartiality

The surveyors should always adopt a neutral role and remember they are not there to be dictated to by their appointing owner or to apply their own personal bias or opinions. Unfortunately, that process/obligation is often overlooked. The surveyor must do what is reasonably necessary to protect the properties integrity by adopting the Acts provisions to achieve the correct outcome for the owners. The surveyor's approach should at all times be impartial and transparent, even more so when appointed as the agreed surveyor. The owners will often try to gain an advantage by discussing matters or disclosing documentation that they feel helps their position whilst claiming it is privileged. This does not apply to a section 10(1)(a) appointment. Unfortunately, some disgruntled owners will vent their views, disappointment, and concern about the surveyor's conduct, when they don't get what they wish. The only way a surveyor can protect themselves from any allegation of bias (perceived or actual) or wrongdoing is to act transparently and set out their procedures from the beginning and follow them religiously. Ensuring all communications are in writing and copied to all parties will demonstrate transparency and impartiality.

11.2.4 Section 10(3) Agreed Surveyors failure to act.

Section 10(3)(a)(b)(c)&(d)

---

394 Manu v Euroview Investments Ltd [2008] 1 EGLR 165.
395 See Appendix A.

If an agreed surveyor-

      (a)   **refuses to act;**
      (b)   **neglects to act for a period of ten days beginning with the day on which either party serves a request on him;**
      (c)   **dies before the dispute is settled; or**
      (d)   **becomes or deems himself incapable of acting,**
  the proceedings for settling such dispute shall begin de novo.

The intention behind this section is clear, it is intended to prevent the matters from being stalled due to a range of events including a surveyor's failure to act promptly. However, sub-section (b) would only be applicable if the appointing owners have in fact been advised that they do have a right to serve a request upon the agreed surveyor to act within 10 days of such request. This again comes down to the implied if not explicit obligations for the surveyors to advise their appointing owners of their statutory rights.[396]

11.3   Section 10(2) Once appointed always appointed

All appointments and selections made under this section shall be in writing and shall not be rescinded by either party.

Section 10(2) is mandatory and upon to the surveyor's appointment being in writing[397] cannot be rescinded, by anyone which includes the Court. Or so the author believed, regrettably, from the author's personnel experiences its application has created difficulties for and disappointingly has on one occasion created a significant miscarriage of justice.[398]

In 2015[399] the Bibizadeh's Counsel[400] surprisingly argued that there was no requirement under the Act to exchange letters of appointments. Therefore, the building owners had not refused or neglected to appoint a surveyor when they refused to disclose a purported letter of appointment for their preferred surveyor. This tactic was employed to avoid a surveyor being appointed under section 10(4). This argument was of course nonsense because the appointment

---

396 See Chapter 1, subsection 11.1, Chapter 13, subsection 13.2.
397 See Chapter 11, subsection 11.13.
398 T. Reeves v R. Young, G. Young & P. Antino [2017] Central London County Court.
399 Dodosh v Bibizadeh [2015] Central London County Court HHJ Bailey (Appeal on preliminary points).
400 Miss H Holmes of Tanfield Chambers.

letter must be disclosed to establish the validity of the appointment, if not why did Parliament include section 10(2)? On this occasion HHJ Bailey reached the proper and sensible conclusion rejecting the suggestion that Mr. Redler had been appointed as the building owner's surveyor.

This is a principal that RICS guidance note[401] advises its members in the following terms: -

> "Appointed surveyors are recommended to provide each other with copies of their written appointment before proceeding with any work to negotiate an award."

There have been instances where surveyors have proceeded without a valid letter of appointment and subsequently their Award has been deemed invalid: -

> "Everything is invalid and the whole process starts de novo and the procedural requirements of the Act are important and the approach of surveyors to those requirements ought not to be casual. It would be a wise precaution for the surveyor of the building owner and the surveyor of the adjoining owner to inspect each other's written appointment before they perform their statutory functions"[402].

The letter of appointment should identify the surveyor by name because the appointment is personal[403] and cannot be a registered company or practice: -

> "Under the Act it is quite clear that an individual has to be appointed. He has to be a person[404] (section 10(5) & (9)(c) reference to death) and under the Act there is the possibility catered for that he may die. It is absolutely clear that he must be an individual".[405]

---

401 7th edition.
402 Gyle-Thompson v Wall Street (Properties) Ltd 1 WLR 123 [1974] 1 ALL ER 295.
403 See Chapter 11, subsection 11.6.
404 Statutory appointment not agency.
405 Loost v Kremer [1997] West London County Court 12 May (Unreported).

If either party to the dispute-

(a)   refuses to appoint a surveyor under subsection (1)(b), or
(b)   neglects to appoint a surveyor under subsection (1)(b) for a period of ten days beginning with the day on which the other party serves a request on him, the other party may make the appointment on his behalf.

Parliament clearly anticipated situations where an owner may refuse or fail to appoint a surveyor and introduced a procedure which allows the requesting surveyor[406] to appoint a surveyor when there is a refusal or neglect to Act. It is not always the adjoining owner that neglects or refuses to appoint a surveyor. Notably, the Act does not explain what constitutes a refusal or neglect to appoint a surveyor, although the consequences and remedy are the same allowing the requesting surveyor to appoint a surveyor on behalf of the defaulting owner. The inclusion of the 10-day provision creates certainty whilst allowing recipient a further period of time to consider their options. In some cases, the neglect can arise by default, for example if the adjoining owners are on holiday.

The Bibizadeh case[407] is indicative of how matters can go horribly wrong when the building owners attempt to manipulate or abuse the Act. The subsequent approach and conduct was astonishing if not bizarre, having served notice they subsequently attempted to deny undertaking notifiable works, to avoid the statutory procedures. When it became clear that their works would trespassed on to the adjoining owners land and advised by a party wall surveyor.[408]

The Bibizadeh's ignored the procedures and started the works and were subjected to an injunction. They refused to appoint a surveyor and appealed the Award served by the adjoining owner's surveyor and the section 10(4) appointed surveyor. They attempted to claim that they had appointed Mr Alistair Redler, another surveyor[409] although had refused through their solicitors to provide a copy of the letter of appointment. The criticism handed down by HHJ Bailey in the judgement is the clearest demonstration of how a

---

406 Request can be made by either the building or adjoining owner's surveyor.
407 Dodosh v Bibizadeh [2015] Central London County Court HHJ Bailey (Appeal on preliminary points).
408 Mr Darren Flight.
409 See Chapter 11, subsection 11.3.

building owner should not conduct themselves. Accordingly, section 10(4) is there to prevent matters from stalling.

11.6   Section 10(5) Incapacity to act

If, before the dispute is settled, a surveyor appointed under paragraph (b) of subsection (1) by a party to the dispute dies, or becomes or deems himself incapable of acting, the party who appointed him may appoint another surveyor in his place with the same power and authority.

The Act[410] recognises the possibility that genuine circumstance may arise where a surveyor is incapable of continuing. In my opinion the surveyors owe a duty of care to all owners to demonstrate solid grounds for doing so.[411] The appropriate test is not simply claiming an incapacity, but having the ability to demonstrate the incapacity that physically prevents the surveyor from continuing with their duties.

When genuine circumstance arises, it is wholly appropriate that the surveyor should deem himself incapable of acting, thus allowing the owners to appoint a replacement surveyor to ensure matters proceed as swiftly as possible. Regrettably, it is a sad fact that some owners will be overly hostile towards their surveyor, if they feel that they are not achieving what they want. Irrespective of the owner's conduct, it is both unprofessional and unacceptable for a surveyor to accede to external pressures and tactics and simply walk away under section 10(5). In such circumstances the surveyor should record the concerns and incidents in writing to all owners for future reference.

If a deemed incapacity is claimed and the grounds are not genuine, the remaining surveyor must register their objections with the surveyor and the owners. The surveyor can serve a section 10(6) or 10(7) request and proceed *ex parte* after the expiry of 10- days (if the latter) or join with the third Surveyor[412]. If the owners attempt to appoint a surveyor where the grounds for the deemed incapacity have been challenged, the surveyor has a difficult decision to make, he can continue as above or join with the replacement surveyor and continue with the statutory procedures. However, in order to protect his appointing owners' position, the surveyor must make it clear that his continued activity is

---

410 See Chapter 11, subsection 11.2.4 and 11.9.
411 Dodosh v Bibizadeh [2015] Central London County Court HHJ Bailey (Appeal on preliminary points).
412 Chapter 11, subsection 11.7.

without prejudice to his contention that the grounds given by the first surveyor are invalid and reserve the owners position.   To ensure the validity of any subsequent appointment, the same procedures for appointing the replacement surveyor applies. If the deceased surveyor was appointed under section 10(4), a new section 10(4) notice must be served. In the alternative, the two surviving surveyors can complete the statutory process with an Award and leave it for the aggrieved party to appeal.   The author having been involved in three recent cases[413] (all before HHJ Bailey), where the issue of a deemed incapacity has been a preliminary point of contention within these cases and a fourth[414] again before HHJ Bailey but stayed. Interestingly in the Bibizadeh case HHJ Bailey ruled[415] *"Miss Holmes submits that for a surveyor to deem himself incapable of acting does require a proper basis and I entirely agree"*.

HHJ Bailey specifically notes at para 18: -

> "It seems that Mr. Flight took his duties seriously, and visited the site at the rear of 50 & 48 Levett Gardens, Ilford during the first week of August. In doing so he incurred the ire of Mr. & Mrs. Bibizadeh. On the 10th August 2014 they sent him an email, copied to Ms Dodosh as the adjoining owner expressing **extreme disappointment that he adopted a "jumped the gun" attitude and had failed to follow the RICS' professional protocol**. They complained that it is the adjoining owner who should have completed the acknowledgement notice form and returned it to them so that ..."

HHJ Bailey commented upon Mr. Flight's response that the building owner's felt that he had acted inappropriately, and seeking to explain that as far as he was concerned, he had acted properly.   HHJ Bailey noted although he wrote in such terms to Mr. & Mrs. Bibizadeh, Mr. Flight was plainly concerned as to his position.   Mr. Flight then deemed himself incapable of acting.   HHJ Bailey continued at paragraphs 82 with specific reference to Mr. Flight's statement: -

---

413 Sell & Sell v Mills & O'Callaghan – Kingston Upon Thames CC A00KT940 Mills & Mills v Savage & Savage [2016] Central London County Court, and Bibizadeh & Bibizadeh v Dodosh [2015] Central London County Court.
414 Takhar, Takhar & Takhar v Mohamed & Mohamed [2016] Central London County Court.
415 Paragraph 85 of the judgement.

> "I am exercising my rights under section 10(5), and
> hereby rescind my appointment."

HHJ Bailey was clearly sceptical and critical of that statement at paragraph 83 stating: -

> "It is difficult to accept that final comment at face value.
> Mr. Flight had no right to rescind his appointment ...."

Astonishingly, at Court the Bibizadeh's counsel claimed that Mr Flight was their appointed surveyor in an attempt to appeal the Award was justifiably questioned at para 86 by HHJ Bailey who records: -

> "It sits ill in the mouth of the building owners to
> complain that their letter of 10th August led to
> Mr. Flight deeming himself incapable of acting,
> and then inserting that he was in fact still
> capable of acting."

A paragraph 87 Judge Bailey raises a pertinent point that surveyors should have sufficient confidence: -

> "In circumstances where, as here, a party wall
> surveyor receives a letter in terms such as those
> in the letter of the 10th August 2014 one might
> hope that he had sufficient confidence to
> continue to act, notwithstanding the attitude of
> the building owners."

When there is such clear criticism handed down by the Court in regards to the surveyor resigning from their appointment albeit in the face of such aggressive and unacceptable behaviour, whilst the surveyors are right to be concerned, they should stand up to such behaviour.

Even when the Bibizadeh's made a complaint to the RICS[416] alleging Mr Flight had acted incorrectly, (in my opinion he had not) which has such serious

---

416 Mr Daren Flight.

implications, cannot be seen as anything other than an attempt to bully, intimidate and/or threaten the surveyor, something RICS refuse to acknowledge.

However, the issue of deemed incapacity was covered in 'fog' in the Mills v Sell, and Savage cases. The building owner's surveyor[417] deemed himself incapable of acting upon a clear request from the building owner's that he do so because they wanted to represent themselves for financial reasons. Rather bizarrely in this judgement, HHJ Bailey held an altogether inconsistent and contradictory view to his decision in the Bibizadeh case:

> "I see no words in the statute that would indicate that a party-appointed surveyor may only deem himself incapable of acting on proper grounds and if what constitutes such grounds. My inclination would be to hold that it is entirely a matter for the surveyor to decide whether he wishes to resign by deeming himself incapable of acting and he may do so on whatever ground seems appropriate to him.[418]"

This inconsistency within HHJ Bailey's decisions causes further difficulties for the surveying community. Indeed, on detailed analysis of the judgement, HHJ Bailey wrongly held that the party wall matters were complete at the time the deemed incapacity arose. Quite how the learned judge formed this view (because it was not raised in evidence) remains a mystery. It is of course disappointing that HHJ Bailey overlooked the expressed wording of section 10(2), because the grounds relied on for the building surveyor to deem himself incapable amounted to rescission of the surveyor's appointment, and not a genuine incapacity. Charles Dawson[419] believed that the grounds relied upon by the building owner's surveyor did not satisfy the genuine incapacity.

11.7   Section 10(6) and (7) Refusal and/or Neglect to act effectively

The underlying principle behind both section 10(6) & (7) is that Parliament was live to the possibility that a surveyor's conduct should not unreasonably delay the service of an Award by refusing and/or neglecting to engage with the process. Accordingly, the intent behind both sections 10(6) and (7) is to provide

---

417 James Hopkins MRICS of Talus Partnership.
418 Paragraph 90 of Sell & Sell v Mills & O'Callaghan – Kingston Upon Thames CC A00KT940 Mills & Mills v Savage & Savage [2016] Central London County Court.
419 Third Surveyor and Former President of Faculty of Party Wall Surveyors.

a mechanism that enables matters to proceed ex parte[420] when a surveyor either refuses or neglects to act effectively. Regrettably the Act does not define what constitutes a refusal or neglect, and it is therefore open to broad interpretation (as is much of the Act) but the following would qualify as would refusal or a neglect to act: -

(1). Silence;
(2). An oral discussion resulting in refusal;
(3). A written communication setting out a refusal; and
(4). An improper use of section 10(5).[421]

One significant difference between sections 10(6) and (7) is that the former bites as soon as the request is made, the latter requires a 10-day time period to pass. Caution should be exercised before proceeding ex parte because there is an increased probability that an owner may appeal an ex parte Award. Whether they are ultimately successful or not will turn on whether it can be demonstrated that a surveyor had refused and/or neglected to act effectively upon a request. There are cases[422] where the Courts have recognised a refusal and/or neglect and rejected the appeal and quite rightly so.

11.7.1   Section 10(6) (a) & (b) A Refusal to Act

If a surveyor-

> *(a)   appointed under paragraph (b) of subsection (1) by a party to the dispute; or*

> *(a)   appointed under subsection (4) or (5),*
> *refuses to act effectively, the surveyor of the other party may proceed to act ex parte and anything so done by him shall be as effectual as if he had been an agreed surveyor.*

In Bansal v Myers[423] the adjoining owner's surveyor[424] invited the building owner's surveyor to discuss his fees in accordance with section 10(13). The surveyors' response was *"discuss your fees with the building owner"*. This was considered a refusal to act effectively, because the fees are quite clearly not a matter for either the building or adjoining owners, and remain within the surveyor's jurisdiction under both sections 10(12) & (13). The only option open

---

420 See Section 2.11.
421 Sell & Sell v Mills & O'Callaghan – Kingston Upon Thames CC A00KT940 Mills & Mills v Savage & Savage [2016] Central London County Court.
422 Bansal v Myers [2007] Romford County Court Unreported.
423 Bansal v Myers [2007] Romford County Court Unreported.
424 Mr. Philip Antino BSc (Hons), MSc, MRes, MRICS, ICIOB FCABE.

to the adjoining owner's surveyor was to serve an ex parte Award settling his fees. The building owner appealed and HHJ Platt, rejected the appeal on the following point: -

> "The building owner's play no part in determining the surveyor's fees"

Therefore, the building owner's surveyor's response was a clear refusal to act effectively and the Award was upheld. In a more recent case, HHJ Marshall held[425] that Mr. Lai's demand for a new notice under section 6 *"Was a refusal to act on the original section 6 notice."* The right to proceed ex parte would turn on whether the first section 6 notice was valid. If so, Mr. Lai's response was a refusal to act effectively. The Court held that the original notice was valid, therefore, as soon as the refusal arises the requesting surveyor could proceed ex parte and settle the request as if he were the agreed surveyor.[426]

11.7.2 Section 10(7) (a) & (b) A Neglect to Act

If a surveyor-

    (a)   *appointed under paragraph (b) of subsection (1) by a party to the dispute; or*

    (b)   *appointed under subsection (4) or (5),*

neglects to act effectively for a period of ten days beginning with the day on which either party or the surveyor of the other party serves a request on him, the surveyor of the other party may proceed to act ex parte, in respect of the subject matter of the request and anything so done by him shall be as effectual as if he had been an agreed surveyor.

Before proceeding under section 10(7), in addition to points (1-4) above the requesting surveyor must be able to demonstrate the date that the request was received. The 10-day request should period to respond in the same way as serving a notice.[427] Accordingly, there are two additional elements that must be demonstrated. The expiry of the statutory 10-day period is mandatory. The

---

425 Paragraph 122 of the judgment.
426 Chapter 12, subsection 12.2.
427 CPR Part 6 Service of Documents R6.26.

second is the requesting surveyor's ability to demonstrate that the request was ignored or not properly addressed. Any response received in the interim period should be considered very carefully. Because the ten-day request period does not require the requesting surveyor to proceed forthwith. The requesting surveyor is entitled to proceed at any time after the ten days but thereafter, the recipient of the request can respond at any time prior to any ex parte Award being served. This was the only matter in the Court of Appeal[428] case which held that post expiry of the ten-day period, the building owner's surveyors[429] response was sufficient to stop the ex parte rights biting. On appeal initially HHJ Hand[430] held that (i) the adjoining owner's surveyor's request under section 10(7) dated 21st December triggered the ten-day period, and (ii) the building owner's surveyor's response was outside the ten-day period and thus invalid.

The building owners were granted permission to take the matter before the Court of Appeal[431] on the basis that HHJ Hand judgement raised important points of principle under the Act. Although their Lordships[432] held that the resolution of the dispute in fact turned on the particular facts rather than on points of principle. Their Lordships[433] had one issue to address (and nothing to do with fees) observing that the requesting surveyor took over a month following the request before proceeding ex parte, during which time the recipient building owner surveyor[434] had engaged with the third surveyor[435] under section 10(10) and jointly served an Award. Thus, removing the adjoining owners' surveyors right to act ex parte. Their Lordships held that the ten-day period did not limit either parties' ability to respond or indeed proceed ex parte, in essence time was at large. In this case it just so happened that the building owner's surveyor adopted section 10(10) before the requesting surveyor proceeded ex parte and their Lordships overturned HHJ Hand QC earlier judgement.

The important lesson to be learnt from this case is that it emphasises the importance of proceeding forthwith after the expiry of the ten-day period. Had the adjoining owner's surveyor acted immediately and served his Award, the building owner's surveyor and third surveyor could not have joined in an Award. The moral is that if you delay you lose the right, so do not make requests unless you are in a position to follow them through.

---

428 Patel & Patel v Peters, Peters, at al [2014] EWCA Civ 335.
429 Mr. Justin Burns MRICS.
430 Paragraph 46(i) – (iv) of the Judgment.
431 High Court.
432 Para 22 of the Judgment.
433 Lord Justice Richards, Lord Justice Beatson and Lord Justice Briggs.
434 Mr. Justin Burns.
435 Mr. Alex Frame.

11.8　Section 10(8) (a) & (b) Unable to agree on the third surveyor

If either surveyor appointed under subsection (1)(b) by a party to the despite refuses to select a third surveyor under subsection (1) or (9), or neglects to do so for a period of ten days beginning with the day on which the other surveyor serves a request on him-

(a)　　the appointing officer; or

(b)　　in cases where the relevant appointing officer or his employer is a party to the dispute, the Secretary of State.

may other application of either surveyor select a third surveyor who shall have the same power and authority as if he had been selected under subsection (1) or subsection (9).

This follows section 10(1)(b) being trigger but not resolved, Parliament anticipated the possibility that the surveyors may not reach an agreement on the selection of the third surveyor and therefore incorporated an alternative independent selection process. In theory the first option (a) should be the more efficient of the two options with a letter/email to the local authority appointing officer. Option (b) is likely to be extremely difficult to achieve and most certainly time consuming. The Act (not unsurprisingly is silent on the prescribed format for contacting the local authority, although there is an implied obligation that the surveyors should act with transparency and in my view advise the appropriate surveyors. Silence will create justified suspicion.[436] Any contact with the local authority should be in writing and also copied to their opposite surveyor disappointingly some surveyors do not recognise this practice[437]. The information relayed to the appointing officer should include: -

(ii)　　The names and addresses of the building and adjoining owners;

(iii)　　The appointed surveyors contact details;

(iv)　　The letters of appointments and notices; and

(v)　　The names of the surveyors rejected as a suitable third Surveyor.

The appointing officer is not required to check the request or documentation for validity, that is and remains at all times the surveyor's duty, and the appointing officer should rely on the information when selecting the third surveyor. Adopting (v) should ensure that the appointing officer does not inadvertently select a previously rejected surveyor. However, the appointing officer is at

---

436 See Chapter 1, subsection 1.10.4.
437 Mr Adam Cakebread and Mr Kevin Turner.

liberty to appoint anyone he/she so choose. Therefore, if either of the two surveyors have concerns regarding the selected surveyor, they should raise these points at the earliest opportunity with the surveyor and request they deem themselves incapable of acting under section 10(9)[438].

11.8.1 Refusal to select a third surveyor

It does not naturally follow that section 10(8) will achieve results. Indeed, in a recent case, [439] Mr. Nicholas Isaac Q.C. had claimed that following service of an Award under section 10(14) the tribunal were *"Functus Officio"* despite the fact that there was inter alia damage caused to the adjoining owner's property and following Mr. Redler's deemed incapacity under section 10(9) the surveyors had no further standing under their statutory appointment and/or selections to resolve 'any matter arising after or incidental' to the Award. This is in my view is and remains a non-sensical position, and wholly without merit. Given the intent of section 10(12)(c)[440] it is on any literal reading clear that the surveyors jurisdiction continues, until **all matters** arising out of **or incidental to the Act** are resolved. Damage can only arise form or be incidental too the works and therefore satisfies both triggers.

Of greater concern was Mr. Isaac's ability to undermine and/or ignore his opinions expressed within his book[441] where in clear and unequivocal terms he suggests at paragraph 8-38: -

> "The appointed party wall surveyors **have continuing authority to make multiple Awards**. At paragraph 8-39 it is well established practice under the Act for **multiple awards to be made by the same tribunal of surveyors**."

Bickford-Smith[442] expresses a similar opinion at paragraphs 8.42-8.43 which of course on any literal and sensible reading of the Act is wholly correct. Mr. Isaac's opinion was sent to Mr. Notta[443] claiming that there were no disputes and therefore no jurisdiction for Mr. Notta to make a selection under section 10(8). Mr. Isaac blatantly ignoring the fact that the building owners and adjoining owners' surveyors had both agreed that a replacement third surveyor

---

438 See Chapter 11, subsection 11.9.
439 Zaman v Zala (2020) Central London County Court F20CL049.
440 See Chapter 11, subsection 11.12.
441 Isaac, N. (2014) "The law and Practice of Party Walls" Property Publishing.
442 Bickford-Smith, S. and Sydenham, C. (1997) "Party Walls Law and Practice" Jordan Publishing Ltd.
443 Head of Building Control London Borough of Redbridge.

should be selected, to ensure that the tribunal was complete and that the two surveyors could settle the **outstanding disputes**!

Shockingly, Mr. Notta refused to select a third surveyor claiming there was no dispute. This in turn raised an incredibly important point of law. Is an appointing officer entitled to make such a determination and in so doing deprive an owner of their statutory right to have a dispute referred to the surveyors and/or the third surveyor? Of course, the obvious and common-sense answer has to be no. The correct and only course of action that Mr. Notta should have taken was to make the selection completing his statutory duty and then let the owners argue the issue at Court. Mr. Notta's actions were clearly bias towards the adjoining owner's statutory rights and contrary to the rules of natural justice.[444]

Indeed, on the simple reading and understanding of the explicit wording of various sections[445] within the Act it is abundantly clear that the surveyor's jurisdiction continues post service of the Award. These sections are included within the Act and are necessary to deal with matters after the Award has been served as well as some of them applying during and prior to the Award. If there were no ongoing jurisdictional powers afforded to the surveyors, any dispute arising after the commencement of the works could not be resolved under the statutory legislation ergo no addendum Awards.

11.9 Section 10(9) (a) (b) & (c) Third surveyor's refusal/failure to act

If a third surveyor selected under subsection (1) (b)

(a)	*refuses to act;*
(b)	*neglects to act for a period of ten days beginning with the day on which either party or the surveyor appointed by either party serves a request on him; or*
(c)	*dies, or becomes or deems himself incapable of acting, before the dispute is settled,*

the other two of the three surveyors shall forthwith select another surveyor in his place with the same power and authority.

Parliament's inclusion of this section is consistent with the principal under section 10(5), and the same rationale applies. The underlying ethos of the Act is to ensure that both building and adjoining owners' rights are protected within an established provisions that ensures matters proceed without any unnecessary

---

444 See Chapter 1.
445 See sections 1(7) and (8), 6(10), 7(2), 8(5) & (6), 10(1), 10(8), 10(10), 10(12)(c), 10(13)(c) and 11(8).

or minimal inconvenience. There are numerous circumstances that give rise to a valid incapacity such as conflict of interest, bias towards an owner/surveyor.[446]

11.10 Section 10(10) Surveyor's jurisdiction

Section 10(10) (a)&(b)

The agreed surveyor or as the case may be the three surveyors or any two of them shall settle by award any matter-

> *(a)   which is connected with any work to which this Act relates, and*
>
> *(b)   which is in dispute between the building owner and the adjoining owner.*

An Award is the document produced by the surveyors (in their various capacities) that effectively sets out the notifiable works and costs and/or works incidental to or arising out of the notifiable works that will be undertaken and any other matter related to the works such as security[447]. The building owner's surveyor will in normal circumstances prepare and send fair copies of the Award which should include the relevant drawings, a schedule of condition (if recorded) including photographs to the adjoining owner's surveyor for agreement. When the adjoining owner's surveyor is satisfied, they would sign and serve the Award on their appointing owners and return signed copies to the building owner's surveyor to serve upon their building owners.

The surveyors' jurisdiction to determine *'any matter'* connected to the work allows any two of the three surveyors to join together and serve an Award[448], on a broad basis explicitly excluding one of the surveyors (without justified reason) would give rise to an appeal.[449] Once the Award has been served, the surveyor's involvement is suspended until anything within the Award, such as undertaking an interim or a final inspection or a dispute arises following commencement of the works. Surveyors can issue multiple Awards[450] especially on large construction projects. For example, an Award allowing the excavations to commence whilst other superstructure works are finalised.

---

446 See Chapter 1, subsection 1.10.4.
447 See Chapter 10, subsection 10.12.
448 Patel and Patel v Peters, Peters, Levy et al [2014] EWCA Civ 335
449 Ferguson & Ferguson v Lloyd-Baker (2017) County Court at Central London.
450 See Chapter 11, subsection 11.9.

A somewhat archaic practice originally perpetrated by the P&T[451] is the misconceived practice that the appointed surveyors should retain unsigned copies of the Award. An unsigned Award has no value to anyone, especially the surveyors. It could not be used in enforcement proceedings to recover unpaid fees.[452] Furthermore, given that the surveyors have to sign at least two Awards, one for each of the appointing owners. Another archaic and misconceived concept is that the surveyors' signatures are witnessed, an Award is not a deed and therefore does not require witnessing.

11.10.1 Retrospective awards

There are generally three reasons why building works start prior to the service of notice: -

(1). Ignorance of the Act;
(2). To avoid the costs and time implications;
(3). To do work that is not permissible under the Act.

Point (1) is thankfully is now quite rare as the professionals and public are better informed of their obligations, however there are always exception to the rule.[453] When the building owners have not served notice, the adjoining owners should immediately request that the works are halted[454] and that no works will continue until notice is served in compliance with the Act. This approach is the most sensible, economical and pragmatic way of reconciling the statutory breaches.[455]   However, even if the building owners agree, one should be ready to instruct solicitors, because it is not unknown for building owners[456] to renege on the undertaking. If the building owner refuses to stop, the only legal remedy is to seek injunctive relief.[457]   How the party wall matters are reconciled after the injunction will turn on the circumstances of each case. Given that the Act is silent on retrospective Awards, the surveyors do not have jurisdiction (unless the owners agree) to retrospectively determine notifiable works completed before their appointment, hence the reason why some owners try to complete

---

451 Pyramus &Thisbe Club.
452 See Chapter 16.
453 Peter J Edmond v Nicholas Bartholomew Denham & Helen Julie Seekings-Denham (2021) H00PE335.
454 See Chapter 19.
455 Dodosh v Bibizadeh [2014] County Court at Romford, Sell & Sell v Mills & O'Callaghan [2014], Rusciani v Kumar and Sharma (2013) County Court at Chelmsford.
456 Dodosh v Bibizadeh [2014] County Court at Romford.
457 Rusciani v Kumar and Sharma (2013) County Court at Chelmsford, Dodosh v Bibizadeh (2014) County Court at Romford.

the works before the injunction is granted. They can only resolve any outstanding matters following service of notices.[458]

11.10.2   No notice, works complete

If the works are complete and no damage has occurred the adjoining owners have limited options, the surveyors can only serve a retrospective Award by agreement between the owners. If the owners do not agree then the works remain a technical breach of the Act. If damage is caused the only remedy available is at common law, as held in Woodhouse v Consolidated[459] where the party wall collapsed before surveyors (all three) had been appointed and the Court held that the tribunal[460] had no jurisdiction under section 55(k) other than to determine liability and the cost of the remaining notifiable works not yet commenced under the Act. The surveyors Award on liability and costs of the collapsed wall was rejected on appeal and the owners had to revert to common law to recover their damages.

11.10.3   No notice, dispute not crystallised

In one of the earliest cases[461] under the current Act, the Appeal considered the extent of the surveyor's jurisdiction to make a retrospective Award and concluded that the absence of a notice did not entitle the surveyors to retrospectively determine the matters. This decision is in line with the Woodhouse case, and clearly logical. HHJ Evans was clear on this very point; -

> "The issue raised in the present case is whether the appellants liability at common law is either excluded or reduced by the provisions of the Act, which he invoked, eventually, after the nuisance had arisen. I would have no hesitation in rejecting this submission even without reference to authority, because, in my judgment, there is nothing in the Act which can be said to have this effect[462].

---

458 Louis v Sadiq [1997] 1 EGLR 136; (1998) 59 Con LR 127 and Woodhouse v Consolidated Property Corporation Ltd [1993] 19 EG 134.
459 Woodhouse v Consolidated Property Corporation Ltd [1993] 19 EG 134.
460 All three.
461 Louis v Sadiq [1997] 1 EGLR 136; (1998) 59 Con LR 127.
462 Louis v Sadiq [1997] 1 EGLR 136; (1998) 59 Con LR 127/

Accordingly, Mr. Sadiq was liable for the consequential damages and losses arising out of the unlawful works at common law. Following service of notice for the outstanding notifiable works, Mr. Sadiq was entitled to rely upon the Act for protection (and limited liability) for the outstanding matters. This approach was adopted in a recent case[463] where HHJ Murfitt recorded:

> "Bearing in mind that they were in litigation by this stage, their failure to consider any party wall notice or indeed other communications with the Claimant before they did so, seems to me indicative of their dismissive approach to the Claimant's concerns, and of their cavalier regard for the terms of the injunction to which they were subject……..Mr Antino wrote to Mr. Lomas making it clear that " your appointing owners have commenced works which should not have been started without an Award in position, this was clearly stated in the injunction and that injunction is now subject to enforcement proceedings against your appointing owners. I have therefore deleted those works within the Award that you are seeking to **retrospectively award and legalise.**"

11.10.4   Notice served, dispute crystallised, refusal to act.

This situation is substantively different from a failure to serve notice and was debated at great length and cost in the Bibizadeh case.[464] The building owners had personally (never a good thing) prepared and served notice under section 6(1) and 1(5). Although wrongly suggesting the name of a practice for an agreed surveyor. The adjoining owner in good faith, contacted the practice and subsequently appointed a surveyor.[465] Thus, crystallising the dispute and the Act having taken effect. The surveyor correctly wrote to the building owner's raising observations regarding the legality of the proposed works and a potential trespass, to which the building owners took exception. The building owners then purported to withdrew the notices claiming the Act did not apply.[466] Unilaterally, they commenced excavations and demolition works

---

463 Rusciani v Kumar and Sharma (2013) County Court at Chelmsford.
464 Dodosh v Bibizadeh (2014) County Court at Romford.
465 Mr. Daren Flight MRICS.
466 See Chapter 11, subsection 11.5.

which included pulling down the adjoining owner's fence and depositing it on her driveway and then erected a temporary hoarding diagonally across the boundary which they securely fixed to the rear elevation of the adjoining owner's extension. Thus, creating a trespass, nuisance, and damage to the adjoining owner's rendering, herb garden and patio.

The building owners were asked to stop works and comply with the procedures under section 6(1) and 1(5) or an injunction would be sought. The building owner's stopped work and took advice from another RICS surveyor whose first report confirmed *"the Party Wall Act applies and you should serve notice immediately"*. For reasons that were never explained, that advice was ignored and the works continued not surprisingly an injunction was obtained.

The Bibizadeh's applied for the injunction to be lifted, arguing that the Act did not apply and even if it did, it could not be applied retrospectively citing Woodhouse v Consolidated. Counsel for the building owner wrongly suggested that the appropriate remedy would have been to claim for damages at common law. Unfortunately, Counsel for the Bibizadeh's had not understood the subtle distinction between Woodhouse v Consolidated and the Dodosh case. In Woodhouse the dispute had not been crystallised when the damage occurred, whereas in Dodosh the dispute had crystallised upon service of notice and Mr. Flights appointment.   It was successfully argued by Ms Dodosh Counsel[467] that the injunction was reasonable because: -

(a) Dissent had occurred;
(b) The works were incomplete;
(c) A surveyor was appointed;
(d) Further notifiable works were intended; and
(e) The adjoining owners were entitled to the protection provided by the statutory legislation.

One would have hoped that the above case would have brought an end to the building owners going behind the Act following service of notice. In a recent case the defendants[468] served notice through their surveyor, the applicant did not accept the accuracy of the drawings and no satisfactory response was received. A second set of notices were served one month later and whilst a dialogue began no consent or agreement was reached. In fact, the adjoining owner made it clear that he was taking legal advice. The defendants started the works causing damage, trespass and also refused to remove their scaffolding from the applicant's land, and also used the adjoining owners garage roof as an access platform. Mr. Antino was instructed and on attendance the defendants

---

467 Mr. Richard Power Head of Lamb Chambers.
468 Peter J Edmond v Nicholas Bartholomew Denham & Helen Julie Seekings-Denham (2021) H00PE335/

gave assurance that no further works would proceed until the party wall matters were completed. Later that day contractors worked late into the evening trying to finish the notifiable works to avoid an injunction.

The strategy adopted by the defendants mirrored that of the Bibizadeh's. The injunction[469] was heard by Recorder Anne McAllister via zoom due to covid restrictions. The Defendants instructed Mr. Stuart Frame under direct access, the applicant instructed Mr. Michael Callaghan[470] and Mr. Daniel Attridge of Trinity Chambers.[471] Mr. Frame argued that the injunction was just a fee earning exercise and should have been dealt with under ADR. Mr Frame is simply wrong Mr Edmond is entitled to his common law. Mr. Attridge countered that the applicant had no alternative but to seek an injunction when the defendants had made it clear that they would not stop the works unless an injunction was obtained. Mr. Frame's arguments were rejected and the injunction was upheld when the defendants giving the appropriate legal undertakings not to do any notifiable works. Costs were awarded against the defendants.

These two cases emphasize that the Courts will not ignore the Act and/or those who seek to abuse the law and to do so will be exposed to considerable costs and the ignominy of being brought before the Court.

In 2021, another injunction was obtained when developers commenced substantial works without notice.[472] Claiming the works were not notifiable.

11.10.5   Consent prior to damage

If the adjoining owner's consent to the works they are not prevented from calling upon the Act and appointing surveyors at a later date to resolve: -

(a) Any dispute;
(b) Any damage caused to their property; and
(c) Any variation to the agreed works.

This approach was adopted in Onigbanjo[473] when the building owner accepted liability for damage although, the cost of repairing the damage could not be

---

469 See Chapter 18.
470 callaghanm@gepp.co.uk of www.geppsolicitors.co.uk.
471 https://www.trinitychambers.com/team/daniel-attridge.
472 Goodmans Autos Ltd v Maverstone Properties Ltd & Byoot Develop Ltd (2021) County Court at Central London H02CL868.
473 Onigbanjo, A. v Mr. & Mrs Pearson [2008] The Mayors and City of London Court.

agreed. The adjoining owner appointed a surveyor, who requested the building owner to appoint a surveyor. The building owner claimed the Act did not apply because consent had been given. Thus, the remedy for the damage was at common law and outside the Act's jurisdiction. The adjoining owner's surveyor served a section 10(4)[474] request and after 10-days appointed a surveyor on behalf of the building owner. The two surveyors served an Award dealing with the costs. The Award was appealed but rejected on the basis that consent was given on the implied condition and expectation that the works would be carried out to the appropriate standards. More importantly the adjoining owner's property would not be damaged by the building owners works. It was held that the damage was a breach of the consent and therefore the adjoining owners were entitled to rely on the Act to resolve the dispute.

11.10.6 Change of ownership and ongoing liability

The adjoining owner[475] obtained an injunction, notices were served and each owner appointed a surveyor and they selected a third Surveyor. Following a deemed incapacity to Act[476] the building owner's appointed Mr. Kevin O'Callaghan[477] as their surveyor. If matters were not complicated enough, the building owner then sold the property to their surveyor/father-in-law, who had to deem himself incapable of acting because owners cannot represent themselves. Given that an Award travels with the property the new building owner's rights to continue with the works were inherited. Although the liabilities awarded against the previous building owner for damage remained with the previous owners. In such cases, the injunction restraining the previous building owner from carrying out the notifiable building works fell away and did not bind the successor-in-title. In such cases, the adjoining owner would have to obtain a second injunction restraining the successor-in-title, if they refused to serve the notices and adopt the Act. The compensation, legal costs, costs for rectifying damage, and the appointed surveyor's fees prior to the sale of the property all remained with the first building owner, because the sale does not remove their liability.

11.10.7 Anticipated Awards

Because surveyors have no legal jurisdiction to act retrospectively (unless the owners agree), it therefore follows that they do not have jurisdiction to determine future or anticipated works. The surveyor's jurisdiction only flows

---

474 See Chapter 11, subsection 11.5.
475 Sell v Mills & Mrs Mills nee O'Callaghan [2104].
476 Chapter 11, subsection 11.5.
477 Father-in-law and Father to the building owners respectively.

from a valid notice to undertake known notifiable works set out within the notices. In Leadbetter v Marylebone[478] the surveyors determined not only the right to carry out future works but works unrelated to the notices. The Court ruled that the appointed surveyors did not have jurisdiction to adjudicate on future (unknown or suspected) works. There are various reasons, but perhaps the most obvious is that anticipated works may place a liability on future owners, or interfere with the property rights of future adjoining owners. This point was based on the premise that the wall might fail in 10-20 years. Therefore, the adjoining owner sought to protect themselves from any future costs by having an ongoing liability awarded against the building owner. This approach was sensibly rejected on appeal because the surveyor's jurisdiction to Award damages and/or compensation must flow from an actual loss and not a perceived or anticipated loss which is therefore not recoverable under the Act or indeed under common law.

11.10.8   Permissive Awards

A permissive Award is intended to record the circumstances surrounding outstanding works where an owner is not complying with the Act or engaging with the surveyors' requests. The surveyors have an obligation to record these outstanding issues to protect themselves from criticism and/or a possible negligence claim.[479] It is not for the surveyors to force the owners to comply, but if an owner's conduct is preventing the outstanding matters that require resolution that should be recorded in an Award and served upon the owners. In Bibizadeh, the two surveyors[480] served a permissive Award recording the outstanding issues to protect themselves from any alleged negligence. The Bibizadeh's rather surprisingly wrote directly to HHJ Bailey[481] outside of any legal proceedings and he subsequently wrote to both surveyors demanding an explanation (which he had no right to do so) and threatened to order them to appear before him. HHJ Bailey appeared incensed. It was not a matter for him to comment upon indeed he had shockingly jumped to the wrong conclusion and was now acting as an advocate for the Bibizadeh's. Both surveyors indulged HHJ Baileys improper conduct and provided a written explanation for serving permissive Award. HHJ Bailey accepted the surveyors were fully entitled to protect themselves from any potential allegation of negligence and that they had complied with their statutory duties and dealt with all outstanding issues. Quite properly HHJ Bailey advised the Bibizadeh's not to appeal the Award.

---

478 Leadbetter v Marylebone Corporation [No. 1] [1904] 2 KB 893.
479 See Chapter 1, subsection 1.7.
480 Mr. Philip Antino and Mr. Ray Stevens.
481 HHJ Bailey started to give legal advice to the Bibizadeh's outside of any active litigation.

11.10.9   Addendum Awards

The surveyor's jurisdiction flows from the explicit wording of various sections of the Act[482] for example when the notifiable works change, damage is caused or unnecessary inconvenience is caused. These are all remain within the tribunal's jurisdiction and should at first instance be dealt with by the surveyors under section 10(12).

11.10.10   Surveyor's exposure to costs

Unlike arbitration[483] and/or adjudication[484] the party wall surveyor has no immunity and can and is now commonly exposed to serious costs when an Award is appealed.[485] The following applies to any Award served under either section 10(10), (11), and/or (14). The threat of substantial costs is a growing tactic adopted by certain barristers in order to intimidate the surveyors into agreeing to set aside or withdraw their Award, and/or the indeed owners.[486] When appealing an Award[487] the surveyors should if the procedures were adopted properly by Counsel be joined as respondents to the appeal. This tactic first came to prominence in 2016[488] and 2017[489] and more recently in 2021.[490]

In relation to the 2016 tactics, it worked because the surveyor thought he had not done anything wrong it was withdrawn to avoid the risk of exposure to many thousands of pounds in costs. In the most recent case in 2021 quite ironically Counsel[491] for the building owner had joined the surveyors one of which was a previous client.[492] In the 2021 case the fourth respondent stood his ground and he should be commended for that. He believed wholeheartedly in his Award and that he had jurisdiction but the matter went to Court. Despite reading the transcript it appears that Counsel had adopted what is fast becoming one of the most common grounds for challenging an Award by claiming that there was no dispute between the building and adjoining owners.[493] However, having discussed the matter with the fourth respondent he was asked by an owner's solicitor to deal with the damages. The surveyors would not have made

---

482 See Chapter 11, subsection 11.12 & 11.13.
483 The Arbitration Act 1996 (England & Wales)
484 The Housing Grants, Construction and Regeneration Act 1996
485 Evans v Paterson, (1) McGeevy-Harris (2), Newton (3) & McAllister (4) [2021] In the County Court at Central London G20CL068
486 Mohamed & Mohamed v Takhar, Takhar, & Takhar [2016] County Court at Central London.
487 See section 11.17
488 Mills & Mills v Savage & Savage [2016] County Court at Central London (Case No 1).
489 Reeves v Young, Young & Antino [2017] County Court at Central London.
490 Evans v Paterson, (1) McGeevy-Harris (2), Newton (3) &McAllister (4) [2021] In the County Court at Central London G20CL068
491 Mr. Stuart Frame of Tanfield Chambers.
492 Farrs Lane v Bristol Magistrates Court (2016) EWHC
493 Adopted in the Mohammed case.

an Award if they were not made aware of a dispute, and this Award was a considerable time after the Parent Award had been served. So, it must naturally follow that somewhere along the line, one of the owners had contacted the surveyors and said they were in dispute and quite properly involved the surveyors.

Quite how the decision was reached that there was no dispute is unclear, but that was the argument that the Judge upheld the appeal. This exposed the fourth respondent because he had quite properly stood his ground to substantial costs. The problem with this tactic is that it appears to be adopted with wild abandonment. |In another 2021 case[494] the same barrister (Mr Frame) that had been involved in all of the other cases referred to above had wrongly joined the author[495] as a second respondent. This was very surprising because the appeal was of a third surveyors award[496] whereas Dr Antino was simply the adjoining owner's surveyor. This was a fatal and serious error in Mr. Frame's strategy and exposed Mr. Frame's clients (the building owners) to considerable costs and litigation. There was resistance in the first instance and an allegation that they were entitled to include Dr Antino to protect themselves against costs, (a wholly unsupportable and irrational argument). Dr Antino instructed solicitors who wrote to the building owners advising that unless they agreed to a discontinuance, against Dr Antino an application will be made to the Court to seek a Court Order removing Dr Antino as a respondent. The building owners had to accept that Mr. frames approach was wrong in law and agree to a discontinuance and pay Dr Antino's legal costs. The building owners had been unnecessarily exposed to additional costs because of the mistake made by their barrister Mr. Stuart Frame of Tanfield Chambers.

11.11 Section 10(11) Third surveyor referral

Either of the parties or either of the surveyors appointed by the parties may call upon the third surveyor selected in pursuant of this section to determine the disputed matters and he shall make the necessary Award.

Continuing Parliament's intention of ensuring the works are not unreasonably delayed, either of the surveyors and/or owners may make a referral to the third Surveyor. Regrettably the latter is only achievable if the owners have been made aware of their rights. Section 10(11) therefore imposes an implied obligation upon the surveyors to advise the owners of the third surveyors' identity and to advise them of their statutory right under section 10(11). Regrettably a large number of surveyors do not inform their appointing owners

---

494 Capper, M (1) and Capper, R (2) v Macey, B (1) & Antino, P. (2) – (2021) The County Court at Central London H20CL135
495 Dr P Antino
496 Mr. Mazalla-Tomlinson, Practising Barrister

of the identity and/or role of the third Surveyor, thus, depriving the owners from exercising their right to make a referral. Furthermore, the majority of surveyors do not inform the third surveyor of his selection[497] until a dispute arises which in itself can also create difficulties.

The Act is silent on how the referral process should proceed and I am constantly amazed at the differences in the various approaches adopted by the party wall surveyors when referring a matter[498] and indeed how a third surveyor approaches the referral also differs. It is not, in my mind a complicated process, indeed there are similarities with adjudication and arbitration. Accordingly, it is important that the third surveyor ensures that the rules of natural justice are observed.[499] Therefore, any contact with the third surveyor should be copied to the opposite surveyor and in turn the surveyors should ensure that their owners are fully informed and updated as matters progress, because the outcome of any referral could have dire consequences for them and they have a right to be informed of the potential risks. I have produced a flow chart[500] setting out the basic the process to follow but of course the complexities of the case will ultimately determine the final structure and time frame.

11.11.1 The referral process

Stage I

The referring party[501] should on first contact provide the third surveyor with copies of the surveyor's letters of appointment, copies of the notices, drawings and any correspondence which confirms the selection of the third surveyor. If section 10(4) has been adopted then all correspondence leading up to the appointment the surveyor including correspondence to the non-responsive owner should also be provided. It is not necessary at this stage to set out the issues or indeed provide any detailed submissions. The initial contact is simply to establish the third surveyors' agreement that he/she is satisfied that their selection is valid and that they have jurisdiction to hear the referral before moving onto Stage II would apply.

Stage II

As soon as a third surveyor has accepted a referral, he/she must treat the referral as the most important project in their diary. The Third Surveyor should issue clear directions setting out the referral process, so the parties understand what

---

497 See Chapter 11, subsection 11.2.1.
498 7th Edition.
499 See Chapter 1, subsection 1.9.
500 See Chapter 21, subsection 21.14.
501 Either owner or surveyor.

they have to do and more importantly the timeframe. There is no value to the owners in delaying the dispute. There is an implied, if not an explicit duty of care to deal with the dispute as swiftly as possible and thus as economically as possible.[502]

The following is general outline of how the third surveyor should conduct the referral[503]: -

1)   TS request the points in dispute;
2)   Advise on potential costs and any personal circumstances (conflict) that may delay the resolution i.e., holidays;
3)   Request that all submissions[504] are in writing simultaneously copied to the other party.
4)   Confirm any ex parte contact will not be acceptable;
5)   All communications shall be in writing either electronically or by post and simultaneously copied to the opposite surveyor
6)   Set out the time frame for the resolution of the dispute as follows: -

    a.   The referring party to make the submissions within 14 days[505];
    b.   The responding party to reply within 14 days;
    c.   The referring party to provide a rejoinder within 7 days,
    d.   The responding party to provide a surrejoinder within 7 days
    e.   The referring party to provide a rebutter within 7 days,

7)   On receipt of the parties' submissions the third surveyor may issue further directions requesting clarification on any points, or where necessary and appropriate raise questions and/or arrange a site inspection;
8)   The third surveyor may if he/she considers it appropriate take advice from a third party such as structural engineer, quantity surveyor, and/or legal advice where appropriate;
9)   The third Surveyor should give explanations for his decision and append information/points/documentation relied upon in reaching the decision to the Award;
10)   Set out the time frame for service of the Award i.e., 14 days; and
11)   Shall simultaneously serve the Award upon the owners and their surveyors to ensure the fourteen-day appeal period commences simultaneously.

---

502 See Chapter 8, subsection 8.2.
503 Is not intended to be definitive.
504 Verbal or written.
505 The timing is open to the third surveyor to determine.

Ultimately, it is for the third surveyor to determine how he/she conducts the referral but the above structure (1-11) is a helpful guide. The parties can ask the third surveyor to vary the structure and issue amended directions. All reasonable requests should be considered on their merit and should not be unreasonably refused. The third surveyor must be able to demonstrate impartiality, diligence, fairness and transparency. Referrals will vary in complexity and therefore require varying degrees of time and resources. It may be necessary to carry out a site inspection, or alternatively simply rely upon written submissions (a zoom meeting may be of assistance). Some referrals may have multiple issues, and it is not unusual to resolve the issues in stages so that the notifiable work can proceed. Thus, leaving the more complicated and technical issues for a later date. The third surveyor may call upon external expertise and for example instruct Counsel to provide a legal opinion. In these circumstances the third surveyor should make clear within the Award by stating, *"this is a point of law, I have taken Counsel's opinion on this and have reached a decision that I believe is within my powers to determine, and will leave it to the parties to decide whether to appeal the Award"*. Including Counsel's opinion as an appendix to the Award is a sensible precaution however that would depend on the Counsel.

11.11.2 Third surveyor duty of care

It is not unknown for a party to challenge an Award by claiming that third surveyor selection is invalid[506] and should be live to the possibility that their Award will be appealed. Having been satisfied that their selection is valid does not necessarily mean that the grounds of appeal will be rejected, sadly the Courts do not always reach the correct decision. This was evident in the Reeves Case, where the building owner's Counsel[507] only argument was to allege that the third surveyor[508] named in the parent Award was not validly selected and sought a declaration of invalidity.[509] It was claimed that the section 10(1)(b) appointed surveyors[510] had prior to their Award discussed (but not appointed in writing) selecting Mr. Alistair Redler as the third surveyor. They chose not to and selected Mr. Philip Antino in writing (in the Award) as the third surveyor.

The third surveyor should be selected with care; dealing with contentious party wall matters requires experience and knowledge of the Act, and more importantly honesty and integrity. In 2019 I became aware of a building owner

---

506 T. Reeves v R. Young, G. Young & P. Antino [2017] Central London County Court.
507 Mr. Stuart Frame.
508 Mr. Philip Antino.
509 Reeves v Young, Young & Antino [2017] County Court at Central London.
510 Mr. James Gold and Mr. Jon Westway of Vincent Brown.

having ex parte discussions with the third surveyor.[511] The third surveyor emailed the building owner telling him not to tell the surveyors that he was talking to the third surveyor. This is plainly wrong and the clearest lack of integrity and bias.[512] In 2021 on another matter, I caught the same third surveyor denying having had any his ex parte conversations with the building owner's surveyor.[513] The building owner's surveyor when asked for disclosure of all communications with Mr Alex Frame confirmed in an email that he had a conversation with the third surveyor. It falls upon the third surveyor to properly record all contact and to immediately notify all parties of the extent of any discussions or private correspondence.[514]

The third surveyor has both an implied and explicit duty of care to be transparent, impartial and honest. If one of the surveyors contacts the third surveyor, he/she should simultaneously provide the opposite surveyor with full disclosure.[515] The third surveyor's duty is to resolve the dispute, the manner in which they go about resolving the dispute is entirely for the surveyor to determine but they should exercise caution, if they are to avoid an appeal. It is always helpful if the third surveyor also has experience of Adjudication and Arbitration procedures. Mr Frame did not in fact to be clear he denied any communication had taken place.

11.12 Section 10(12) Matters arising out of or incidental to an Award

An Award may determine-

(a)   *the right to execute any work;*
(b)   *the time and manner of executing any work; and*
(c)   *any other matter arising out of or incidental to the dispute including the costs of making the Award;*
but any period appointed by the Award for executing any work shall not unless otherwise agreed between the building owner and the adjoining owner begin to run until after the expiration of the period prescribed by this Act for serve of the notice in respect of which the dispute raises or is deemed to have arisen.

---

511 Mr. Alex Frame.
512 See Chapter 1, subsection 1.10.
513 Mr Kevin Turner.
514 Emails, letters, faxes.
515 See Chapter 1, subsection 1.10.4.

Subsections (a) and (b) are free of ambiguity, however, the explicit wording of subsection (c) is not generally accepted.[516] In my opinion this establishes the surveyors ongoing jurisdiction post service of the parent Award. On the literal meaning of the English language, the inclusion of the words "arising out of" and "incidental to" can only apply after the works have been commenced. There can be no doubt that the surveyor's jurisdiction is ongoing until (contrary to Mr. Isaac's interpretation) such time as the owners agree that all matters covered under the statutory legislation are resolved to the satisfaction of all owners. Accordingly, the provisions created by section 10(12) should not be overlooked or underestimated by surveyors, barristers and indeed the Courts. It explicitly provides the surveyors with very broad jurisdiction allowing them to determine a whole range of matters including but not limited to their fees.

11.12.1 Interim Inspections

It is common practice for surveyors to include within the Award their costs for an interim or a final inspection. However, this is not always justified, for example, excavations are subject to building control approval, if unforeseen problems, such as unstable ground conditions are identified requiring the foundation depth to be increased, the building inspector and/or engineers will determine the appropriate depth. The party wall surveyors only involvement is to be notified of any changes to the notifiable works and to consider the implications. In some instances, they should request further drawings under 6(6) and 6(9) to record the changes but that does necessarily require an addendum Award. An interim inspection is not necessarily justified because the surveyors do not design or manage the works. There may be situations where interim inspections are necessary, for example to check the cutting in of beam to ensure it does not project past the centre of the party wall.

11.13   Section 10(13) Reasonable costs

The reasonable costs incurred in-

(a)   making or obtaining an Award under this section;
(b)   reasonable inspections of work to which the Award relates;
and
(c)   any other matter arising out of the dispute,

shall be paid by such of the parties as the surveyor or surveyors making the Award determine.

---

516 Zaman v Zala (2020) County Court at Central London HHJ Parfitt.

Whilst it is generally held that the building owner will pay the reasonable costs of obtaining an Award, costs can also be awarded against the adjoining owners. Obviously, costs are an emotive subject, especially where the owners have not budgeted for surveyors' fees. The building owner's initial response will be *"why do I have to pay for the adjoining owner's surveyors fees and/or costs"*. The answer is straightforward, the Act authorises the building owner's right to execute notifiable works that may interfere with the adjoining owner's property rights. It should follow that the adjoining owners shall not be exposed to costs because of the building owner's works, also quite naturally should be liable for the reasonable costs incurred on the basis that costs follow the event.

What falls within the term reasonable "costs" is broad and can include checking engineers' fees, and other reasonable and proportionate disbursements incurred in preparing the Award. It has been held that there may be circumstances in which the appointed surveyors also have the power to award payment of non-contentious legal costs.[517] In a recent case it was held *"there can be no doubt that there may be circumstances in which appointed surveyors have the power under section 10 to order payment by one adjoining owner of legal costs reasonably and properly incurred by another.[518]"* In Reeves v Blake, a second Award authorised and directed the content, manner, and timing of work to be carried out by the respondent. In a letter sent to the respondent the surveyor wrote;

> "It is regrettable that the works progressed without settlement of an Award thus giving the adjoining owner little option other than to take legal advice with the work continuing to instigate proceedings to stop the work until such time as an Award had been settled and delivered. Such a set of circumstances involve significant time on the part of both surveyors and solicitors and per the terms of the Award, are recoverable in accordance with section 10(13) of the Act. I enclose herewith the various fee accounts referred to in clause 9 of the Award and would ask that these accounts be discharged directly. My own invoice will be rendered in due course".

---

517 Onigbanjo, A. v Mr. & Mrs Pearson [2008] The Mayors and City of London Court.
518 Reeves v Blake [2009] EWCA C iv 611 P.14.

The surveyors had wrongly determined that the respondents shall forthwith pay the appellants solicitors fees although it was recognised that the costs were for *"contemplated proceedings."* These legal costs were rejected on appeal because they were prepared in anticipation of a refusal to stop, not after any referral. They were avoidable and cannot be recovered.[519] In simple terms the solicitors had jumped the gun and the surveyors clearly got it wrong.

11.13.1 Surveyors contractual relationship

Building owners obviously want to know their potential expenditure before appointing a surveyor. In these instances, it is not uncommon for a surveyor to quote a competitive fixed fee and hoping that they are appointed as an agreed surveyor to limit their time.[520] Therefore, operating under a 'fixed fee' creates a binding contract. The majority of the time, the surveyor will not fully appreciate the extent of the work and/or issues that may be generated by the adjoining owners. The situation vis-à-vis the adjoining owner's surveyors' fees is not bound by that fixed fee approach and inevitably become a highly contentious subject. There is significant disparity between surveyors' hourly rates and how they calculate their fees. Regrettably, a large volume of surveyor's target planning applications as a source of creating work by contacting the adjoining owners and offering their services on the pre-text that the building owners will pay their fees. Unfortunately, that is not how the Act was designed to work. Sections 10(12) and (13) provide the surveyor's powers to determining the reasonable costs payable by the building owner to the adjoining owner. The building owner may not be liable for the full time and effort provided by the adjoining owners surveyor and there may be a shortfall. So, what are the adjoining owners' surveyors' options, quite clearly none, unless he/she has secured terms and conditions of engagement with the adjoining owner when appointed.

Accordingly, if there is a shortfall the surveyor can revert to his terms and conditions for payment. What the surveyor cannot do is to request either the building owner or third surveyor to Award any shortfall against the adjoining owner, because a dispute between an owner and their surveyor is a contractual matter and is not a dispute between the owners. This principle was expressed in a case[521] HHJ Bailey judgment is clear at paragraphs No's 40 and 42 on the adjoining owners' surveyors' legal remedies: -

> *"In the ordinary course of events, however, it is*
> *to be anticipated that the adjoining owners will*
> *pay the fees of their appointed surveyor and any*

519 Midland Bank plc v Bardgrove Property Services Ltd [1991] 2 EGLR 283.
520 See Chapter 11, subsection 11.2.
521 Mohamed v Antino & Stevens (2017) County Court at Central London.

engineer engaged by them, and that the building owners will reimburse them for such payments."

"But there remain the civil courts, both High Court and County Court, where recovery might be made. For the owner-appointed surveyors it will be a matter of contract. It is for the surveyor to ensure that his terms of appointment properly cover the payment of fees."

The earlier case of Dust v Marioni, HHJ Collins CBE, [522] judgment at paragraph 11: -

"The other point which emerges is that, of course, to underline what I have said already, that it only relates to matters which are connected with any work to which the Act relates and which are in dispute between the Building and Adjoining Owner. In other words, the Third Surveyor is not authorised to determine how much a party owes his own surveyor, all the Third Surveyor is entitled to do is to decide how much one Building Owner shall pay the Adjoining Owner. He is not concerned with the contractual dispute between the surveyor and his own client."

It is therefore an important element to the surveyor's successful recovery of their reasonable fees for their justified labour that they have a contract in place with their appointing owners. That of course would also apply to the building owner's surveyor because the circumstances upon which they offered a fixed fee or if indeed work on an hourly rate may not be fully reimbursed for their time. In one case[523] the third surveyor[524] had awarded himself £12,000 in fees, obviously this was appealed.

---

522 Dust v Marioni Greenaway & MacNulty (2004) County Court at Clerkenwell HHJ Collins CBE.
523 Edmond, Edmond & Mulligan v Denham & Seekings-Denham (2021) County Court at Central London (J20CL075).
524 Mr Steve Campbell.

The third surveyors' position is slightly different having been selected and of course is entitled to payment of their fees before releasing their Award, it is nonetheless important that upon receipt of a selection/referral that they should set out their hourly rate, terms and conditions.

Under no circumstances should the surveyors attempt to use the Act to resolve a dispute between an appointing owner and their respective surveyor, that is clearly a contractual matter. Ideally, the contract[525] will also include a dispute resolution procedure to avoid costly litigation.

11.13.2 Demonstrating reasonable fees

Achieving a swift agreement on the surveyor's fees irrespective of whether it is by negotiation between the surveyors or when presenting a fee note to an appointing owner is favourable to all parties. It is imperative that the fees are set out in a clear and concise format. A time sheet (excel spread) that has been meticulously maintained throughout the process will assist in avoiding a dispute or negotiating a resolution. This allows the surveyor to inform the owners or indeed opposing surveyor of their fees at any time. The practice of completing a costs schedule is important for tracking costs and indeed managing the business properly and professionally.

The way in which surveyors present their costs will vary enormously, although a growing number of surveyors have since 2012 adopted the authors approach which is reiterated below. The schedule should include the date of the activity, the hourly rate charged by the surveyor, (generally recorded in 6-minute segments).[526] This is calculated by dividing the hourly rate by ten six-minute segments, for example £350 per hour equates to £35.00 per 6-minute segment. The spreadsheet will automatically calculate the number of segments (time) by the surveyor's rate, disbursements and provide a running sub-total and the VAT liabilities.

11.13.3 Travelling costs and disbursements

One area of constant dispute is the amount that a surveyor can charge for travelling costs when using a company vehicle. This confusion/rejection arises out of the misconceived approach adopted by HMRC's acceptance that an employee can claim 45p per mile from their employer when they use their personal car for commercial activities. The 45p is paid tax free to the employee

---

525 Terms and Conditions.
526 An establish practice with in the legal profession.

and is intended to represent a proportional contribution towards insurance, road tax, fuel, servicing, wear and tear etc. because the car is not always used for commercial purposes the full costs are not recognised by HMRC.

Therefore, the 45p rate per mile is not applicable when an employer provides their employee with a company or pool car where 100% of the costs are paid for by the company.

In this circumstance, it is reasonable for the company to charge a higher level per mile than the HMRC rate because, firstly it is not tax free, secondly it is in recognition of the 100% cost of the fuel, road tax, insurance, servicing, depreciation, finance wear and tear etc.
Therefore, it is not unreasonable for a company to set their own level of charges and are most certainly, not limited to the 45p per mile HMRC rate. Charging upwards of £1 per mile (especially with the fuel costs having gone up some 30% in the last 12 months to reflect their actual cost.

The time incurred for a surveyor to travel to and from a site/meeting is also an allowable cost, and it is not unreasonable to charge 100% of the hourly rate when the time and the date of the meeting is being dictated by a third party.[527] The requesting party must realise that it is unreasonable to put any sort of cap on the level of fee i.e., the time taken multiplied by the hourly rate because the surveyor attending the meeting is doing so at the third party's convenience.

The third party has an obligation to mitigate their liability and should be respectful of the surveyors' other commitments and try to work with them to accommodate a convenient date and appointment time by working to the surveyor's schedule even if it works against their schedule. Arranging for the meeting to take place when they are in the vicinity and therefore reducing the mileage distance chargeable and the time taken is a sensible approach.

The mistaken belief that surveyors can simply say 'well you are not entitled to any more than 30 minutes travelling time' in this day of congestion of congestion is simply unrealistic on a commercial basis. Public transport is erratic and unreliable (especially during Covid) and of course surveyors have a substantial amount of equipment which cannot physically be carried on public transport. Therefore, travelling by road is often the only reasonable way of providing a prompt service. Therefore, in my opinion when the requesting third party is demanding a certain date or time, they must realise that they are exposing their owner to exceptionally higher costs because of their intransigence rather than accommodating the other party's diary.

---

527 Party wall surveyor, building or adjoining owner etc.

11.13.3 Unreasonable Costs

What constitutes unreasonable costs is open to debate, however where a surveyor has failed to provide a level of service commensurate with that of the ordinarily competent surveyor. Then as certain as night follows day, the surveyor cannot expect to be paid their full fee or indeed in some cases anything.

In Delva Patman Redler LLP v D Franses[528] Mr. Franses[529] appointed Mrs. Delva Patman of Delva Patman Redler ("DPR") as his party wall surveyor. The, building owner had served notice on the freeholder but refused to serve notice on Mr. Franses as a lease holder, who's west london Mansion-House apartment was directly below the building owners' apartment. Works commenced without an award in place with Mr. Franses. DPR did not advise Mr. Franses of his right to obtain an injunction and thus, apart from sending a few emails did very little to ensure that Mr. Franses statutory rights were upheld.

The building owner's works, involved cutting into the concrete floor (party structure) and caused significant cracking to the architectural fibrous mouldings, ceiling and indeed in one location pierced all the way through the concrete floor. DPR advised Mr. Franses that because the party wall works had not been triggered, they could do nothing further and then issued an invoice for their fees in the amount of £1,276.50. There was no advice whatsoever of the right to injunct. Mr. Franses instructed Philip Antino who advised him not to pay the fees because the level of service provided did not in his opinion satisfy the test *of the ordinarily competent party wall surveyor.*

DPR issued proceedings to recover their fees of £1,276.50, plus interest of £60.15p and court costs. Mr. Franses filed a defence setting out (1) DPR's failure to provide the appropriate standards and level of service, and (2) the unreasonableness of DPR's fees given they had sent 3 or 4 emails. DPR then offered to reduce their fees to compromise the case. On Philip Antino's advice, Mr. Franses rejected that offer. DPR subsequently and very sensibly withdrew their claim against Mr. Franses without payment for their services.

---

528 Delva Patman Redler LLP v D Franses (2020) - County Court Money Claims Centre G09YJI98.

529 Mr. Franses was 96 years young.

The question is, were DPR fees unreasonable in these circumstances? That's a question that only the reader can form a view about and I make no suggestions either way.

Notwithstanding, credit where credit is due, DPR did withdraw the claim and thus, avoided further distress to a 96 years 'young' Mr Franses and I thank them for that.

However, the issue of unreasonableness does not finish there, the surveyor's hourly rate is often a bone of contention. So how do you determine what is a reasonable hourly rate? The Authors hourly rate[530] is £350.00 plus vat and has been since 2015. Some surveyors charge considerably less, but increase the amount of time they allege to have incurred. When considering my opposite surveyors fees, as the building owners survey, I will look at my own time having done most of the work.[531] If my time is only 8 hours, my opposite surveyor will have a very hard time justifying say 15 hours. So, in this situation who is being reasonable the surveyor who charges less per hour but inflates his time or the surveyor who properly records his time?

In other instances, I have established that some surveyors increase his/her hourly rate when acting for the adjoining owner, on the mistaken belief that the building owners will be paying his fees, in this situation who is being reasonable?

Clearly, it is a problem, but ultimately comes down to the surveyors' morals and integrity.

11.14   Section 10(14) Serving an award

Where the surveyors appointed by the parties make an Award the surveyors shall serve it forthwith on the parties.

Forthwith means immediately[532] surveyors cannot delay service once the Award has been signed, and it has no legal status until it is served, so why delay? The Award can be served on the owners by any of the two surveyors, but service must comply with the procedures set out in section 15[533] unless an alternative

---

530 At the time of writing.
531 Preparing the Award schedule of conditions etc.
532 See Chapter 2, subsection 2.11.
533 See Chapter 3, subsection 3.6.

means has been agreed. Once served the Award is conclusive unless an appeal is filed within 14-days from date of receipt.[534]

11.15 Section 10(15) (a) & (b) Third surveyor's award

Where an Award is made by the third surveyor-

>   *(a)   he shall, after payment of the costs of the Award, serve it forthwith on the parties or their appointed surveyors; and*
>   *(b)   if it is served on their appointed surveyors, they shall serve it forthwith on the parties.*

There may be concerns that one or more of the owners is unlikely to pay the third surveyors' costs when requested. However, does this entitle the third surveyor to request payment on receipt of a referral?   The answer is an unequivocable No.

In some referrals the third surveyor may require expert advice[535] and are exposed to disbursement costs. The right to receive disbursements on account is a long-standing principle within the legal profession, and given that a third surveyor is acting in a quasi-judicial/arbitral position, they should not be required to pay disbursements. But who should pay? and what happens if either both or one of the party's refuses? Is the third surveyor required to pay the disbursement costs in anticipation being paid? These are legitimate questions and should be set out in the third surveyors' terms and conditions.[536]

The third surveyor is the only surveyor entitled to request payment of his fees and/or costs prior to the service of the Award and many do so. However, if the owners refuse to pay the third surveyor, he will never get paid, unless he either progresses a common law action or serves the Award and then enforces the Award after the 14-day appeal period has expired.

Sub-section (b) entitles the third surveyor to serve the Awards on both the surveyors who *"... shall serve it forthwith on the parties."* I always serve my third surveyor awards on the owners, and as a matter of courtesy I provide a signed copy of the Award to the surveyors. Thus, effecting service and establishing the commencement of the simultaneous 14-day appeal process.

11.16 Section 10(16) Award is conclusive

---

534 See Chapter 10, subsections 10.16 & 10.17.
535 Structural engineer, legal advice etc.
536 See Chapter 11, subsection 11.13.1.

The Award shall be conclusive and shall not except as provided by this section be questioned in any Court.

This section is clear and concise, unless an owner files an appeal under section 10(17) or in the alternative apply for a declaration of invalidity the Award is binding, and cannot be overturned at a later date

11.17 Section 10(17) Appealing an award

Either of the parties to the dispute may, within the period of fourteen days beginning with the day on which an Award made under this section is served on him, appeal to the county Court against the Award and the county Court may-

(a)   Rescind the Award or modify it in such manner as the Court thinks fit; and
(b)   make such order as to costs as the Court thinks fit.

Applying the rules of natural justice, the Act that entitles an owner to appeal an Award. Notwithstanding, this right does come with some limitations, the most important of course is the explicit 14-day time period in which the appeal must be filed with the Court, miss this deadline and the Award is binding, or is it?

Historically very few Awards were actually appealed, as recognised by HHJ Platt[537]:

> "It is a tribute to surveyor's profession as a whole and to the members..........in particular that issues over party walls have generally been resolved by a pragmatic and cooperative approach to the provisions of the Act, and consequently appeals to the County Court have been extremely rare."

Regretfully, in recent years it has become the norm to challenge any Award on any basis irrespective of how remote the chances of winning are. Accordingly, the first step is being able to demonstrate when the 14-day period began. It is not negotiable, miss it, and the Award stands.[538] Obtaining a certificate of posting to demonstrate the date of service has historically been all that the surveyors were required to trigger the 14-day period and is relatively straight

---

537 Bansal v Myers [2007] Romford County Court.
538 Zissis v Lukomski & Carter [2006] EWCA C iv 341.

forward process.[539] Sadly, that is no longer the case some Judges[540] such as HHJ Bailey are easily persuaded by an outright denial of having received the Award to justify their appeal outside of the 14-day period.

Adopting the correct legal procedures is critical to securing the appeal within time.[541] In a relatively recent case[542] it was held that CPR 52 and Practice Direction 52D were the correct appeal process. Following the revised CPR Part 52[543] and in particular CPR 52.11, the default position is now that an appeal would generally proceed by way of review and not by rehearing, although there are always exceptions to the rule[544] which would involve hearing new evidence. CPR 52.4(3) provides that unless the appeal Court orders otherwise, an appellant's notice must be served on each respondent as soon as practicable and in any event not later than 7 days. Section 3.4 of Practice Direction 52DPD.4 requires service of the Appellant's notice on the appointed surveyors. The Courts have held that it is important that the appeal is not only filed[545] on time but also correctly, get the process wrong and the Appellant may find themselves without sufficient time to file a revised appeal.

The building owners are entitled to commence the works upon receipt of the Award, although, I would always advise the owners to wait for the appeal period to expire before commencing any of the notifiable works to avoid incurring potentially avoidable and abortive building costs if the appeal is upheld.

11.17.1   Complying with practice direction 52DPD.4

Section 3.4 of 52 DPD.4 requires the surveyor's to be served with the notice of appeal to allow the surveyor the opportunity to defend the Award, which of course is one of the rules of natural justice giving a party the right to be heard. Regrettably, it does not follow that all Judges or indeed barristers[546] are live to this principle or indeed will ensure that the surveyors right to heard is upheld.[547] In this case the building owner's legal team[548] failed to comply with section 3.4

---

539 CPR Part 06 r.6.26.
540 Mills & Mills v Savage & Savage [2016] Central London County Court.
541 Riley Gowler Ltd v National Hospital Board of Governors [1969] 3 ALL ER 1401.
542 Zissis v Lukomski & Carter [2006] EWCA C iv 341.
543 1st October 2012.
544 Capper, M (1) and Capper, R (2) v Macey, B (1) & Antino, P. (2) – (2021) The County Court at Central London H20CL135
545 Zaman v Zala (2020) County Court at Central London HHJ Parfitt.
546 Mr. S Frame of Tanfield Chambers in Capper v Macey.
547 Kultar & Sohanpal v Humble & Humble (2020) Central London County Court.
548 Mr. Paul Dunbar and Mr. Nick Isaac QC.

of Practice Direction 52DPD.4 within the 14-day appeal period[549] and did not serve the appeal on both the adjoining owner's surveyor and the section 10(4) building owners' appointed surveyor.

11.17.2 Setting an Award aside

As an alternative to appealing or seeking a declaration of invalidity, the owners can jointly agree not to be bound by the Award. However, they would not avoid the liability for any costs stated within the Award or under their contractual obligations. If the Award is not appealed, the surveyors can recover their costs. If they remain unpaid and/or refer to their terms and conditions of engagement to recover payment directly from their owner.

11.17.3 Ultra vires

A common ground for appealing an Award is to argue that the Award is ultra vires because of a technical (actual or perceived/manufactured) issue and is not restricted by the 14-day time period.[550] The appellant should set out their concerns clearly and concisely before commencing proceedings, seeking the other sides agreement. If there is no agreement, a declaration for relief is the only alternative option available outside the 14-day period.

Demonstrating an Award or any part of it is ultra vires is challenging and will turn on the specifics of each case. A common defence include *inter alia* the Award was never received, the surveyors lack jurisdiction or the owners have contracted out of the Act[551]. One would hope the Courts would treat any such claim with considerable suspicion, and place the emphasis upon the appellant to demonstrate that the Award was never received. Disappointingly, HHJ Bailey has on occasions[552] held that the building owners had not received the Awards. This was somewhat bizarre, given that there were certificates of postings for separate Awards, and every other party involved received their Award except allegedly for the recipient. All having been posted on the same day. In one case on oath the building owner[553] accepted that post was delivered to a communal hall and might have been picked up by another resident. HHJ Bailey's decision did not appear to recognise that admission and/or to recognise section 15 only required service to the last known address as sufficient.

---

549 See Chapter 10, subsection 10.14.
550 Section 10(17).
551 Mohamed & Mohamed v Antino & Stevens [2017] County Court at Central London.
552 Mills & Mills v Savage & Savage [2016] Central London County Court.
553 Mills & Mills v Savage & Savage [2016] Central London County Court.

In my opinion HHJ Bailey should have recognised that service had been properly served and dismissed the two appeals on the grounds that they were out of time. A defendant should be able to defend such a claim when they have a certificate of posting[554] and the provisions that follow CPR Part 36. With such documentary evidence the appellant should have a very difficult time proving that the service was not affected. An Award or any part thereof may be challenged on the grounds that it is outside the surveyors' jurisdiction[555].

Given the provisions under sections 10(12)(c) & (13) provides broad powers to the surveyor to determine a wide range of issues. The only proviso being that the issue must be *"arising out of or incidental to the dispute……"* and/or *"any other matter arising out of the dispute"*.[556] The surveyors should always remember that an appeal is generally is a review unless the Court directs otherwise[557] thus allowing additional documentation to be submitted. Any appeal should be based on the contents of the Award and if lacking information to support the reasonableness and more importantly the rationale behind the surveyor's decision, the appeal is likely to be successful.[558]

11.17.4 Abuse of due process

The ongoing and acrimonious relationship between the Mohamed and Takhar families first commenced in 2015 and was continuing into late 2021 and beyond. In 2017 the Mohamed and Takhar's had sought an injunction against two surveyors[559] to stop them proceeding under the Party Wall Act to determine their fees. The assertation raised by the Mohamed's (the Takhar's did not take part in the injunction) was to claim that both had both contracted out of the Act, therefore removing the surveyor's jurisdiction. HHJ Bailey was persuaded by this argument, but was it true? Or another misleading statement by the Mohamed's then Counsel Mr Isaac. An independent expert, was appointed to resolve the disputes.

As with many things in life, karma has a habit of turning full circle and in late 2021, the Mohamed's realised that their rejection of the Act had drastically backfired, when the independent expert's report awarded substantial damages and costs in favour of the Takhar's.

---

554 Mills & Mills v Savage & Savage [2016] Central London County Court, Sell & Sell v Mills & O'Callaghan – Kingston Upon Thames CC A00KT940.
555 Bansal v Myers [2007] Romford County Court Unreported.
556 See Chapter 11, section 11.12.
557 Capper, M (1) and Capper, R (2) v Macey, B (1) & Antino, P. (2) – (2021) The County Court at Central London H20CL135
558 Capper, M (1) and Capper, R (2) v Macey, B (1) & Antino, P. (2) – (2021) The County Court at Central London H20CL135
559 Mohamed & Mohamed v Antino & Stevens [2017] County Court at Central London.

The Mohamed's now represented by Mr Stuart Frame wanted to appeal the experts determination. Mr Frame's tactic was to appeal the independent experts award under section 10(17) claiming that it is a party wall matter. This of course was plainly contrary to the position adopted in 2017. The Takhar's were represented by Counsel[560] and Solicitor[561] both eminently experienced and knowledgeable in this area of law and indeed were fully familiar with the grounds argued at the injunction hearing.

A preliminary hearing before HHJ Parfitt, Counsel for the Takhar's[562] referred the Judge to the 2017 injunction hearing. HHJ Parfitt was justifiably concerned and indeed at paragraph 26 of the Judgment[563] made a startling observation that the Court was either being misled in 2017 or misled in 2021!!! The application by the Mohamed's was struck out although they were given leave to file a fresh appeal under CPR procedures, but not under the Party Wall Act. It is extremely difficult to understand how the Mohamed's and/or Mr Frame could even begin to remotely believe that they would be successful.

---

560 Mr. David Mayall of Lamb Chambers.
561 Mr. Ashley Bean of Thirsk Winton LLP.
562 Mr. David Mayall.
563 Mohamed & Lahrie v Takhar & Takhar & Takhar (2021) in the County Court of Central London TCC G20CL122

CHAPTER 12

12.0   Section 11: – Expenses

12.1   Introduction

One of the most provocative issues that the surveyors are asked to decide upon are the costs generated through the administration of the Act. Contrary to popular belief, it is not necessarily the building owner's that is always liable for the costs/expenses incurred. The Act provides the adjoining owners with rights to request works and/or in some circumstances the parties conduct can influence who the surveyors award costs against.

12.2   Section 11(1)(2) and (3) Costs

(1)   Except as provided under this section expenses of work under this Act shall be defrayed by the building owner.
(2)   Any dispute as to responsibility for expenses shall be settled as provided in section 10.
(3)   An expense mentioned in section 1(3)(b) shall be defrayed as there mentioned.

This section reinforces the general principle that the costs of executing the works and *inter alia* the adjoining owner's surveyors' reasonable costs and disbursements are paid by the building owner. The Act quite properly does not define what is a reasonable cost or impose any limitations, that remains within the surveyor's jurisdiction to determine. Where a claim for expenses arises, the appointed surveyors will determine the reasonableness of the request taking into account the party's actions and conduct when apportioning liability. It is therefore important that the surveyors proactively advise the owners about the potential exposure to costs being awarded against them. A surveyor's failure to participate in negotiations regarding costs on receipt of a request will entitle the requesting surveyor[564] to proceed *ex parte,* and determine both the costs and liability leaving the parties with the only option t to appeal the Award.[565]

12.3   Section 11(4)(a) & (b) Owners benefits and responsibility

---

564 Bansal v Myers [2007] Romford County Court Unreported.
565 See Chapter 11, subsection 11.17.

Where work carried out in exercise of the right mentioned in section 2(2)(a), and the work is necessary on account of defect or want of repair of the structure or wall concerned, the expenses shall be defrayed by the building owner and the adjoining owner in such proportion as has regard to-

(a)   the use which the owners respectively make or may make of the structure or wall concerned; and
(b)   responsibility for the defect or want of repair concerned, if more than one owner makes use of the structure or wall concerned.

In my first edition I advised that when the building owners intend to raise a type (a) party wall which is solely for their benefit they have to accept responsibility for any/all costs necessary to ensure the existing wall is sufficient for the proposed increased height. This may include underpinning or demolition and reconstruction. It was 8 years before this opinion was unsuccessfully challenged.[566]   HHJ Parfitt rejected Counsel's[567] submissions that the adjoining owners should contribute to the costs of works to the party wall which the building owners structural engineer requested to support the increased loads created by the raising of the wall. It is not until the adjoining owner decides to enclose upon or adopt the raised section of wall, that they obtain a benefit and become liable to a proportion of the costs. At which time the adjoining owner becomes the building owner and is required to serve notice under section 2(2)(a).

If after completion of section 2(2)(a) works the building owner sells their property prior to any enclosure by the adjoining owner then in my view they are not entitled to a contribution towards the cost of the wall after the sale has completed. This is based on the principle that when the first building owner sold their property, its value was calculated as being inclusive of the whole cost of the increased height/use of the wall and therefore has already been compensated by the purchaser.[568]   It is the new owner who inherits the right to receive a 50% contribution for the future enclosure upon the wall.[569]

---

566 Maddow v Fernandez (2020) TCC.
567 Mr. Isaac Q.C.
568 See Chapter 13, subsection 13.10.
569 See Chapter 12, subsection 12.4.

12.4   Section 11(5)(a) & (b) Proportional use and costs

Where work is carried out in exercise of the right mentioned in section 2(2)(b) the expenses shall be defrayed by the building owner and the adjoining owner in such proportion as has regard to-

(a)   the use which the owners respectively make or may make of the structure or wall concerned; and

(b)   responsibility for the defect or want of repair concerned, if more than one owner makes use of the structure or wall concerned.

This section is explicit when determining liability for the costs, the surveyors shall have regard to the purpose of the works, and the benefit that each owner will obtain from the works. Where works of repair are necessary the liability is split proportionally between the owners. The surveyors can request contractors to give independent estimates and/or to instruct a quantity surveyor to provide assistance if the party wall surveyors are in dispute over the reasonableness of the contribution being claimed.

12.5   Section 11(6) Disturbance and inconvenience

Where the adjoining premises are laid open in exercise of the right mentioned in section 2(2)(e) a fair allowance in respect of disturbance and inconvenience shall be paid by the building owner to the adjoining owner or occupier.

Determining the degree of *"fair allowance* for any inconvenience and/or disturbance"[570] is subjective and must be relevant to the degree of inconvenience and the compensation must be reasonable.[571] For example, if the adjoining owners have to move out of their premises, whilst the works are undertaken the alternative accommodation costs together with out-of-pocket expenses could include dining out[572] or increased travelling costs to work, costs of packing and relocating furniture. It may also be reasonable to award a nominal daily rate for the general inconvenience, disturbance and loss of their use of their home. The surveyors must adopt a pragmatic, impartial and sensible approach to dealing with the issue of compensation. However, the compensation must not be punitive although given the recent judgement[573] the Courts will consider awarding substantial damages for unreasonable conduct.

---

570 Emms v Polya [1973] 227 EG 1659.
571 See Chapter 8.
572 If moved to a hotel.
573 Jones & Lovegrove v Ruth & Ruth [2012} EWHC 1538 and in the Court of Appeal [2011].

12.6   Section 11(7)(a) & (b) Altering the height of the wall

Where a building owner proposes to reduce the height of a party wall or party fence wall under section 2(2)(m) the adjoining owner may serve a counter notice under section 4 requiring the building owner to maintain the existing height of the wall, and in such case the adjoining owner shall pay to the building owner a due proportion of the cost of the wall so far as it exceeds-

(a)   two metres in height; or
(b)   the height currently enclosed upon the building of the adjoining owner.

There can be no doubt that the introduction of section 11(7) flows from the decision in Gyle-Thompson[574] where it was held that there was no explicit right under the 1939 Act to reduce the height of the party wall or party fence wall. In Gyle-Thompson, the surveyors had wrongly authorised such works, and compounded this error by numerous procedural irregularities which invalidated the Award. Notwithstanding, this section does not automatically grant the building owner's a right to reduce the height of the wall, because the adjoining owners also have rights and benefits over the original wall. If the adjoining owner can demonstrate that the existing height is relevant to their continued use and enjoyment of the wall, they can successfully prevent the reduction in height.

12.7   Section 11(8) Cash settlement

Where the building owner is required to make good damage under this Act the adjoining owner has a right to require that the expenses of such making good be determined in accordance with section 10 and paid to him in lieu of the carrying out of work to make the damage good.

This section is an extension of section 7, and applies even if consent[575] was given on receipt of notices and. In my opinion, settling the matter with a cash payment is always the most effective way of bringing a claim to its natural conclusion. The surveyors do not have any powers to deny the adjoining owner's a cash settlement, they can only determine the reasonableness of the amount paid and only if the owners are in dispute. The payment should always (in my opinion) be on a full and final basis, therefore eliminating any further liability. The adjoining owners are not obliged to undertake the works, and may spend the cash how they wish.

---

574 Gyle-Thompson v Wall Street (Properties) Ltd 1 WLR 123 [1974] 1 ALL ER 295.
575 Onigbanjo, A. v Mr. & Mrs Pearson [2008] The Mayors and City of London Court.

12.8   Section 11(9)(a) & (b) Adjoining owners' liability to costs

Where-

(a)   works are carried out, and
(b)   some of the works are carried out at the request of the adjoining owner or in pursuance of a requirement made by him,

he shall defray the expenses of carrying out the works requested or required by him.

The adjoining owners have the right to request building owner's carry out certain works. In these circumstances the adjoining owners are responsible for the costs for executing those works and any associated surveyors' and professional fees. However, the building owners cannot charge inflated rates for the works. Similarly, the adjoining owners cannot seek to have the works carried out at a discounted price. The surveyors will determine the reasonableness of the costs if disputed and make the necessary Award.

12.9   Section 11(10)(a) & (b)Special Foundations with Consent

Where-

(a)   consent in writing has been given to the construction of special foundations on land of an adjoining owner; and
(b)   the adjoining owner erects any building or structure and its cost is found to be increased by reason of the existence of the said foundations,

The owner of the building to which the said foundations belong shall, on receiving an account with any necessary invoices and other supporting documents within the period of two months beginning with the day of the completion of the work by the adjoining owner, repay to the adjoining owner so much of the cost as is due to the existence of the said foundations.

This is another reason why special foundations should never be projected onto an adjoining owner's property, because it creates opportunities for future disputes and claims for costs. The projecting foundations can have an adverse effect on the capital value of the adjoining owner's property and/or their ability to undertake certain building works in the future. Because the Act states that *"the said foundations belong"* will always remain with the owner having undertaken the works. Any benefits and/or liabilities will transfer to future owners. The surveyors have an implied if not explicit duty of care to explain and advise the owners of the possible adverse consequences of giving written consent.

12.10   Section 11(11) Benefit in kind

Where use is subsequently made by the adjoining owner of work carried out solely at the expense of the building owner, the adjoining owner shall pay a due proportion of the expenses incurred by the building owner in carrying out that work; and for this purpose, he shall be taken to have incurred expenses calculated by reference to what the cost of the work would be if it were carried out at the time when that subsequent use is made.

Any benefit obtained by the adjoining owners from works carried out by the building owners must be properly compensated by the adjoining owners who are required to contribute up to 50% towards the current cost of executing the works. This section reinforces[576] the principle that neither owner can obtain a material benefit at the adjoining owner's expense.

12.10   Ambulance chasing

Ambulance chasing is a term that originated in the USA, where the ambulance services are privately owned. They monitor emergency radio frequencies to identify incidents and rush to the scene to obtain work. Disappointingly there are a substantial volume of RICS surveyors' who adopt similar tactics, they scan local authority planning applications and then write to the adjoining owners inviting them to appoint them as their party wall surveyor. The carrot they dangle is the suggestion that as the adjoining owner that they will not incur any costs and thus fall into the trap set by these nefarious tactics.[577] When an Award goes against them, the adjoining will find themselves exposed to fees for their surveyor and/or other costs. Quite astonishingly, a substantial number of professional organisations[578] and associations do not consider this approach to obtaining work as unprofessional or lacking in integrity. Property owners should be wary of strangers bearing gifts, there is no such thing as free advice. When approached by these various organisations they should ask themselves, if they were reputable why do they have to resort to such tactics to obtain work?

---

576 Maddow v Fernandez (2020) TCC.
577 See Chapter 11, section 11.11.
578 RICS and FPWS.

CHAPTER 13

13.1   Introduction: - Security for expenses

Section 12(1) objective is all about protecting the adjoining owner by allowing them to request security of expenses before the commencement of notifiable works. The inclusion of the word 'may' create a non-mandatory activity with the singular intention to protect owners from a loss when an owner is unable to satisfy their financial obligations to either pay for repairs or compensation in lieu of executing the repairs that flow from the building owner's notifiable works. It is effectively an extension to section 7[579] and there are no qualifications required to be demonstrated before a request can be made.

Therefore, in my opinion the surveyors have a statutory obligation (in addition to their expressed and/or implied duty of care) to advise the owners of their right to request security in the first instance. Unfortunately, this approach is not recognised by some organisations,[580] or indeed some party wall surveyors. This raises an important question, how are the owners expected to understand and exercise their rights, if their surveyor is not required to advise them of their rights. An appointed surveyor can never be criticised for providing advice, but will certainly be criticised (possibly sued for negligence)[581] if they have not given the correct advice that the ordinarily competent surveyor should have given, and moreover is deemed to be reasonably foreseeable and necessary for the adjoining owner to decide whether to exercise their statutory right and to mitigate any potential loss.

Surprisingly when a request is made by an adjoining owner. I have encountered a number of excuses such as "my owner is a wealthy person and will be able to pay for any damage" and "my owner owns his house, and is obviously spending a lot of money on the extension or alterations and therefore can pay any damage".

Well for reasons which hopefully are set out below, statements like that are simply irrelevant to the statutory right to make the request. What some surveyors do not appear to appreciate and this is fundamental to the application of section 12(1) it does not matter what the surveyors believe their owners financial position or background is. It is a statutory right laid down by Parliament which allows an owner to make a request for security of expenses. It

---

579 See Chapter 8.
580 RICS 7th Edition (2020) Guidance Notes "Party Wall Legislation and Procedure" Section 8.8.
581 See Chapter, subsection 1.7.

does not fall into the surveyor's jurisdiction to refuse the request, and that is abundantly clear from the literal reading of section 12(1). It is only when there is a dispute as to the amount that it falls upon the surveyors and it is not for the surveyors to say that they cannot have security, the surveyors have to determine a reasonable amount of security.

13.2   Section 12(1) Adjoining owner's security

An adjoining owner may serve a notice requiring the building owner before he begins any work in the exercise of the rights conferred by this Act to give such security as may be agreed between the owners or in the event of dispute determined in accordance with section 10.

Parliament's intention to include a non-mandatory right leaving it open to the adjoining owner to decide whether they wish to request security and if so, they must do it before the works commence. The party wall surveyor should advise their respective owners so they are fully appraised of all their statutory rights.

Accordingly, the surveyor must advise the adjoining owner of their right to request security, and a failure to do so could potentially expose the surveyor[582] to a negligence claim. Surprisingly, this approach is not universally accepted, RICS whilst promoting their organisation and members as operating to the highest standards of professionalism and integrity to protect the public, controversially, in their guidance on party wall matters states the complete opposite: -

> "The surveyor is not statutorily obliged to advise the appointing owner on security of expenses issues, unless there is a dispute in respect of requested security."

> and

> "Requests for security for expenses are not appropriate for a general risk of damage caused by failure to follow the terms of an award or accidental damage."[583]

---

582 See Chapter 1, subsection 1.7.
583 RICS 7th Edition (2020) Guidance Notes "Party Wall Legislation and Procedure" Section 8.8.

The RICS's first statement is non-sensical. This approach is diametrically opposite to the surveyor's statutory appointment and implied duty of care to act with transparency and impartiality. How can an adjoining owner possibly know what their rights are, if they have not been advised of their right under section 12(1)? By implication and on the literal reading of section 12(1) the party wall surveyor owes an implied, if not explicit duty of care to the appointing owners to inform them of all their rights.

The second statement introduces a qualification that simply does not exist within the clear and explicit wording of section 12(1) or any section of the Act. RICS guidance attempts to remove an adjoining owners' statutory right to protect themselves against any potential failure to pay damages. It is not as RICS suggest limited to *"failure to follow the terms of an award or accidental damage."* Parliament did not deem it necessary to include any limitation and therefore, it is not open to the RICS or their members to go behind or indeed to attempt to rewrite the Act. The decision rests with the adjoining owner and that can only arise if the surveyors have advised them of the right to do so. A failure to do so can expose them to a negligence claim.

The intention behind parliament's introduction of the security request is to protect the adjoining owner when the building owner does not have sufficient resources to complete the works and/or from being drawn into unnecessary inconvenience such as litigation or ADR to recover any losses which is in line with the obligations created within section 7.[584]

Given the RICS guidance, it is not unsurprising that there are conflicting opinions on when and how the right to request security can/should be applied. Indeed, the confusion is not limited to RICS members, as recently as 2021, the building owner's surveyor expressed his position following an adjoining owner's request for security: -

> *"I am in agreement with my appointing owner and can see no valid reason or justification for an Award of SFE, and I trust that as the matter is now with the surveyors, you are in agreement with me in that regard."* and *"However, should you be minded that there is such justification, can I please ask you to set out that justification."* Thirteen days later the surveyor continued *"The removal of a chimney breast does not give rise to circumstances that require an Award of security for expenses."*

---

584 See Chapter 8.

Regrettably, this RICS surveyors' interpretation/opinion is not a rational or a logical interpretation of section 12(1), because: -

(i) The Act does not require the adjoining owner or their surveyor to give any reason or justification for the request, it is a statutory right;
(ii) The surveyors do not have the right to introduce any limitations on when, how or indeed why security should be given;
(iii) The surveyors are not required to introduce any reason or justification so long as the security relates to the notifiable works such as the chimney breast removal under section 2(2) (g);
(iv) If the owners are in dispute the surveyor's jurisdiction is limited to two functions, firstly, determining a reasonable amount of security and secondly, how that will be secured/held;[585] and
(v) The surveyor's opinion sought to deprive the adjoining owner of their statutory rights which cannot be lawful.

Regrettably, in this party wall matter the adjoining owner did not want to challenge this through the courts, a decision they later regretted. The request for security is not open to interpretation, it is explicit and once raised must be assessed, even if the surveyors determine a nominal amount. The surveyors should be very cautious about the how they address and calculate any request for security. If the surveyors apply common sense, they should be able to reach agreement on a reasonable level of security. However, it is important that the surveyors remember that their right to determine security only relates to the notifiable works and not any ancillary works.

13.2.1 Possible negligence

A failure to notify the owners of their statutory right under section 12(1) can have devastating consequences for both the surveyors and owners. In one case the author was acting as an expert in respect of a negligence[586] claim against an RICS member who had accepted a section 10(1)(a) appointment. Following service of the Award, substantial structural damage was caused to the adjoining owners property. The agreed surveyor correctly produced an addendum Award requiring the building owner to pay circa £30,000 in lieu of the damage.[587] The building owner was a developer (company A) and were either unwilling or unable to pay the costs. They subsequently sold the development site at a reduced value to 'company B' owned by the same people as company A and then put 'company A' into voluntary liquidation leaving the adjoining owner with no means of recovering the damages from 'company A'.

---

585 Escrow account, bond, insurance policy, cash deposit.
586 See Chapter 1, subsection 1.7.
587 Section 11(8).

The parent Award remained valid allowing the new owner 'company B' to proceed with the works. Company B rejected liability. The adjoining owner was advised to make a claim under his household buildings insurance policy, which not unsurprisingly was rejected in the first instance, but after some difficult negotiations accepted liability.

The insurers wanted to recover or minimise their loss and instructed solicitors, who subsequently instructed the author to produce a CPR part 35 experts report on the liability claim against the agreed surveyor. Because the agreed surveyor[588] had not advised/informed the adjoining owner of his right to request security of expenses, the author considered that the agreed surveyor had not demonstrated and or executed his professional services, applying the test being "the standard of the ordinarily competent party wall surveyor". Consequently, depriving the adjoining owner of the right to protect himself from any loss. In the author's opinion, the agreed surveyor had failed to comply with his statutory duty when he failed to advise the adjoining owner of the section 12(1) right to request security. The adjoining owner's insurers pursued a claim against the agreed surveyor's Professional Indemnity Insurance ("PII"). The PII insurers assessed their potential liability and chances of winning in Court, they negotiated a settlement with a non-disclosure clause. Hence the reason why I am unable to disclose the identity of the parties involved in this matter.

Approximately 18 months later. that I was appointed as a building owners party wall surveyor and the agreed surveyor (in the aforementioned narrative) was the adjoining owner's surveyor. The reception I received was less than cordial and he made it quite clear that following the claim, his insurance premiums had increased by 25%, and that he was unable to obtain alternative cover from other insurers. Therefore, this surveyor was indirectly (through the increased premiums) paying for the adjoining owner's loss[589] and not his insurers.

I explained that had he advised the adjoining owner of their right to request section 12(1) security and even if the adjoining owner had failed to exercise his right, or in the event that security was requested and he had awarded a reasonable amount even if it was less than the value of the damage, he could not have been liable because he had discharged his profession duty of care. One simple letter would have avoided a substantial amount of stress and costs. Not unsurprisingly, the adjoining owner made a request for security the very next day, and the matter was resolved.

Therefore, my advice to all surveyors is **not to** ignore the implied duty of care to advise the owner of their right to request security or as in the position[590]

---

588 A surveyor located in the Manchester area.
589 Insurance companies never lose.
590 Mr. Mike Harry FFPWS in email dated 04.05.21 and 17.05.21.

adopted by one surveyor challenge a legitimate request on the spurious grounds.

13.2.2 Letters of comfort

The concept of offering/providing 'a letter of comfort' in place of security of expenses is a red herring and appears to have been hijacked by some party wall surveyors who do not understand either the section 12 (1) procedures and more alarmingly the concept and function of a comfort letter.

The use of comfort letters was initially developed and introduced by the Government when seeking to procure construction tenders and services. As one can imagine preparing tenders for infrastructure projects like Crossrail, HS2, and HMS Queen Elizabeth II aircraft carrier (to name but a few examples are eyewatering). Consequently, contractors are reluctant to speculate and incur these upfront and unrecoverable costs if they are subsequently found not to meet a particular requirement of the Client. So, the letter of comfort was developed to firstly confirm that the contractor already meets all of the client's specific requirements, and if their tender is the most competitive will be awarded the project. In some instances, the comfort letter will also include a contribution towards their tendering costs even if they are unsuccessful.

For some unfathomable reason some surveyors[591] seem to believe that a letter of comfort from an engineer stating that there should not be any damage in some way satisfies the section 12(1) statutory security. The general wording that seems to be suggested is as follows: -

> "The building owner is to maintain or cause the
> contractor(s) to maintain adequate insurance
> against such risks and provide evidence of this
> to the adjoining owner's surveyor before the
> commencement of the works".

This is in my opinion nonsensical and does not provide the adjoining owner with any protection whatsoever. In circumstances where the letter of comfort has been proffered, the surveyor who accepts it exposes themselves to the same potential negligence as set out in 13.2.1 above.

13.2.3 Contractor's insurance

Some surveyors seem to believe that if the building owner's building contractor provides evidence of their public liability insurance that is sufficient to satisfy

---

591 Mr. Mike Harry FFPWS.

section 12(1). How this approach originated and/or evolved is unclear, but it is nonetheless misconceived, because the contractor's insurance provides no protection to an adjoining owner. The contractor's liability is to the building owner who will recover their costs, if liability is accepted by the contractors' insurers. From the adjoining owner's perspective, it is irrelevant whether the contractors are or are not insured, because any damage caused is resolved by the party wall surveyors (if notifiable works) through an Addendum Award.[592] That will place the liability to reimburse/compensate the adjoining owner upon the building owner, not the contractor. The adjoining owner/occupier should not give up their statutory rights on the wrongful assumption that the contractor's insurance company will accept liability and quantum of any claim, because there is no contractual relationship between the contractors and the adjoining owners.

13.3   Section 12(2)(a) & (b) Building owner's security

Where-

(a)   in the exercise of the rights conferred by this Act an adjoining owner requires the building owner to carry out any work the expenses of which are to be defrayed in whole or in part by the adjoining owner; or
(b)   an adjoining owner serves a notice on the building owner under subsection (1),

the building owner may before beginning the work to which the requirement or notice relates serve a notice on the adjoining owner requiring him to give such security as may be agreed between the owners or in the event of dispute determined in accordance with section 10.

If the adjoining owner serves a counter-notice requesting the building owner to do certain works which are for the benefit of the adjoining owner, then all of the costs quite rightly fall upon the adjoining owner. Accordingly, the building owner is entitled to seek the same protection in the event of possible default of payment by the adjoining owner. The adjoining owners should have sufficient funds available to pay for the works and to be prepared to have that money placed as security and prior to the building owner undertaking the works. The principles of set out within section 13.2 above would apply both owners.

13.4   Section 12(3) & (b) Adjoining owners request for building works

---

592 See Chapter 10, subsection 10.10.9.

If within the period of one month beginning with-

(a)   the day on which a notice is served under subsection (2); or
(b)   in the event of dispute, the date of the determination by the surveyor or
surveyors,
the adjoining owner does not comply with the notice or the determination, the
requirement or notice by him to which the building owner's notice under that
subsection relates shall cease to have effect.

This is intended to prevent the building owners from unnecessary delay, disruption or inconvenience. The same principles regarding finality of notice apply, miss the time frame and the adjoining owners lose the right to have the building owner undertake those works. Establishing when the date of the determination occurred is therefore important, but remember this section only applies to notifiable works.

CHAPTER 14

14.0 Sections 13 &14: – Account for work carried out & settlement of account

14.1 Introduction: - Account for work carried out & settlement of account

These two sections address liability for the costs of works requested by the adjoining owners and sets out the procedures that the building owners must adopt in order to ensure payment. Whilst each case will turn on its own merits, this appears to place an unreasonable burden upon the building owners to finance additional works which would not have been anticipated. Accordingly, the building owners are entitled to request security in the event that the adjoining owner does not have the funds to pay for the requested works. Notwithstanding, these owners will only be aware of their rights and the draconian timeframes imposed, if advised by their appointed surveyor. Accordingly, there is both an implied duty of care owed by the surveyors to make their owners aware of the procedures.

14.2 Section 13(1)(a)&(b) & 14(1) adjoining owners' liability

Within the period of two months beginning with the day of the completion of any work executed by a building owner of which the expenses are to be wholly or partially defrayed by an adjoining owner in accordance with section 11 the building owner shall serve on the adjoining owner an account in writing showing-

(a)   particulars and expenses of the work; and
(b)   any deductions to which the adjoining owner or any other person is entitled in respect of old materials or otherwise;

and in preparing the account the works shall be estimated and valued at fair average rates and prices according to the nature of the work, the locality and the cost of labour and materials prevailing at the time when the work is executed.

In my view it is unreasonable to expect the building owner to finance the works requested by the adjoining owners, which in some instances could be substantial. Therefore, a pragmatic approach has to be adopted and of course it is open to the owners to reach any independent agreement. Waiting until the works have been completed and/or then a further period of two months before being able to request and/or be entitled to payment for the works which the building owner has undertaken is unreasonable. Given this draconian practice regarding finality of notice periods the building owner may lose the right to recover any costs incurred under the Act is also unreasonable. Establishing when the day of completion occurs is therefore important, and only applies to notifiable works which will require the surveyor's input. When the account is challenged, the surveyors must adopt a reasonable and pragmatic approach to determine the reasonable costs which should be recorded within an Award.[593] Thus, allowing the Award to be challenged by the owners. If the works are substantial, I would seek a Quantity surveyors' opinion on the cost of the works.

14.3   Section 13(2) adjoining owners' liability to expenses

Within the period of one month beginning with the day of service of the said account the adjoining owner may serve on the building owner a notice stating any objection he may have thereto and thereupon a dispute shall be deemed to have arisen between the parties.

This is not mandatory and if an agreement on the costs under subsection 13(2) is reached is not within the surveyors jurisdiction. In these circumstances absent of any agreement the provisions under section 10 apply. It would not be unreasonable for the building owner to require an agreement on costs and/or indeed payment up front before instructing the builders to proceed with the works requested by and for the sole benefit of the adjoining owner. After all, why should a building owner pay for building works for the benefit of another property owner. Whilst simultaneously exposing themselves to potential litigation or ADR costs or indeed under section 10 to resolve the dispute. Where the adjoining owners are waiting on information to support their objections, they should notify the building owners and/or the surveyors forthwith, and in such circumstances, it would be unreasonable to refuse an extension of time for service of notice or to serve notice subject to full and better particulars to be served in due course.

14.4   Section 13(3) adjoining owners' liability to expenses

If within that period of one month the adjoining owner does not serve notice under subsection (2) he shall be deemed to have no objection to the account.

---

593 Davies & Sleep v Wise [2006] Barnet County Court.

14.5   Section 14(1) & (2) payment of expenses

*(1)   All expenses to be defrayed by an adjoining owner in accordance with
an account served under section 13 shall be paid by the adjoining
owner.*

*(2)   Until an adjoining owner pays to the building owner such expenses
as aforesaid the property in any works executed under this Act to
which the expenses relate shall be vested solely in the building owner.*

If the adjoining owner's fail to settle any accounts that are deemed reasonable under subsection (1) & (2), the building owners retain ownership and can recover the debt through the Magistrate's Court as a Civil Debt[594] once an Award is served.

However, subsection 14(2) is a toothless tiger, because the works undertaken by the building owner could not necessarily be removed and/or if they are removable may incur further costs.

14.6   Costs and disbursements

14.6.1 Protection against costs

Undoubtedly, the most controversial aspect of the Act and whilst section 10 incorporates various provisions for dealing with the costs of administering the Act, there may be occasions where a party will attempt to protect their position when a dispute arises. Litigants or parties in dispute should be aware that even if they do win their referral to the third surveyor[595] it is by no means a certainty that they will recover all of their costs. Therefore, costs should always be a primary concern if not for the aggrieved party most certainly for their surveyors who should provide an estimation of the costs for acting in a section 10(11) referral. The costs will accrue rapidly and may include disbursement costs.[596] Referring a matter to the third surveyor is time consuming and costly.
The difficulties of achieving all costs were demonstrated the Court of Appeal case[597] on liability to pay abortive costs arising from an injunction. The claimants were the freehold owner of Nelson's Yard. The defendants began excavations without serving notice under section 6(1). The claimants were aware of the procedures under the Act and asked the defendant to comply with his statutory obligations and stop works.   The defendant ignored all correspondence, leaving the claimant with no option but to obtain an

---

594 See Chapter 19 subsection 19.2.
595 See Chapter 11, subsection 11.11.
596 Solicitor's, Barristers, Expert witness and Court fees.
597 Nelson's Yard Management Co v Eziefula [2013] EWCA Civ 235.

injunction.[598] The parties then agreed to a stay of proceedings, surveyors were appointed and an Award was served determining that the defendant should pay a modest sum for the damage caused to the claimant's foundations. The injunction proceedings were brought to a conclusion and the Civil Procedures Rules ("CPR") applied. Under CPR 38.6(1) when a claimant seeks a discontinuance order they would pay the other parties' costs. However, that would only apply if, or where the claimant realises that they do not have a case and want to bring matters to a halt.[599]

In Nelsons Yard, the Court ordered the defendant to pay the claimants costs up to the date of filing of his defence, thereafter each party had to pay their own costs. This seems somewhat at odds with the decision[600] where it was held that reasonable legal costs were recoverable from the other side. The claimants felt aggrieved with the judgment and appealed. The Court of Appeal held that the defendant had failed to respond to any of pre-action correspondence, which amounted to unreasonable conduct that justified the Court a departing from the usual rules on costs. The Court of Appeal held that the defendants were liable for the claimants costs up to the point in time when the defence was filed, but not the costs thereafter. The Court's decision was based on the principle that the claimants could have applied to have the defendants defence struck out, which they chose not to do. Therefore, the parties should each pay their own costs thereafter. The important point to remember is that the professionals advising the litigants must be live to the potential exposure to costs.

14.6.2 A Calderbank offer

This principle evolved from a divorce case between Mr. Calderbank and Mrs. Calderbank. Mr Calderbank made an offer at an early stage of the litigation which Mrs. Calderbank rejected and did not better at trial. Therefore, it was argued that she should be liable for all costs from the date the offer was made. A 'Calderbank offer' is therefore an offer to settle on a *without prejudice save as to costs* basis. These offers can be made by either party and at any time during the litigation process. The objective is to apply pressure on the other side to compromise the litigation and settle at a lower level. However, given that the purpose of the injunction is to uphold the entitlement of one party or to undo something and since the primary relief sought is either an injunction or damages in lieu of an injunction, there is seldom very little scope or opportunity for parties to make a Calderbank offer[601] unless it is the costs of the injunction.

---

598 See Chapter 19.
599 Capper, M (1) and Capper, R (2) v Macey, B (1) & Antino, P. (2) – (2021) The County Court at Central London H20CL135.
600 Onigbanjo, A. v Mr. & Mrs Pearson [2008] The Mayors and City of London Court.
601 Cutts v Head [1984] Ch. 290.

The principle works as follows, assuming a claimant is seeking a payment of £5,000 for damages, the defendants may make a calderbank offer of £3,500. If the Court decides that the claimant is entitled to £3,499 or less. The defendants now have a very strong case for recovering all of their costs on an indemnity basis from the time that the offer was made. Conversely, if the claimant is awarded £3,501 or more then the position is reversed and they are now in a strong position for recovering their costs. The Court will not be made aware of the Calderbank offer (other than its existence) and is only disclosed when costs are considered.[602] The offer must be clear of any ambiguity, if there is any doubt, the recipient should seek clarification otherwise they remain at risk on costs.[603] Another important point to note is that a party can make any number of Calderbank offers to increase the pressure on the other party.

14.6.3 Part 36 Offers

Because costs are an intrinsic element of any litigation, CPR allows either party to protect themselves by making a Part 36 offer. The offer must be in writing and must state (without ambiguity) whether it is in settlement of the whole of the claim or which part of the claim it applies to. The offer should also explain whether it takes into account any counterclaim and should also address the question of interest and whether interest is included in the Part 36 offer. If not the rates of interest and the period that the interest applies should be stated. The Part 36 offer should be made not less than 21 days before the start of the trial and it must be clearly expressed that it remains open for acceptance for 21 days. Thereafter, the *'offeree'* may accept it if there is agreement on the liability of costs which have been incurred after the 21 days have expired, or where the Court gives permission.

CPR Part 36 RR.13 and RR.14 sets out the cost consequences when a Part 36 offer is not accepted. If the claimant fails to better the Part 36 offer, they will generally be ordered to pay the other parties' costs from the date that the Part 36 offer could have been accepted (without a Court order) especially if the party betters their own Part 36 offer. The Court has broad powers and may award and enhance the rate of interest and award the costs on an indemnity basis as set out under CPR Part 36 Rule 21.

---

602 Gaunt, J Q.C. and Morgan, P. C.C. (2002) "Gale on Easements" 7th Edition Sweet & Maxwell Ltd P.532.
603 Phillis Trading Ltd v 86 Lordship Road Ltd [2001] 2 E.G.L.R 85; [2001] EWCA Civ 350.

CHAPTER 15

15.0   Section 16: - Offences

15.0   Introduction: -

This section is invariably overlooked by the surveyors who do not advise the owners or occupier(s) of the consequences of refusing or allowing a person to do anything which they are entitled to do under the Act. The Act clearly must have teeth and if adopted properly when an obstruction occurs[604] can ensure compliance with the Act and/or can impose significant penalties on the offending owners/occupier(s).

15.1   Section 16(1) (a)&(b)

If-

(a)   an occupier of land or premises refused to permit a person to do anything which he is entitled to do with regard to the land or premises under section 8(1) or (5); and

(b)   the occupier knows or has reasonable cause to believe that the person is so entitled,

the occupier is guilt of an offence.

In one very frustrating party wall project the building owners were arrested for public order offences following threats of violence.[605] An injunction was obtained and when the building owners breached the injunction on two separate occasions, an application for committal was made by the adjoining owners. Whilst this was an unusual (and is thankfully a rare occurrence), it demonstrates that not all building owners will act rationally and/or reasonably,[606] even after having been ordered by the Court. Furthermore, the obstructive behaviour is not limited to the owners or surveyors but can extend to a solicitor or surveyor knowingly hiding/withholding documents.

---

604 Dodosh v Bibizadeh [2014] County Court at Romford.
605 Rusciani v Kumar and Sharma (2012) County Court of Chelmsford (unreported).
606 See Chapter 1, subsection 1.10.4.

15.4   Section 16(2)(a)&(b) Hindrance

If-

*(a)   a person hinders or obstructs a person in attempting to do
          anything which he is entitled to do with regard to land or
          premises under section 891) or (5); and*
(b)   the first-mentioned person is guilty of an offence.

The surveyors owe the owners a duty of care and should advise them of the consequences of hindering any lawful activities. Subsection (b) would appear to remove any defence to the offence, but if the surveyors have not advised their owners they could and should be criticised by the Court. The owners must be advised of the consequences of any obstructive actions.

15.5   Section 16(3) Conviction

A person guilty of an offence under subsection (1) or (2) is liable on summary conviction to a fine of an amount not exceeding level 3 on the standard scale.

Despite having been involved in some very acrimonious matters the author is not aware of any person being prosecuted thus far. However, if they were, it would be heard in the Magistrates Court and on summary conviction liable to a fine which should not exceed level 3 on the standard scale which is currently £1,000.00. Any appeal against such a conviction would be heard within the Crown Court.

CHAPTER 16

16.0   Section 17: - Recovery of sums

16.1   Introduction

Party wall surveyors are not entitled to payment of their fees prior to service of an Award[607] and unfortunately in some instances owners refuse to pay the fees especially when section 10(4) has been adopted. Therefore, it is only right that the Act includes provisions for enforcing payment. However, this will incur the surveyors further time and legal costs sometimes in excess of what is actually owed. One of the factors that often influences the decision to commence legal action is the uncertainty of recovering legal costs, which is ultimately at the discretion of the Court.

The Act recognises these difficulties with the inclusion of *"any sum payable shall be recoverable as a civil debt"* in the Magistrates Court and the process is substantively different to and more efficient than the traditional small claims Court. Another benefit is the speed in which the Magistrates' Court will/should deal with the complaint which is generally within a matter of weeks as opposed to many months/years if pursued through the County Court.[608]   The process begins when a complaint is laid before the Magistrates which entitles the claimant to recover not only the sum Awarded but provides greater certainty to recover their costs in pursuing the complaint. In the early days of the Act, the Magistrate's Clerks were unaware of the right to serve a complaint (because it was rarely adopted), the Court Clerk would initially resist the application, believing it should be filed within the County Court. Mr. S Brighton[609] advised his colleagues that this was the correct the approach due to section 17. Therefore, allowing the owners and/or surveyors[610] to recover the Awarded sum as a Civil Debt. This does not affect the third surveyor, because he/she is entitled under section 10(11) to request payment of their fees before service of their Award, and very rarely do they have to enforce payment.

16.2   Section 17 Magistrates' Court

---

607 Save for the third surveyor.
608 County Court is overloaded and underfunded.
609 Chief Executive of the Justices' Clerks' Society in 2010.
610 Subject to obtaining a Deed of Assignment.

Any sum payable in pursuance of this Act (otherwise than by way of a fine) shall be recoverable summarily as a civil debt.

The definition of a Civil Debt is found within chapter 43, section 150(1) of *The Magistrates' Courts Act 1980*[611] ("the MCA"): -

"Sum enforceable as a civil debt" means -

(a)   any sum recoverable summarily as a civil debt which is adjudged to be paid by the order of a magistrates' court;

(b)   any other sum expressed by this or any other Act to be so enforceable".

Section 53 of the MCA provides:

"(1)   On the hearing of a complaint, the Court shall, if the defendant appears, state to him the substance of the complaint.

(2)   The court, after hearing the evidence and the parties, shall make the order for which the complaint is made or dismiss the complaint.

(3)   Where a complaint is for an order for the payment of a sum recoverable summarily as a civil debt, ... the Court may make the order with the consent of the defendant without hearing evidence."

Section 58(1) of the MCA 1980 provides:

"A magistrates' Court shall have power to make an order on complaint for the payment of any money recoverable summarily as a civil debt."

16.2.1 Enforcing Recovery of Costs

The majority of Awards will state that the surveyors' costs should be paid direct to the surveyor, it was unclear if this was correct, and the author would recommend enforcing the Award as a civil debt. This is supported by the provisions under section 10(12)(c) & (13)(c) which includes the words *"as the surveyor or surveyors making the Award determine"*. This gives the surveyors the right to Award who shall pay the costs and to who. The issue was clarified

---

by Judicial Review[612] which held that surveyors could indeed award costs to be paid direct to the surveyor. A surveyor[613] appointed under section 10(4), will want to be satisfied that he/she will get paid. Adjoining owners that are reluctant to appoint a surveyor (hence giving rise to the section 10(4) appointment) are unlikely to pay any monies owed to the surveyor. With this degree of uncertainty, why would any surveyor logically accept a section 10(4) appointment? They overcome this uncertainty by producing an Award that requires the owners[614] to pay the surveyors costs directly, leaving the owners to recover the costs where/if applicable.

The approach is as follows: -

Atkin's Court Forms, Vol 19(1), (2), paragraph 246, says as follows: -

> "The distinction between a sum recoverable as a civil debt and a sum enforceable as a civil debt is important because a different procedure applies in each case. Where the sum is recoverable as a civil debt <u>the debt must be proved</u> and an order for payment obtained before further enforcement action may be taken. Where the sum is enforceable as a civil debt the amount of the debt has been established by the Court in other proceedings, usually as part of the adjudication of those proceedings, and no order for payment is necessary as a preliminary step to enforcement".

The provisions of the MCA are procedural in nature and do not change the basis of liability, whilst giving the power to decide whether a debt is due and enforcing such payment. Money payable as a result of an Award under the Act will amount to a 'debt' to the surveyor when the following wording is included with an Award: -

> "The building owners will pay directly to Mr. X (the surveyor) costs of the appointment of £ **[insert fees]** plus VAT in connection with the preparation of this Award".

Because this debt is owed to 'Mr X' and if it is intended to rely upon the MCA to enforce the Award, the surveyor will require a deed of assignment from his/her appointing owner if they want to enforce payment[615] otherwise the appointing owner must become the Claimant.

---

612 Farrs Developments v Bristol Magistrates Court, Judicial Review.
613 Dodosh v Bibizadeh [2014] Romford County Court.
614 Or adjoining owners.
615 Antino v Reeves (2016) Barkingside Magistrates Court, Antino v Stirling Properties Ltd (2016) Barking Magistrates Court S & Antino v Burke & Johnny (2016) Barking Magistrates Court.

To protect themselves a surveyor should set out his terms of engagement with their appointing owners however, this is not necessarily applicable in all cases[616]. Thus, a section 10(4) surveyor should ensure the building owner agrees his terms and conditions. The tribunal[617] are operating under statutory powers within the meaning of Section 10 of the 1996 Act. Whilst, they have a statutory duty, there is no reason why that surveyor cannot also have a contract[618] with an appointing owner (especially under section 10(4) circumstances), the terms and conditions must be set out at the commencement of the contract in the normal way. Furthermore, the principle that a surveyor may owe statutory duties to someone other than his contractual client does not preclude a contract from arising[619] by implicit or explicit means with the appointing owner. CPR Part 35 for example imposes on expert witnesses in litigation an overriding duty to the Court, (not their client) yet there is undeniably a contract between the expert and his client.

CPR Part 35.3 provides:

> *35.3*   *(1)*   *It is the duty of the experts to help the Court on matters within their expertise.*
>
>   *(2)*   *This duty overrides any obligations to the person from whom experts have received instructions or by whom they are paid.*

16.2.2 Recovering costs is expensive

Legal advice should always be obtained before commencing any debt recovery process, but as a general principal, a letter before action setting out the debt and the intention to commence litigation or ADR[620] requesting payment within seven days before filing a claim with the Court should be sent to the debtor. The pre-action letter should set out the remedy sought and what the recipient is required to do to avoid litigation and further costs such as interest which should also be included in the pre-action letter. Demonstrating service of all the documentation will be essential to achieving an order for payment, all correspondence should be properly recorded[621] and evidenced in the bundle[622].

---

616 S.10(4) does not in my view create an appointment between the appointed surveyor and reluctant owner.
617 Surveyors
618 Terms & Conditions.
619 Mr. Richard Power Counsel of Lamb Chambers Temple.
620 If incorporated within the surveyors T&C.
621 Chapter 17, subsection 17.2.
622 The term "Bundle" is used in litigation to refer to the documents relied upon in the action.

If the pre-action letter does not achieve a positive response, the claimant must file a written complaint before the Justices' Clerk at the local Magistrates' Court. The Magistrates' Court (Forms) Rules 1981 suggest either Form 98 or 104; the technically correct version is the latter. Using the prescribed form will eliminate procedural mistakes which may be argued or relied upon by the defendant. The complaint should include a statement that the application is made under section 17 of The Party Wall etc. Act 1996 and include the parties' full names and last known residential address and identify them as either the Defendant or Claimant with their contact details (where known). The bundle should include *inter alia* (i) all notices and letters of appointment (ii) a signed copy of the Award (iii) the pre-action letters requesting payment, (iv) and all correspondence that demonstrates that the defendants ignored the Award and fail to pay the sums so Awarded, (v) proof of posting, (vi) Copies of Fee accounts, (vii) an estimated schedule of the costs in pursuing the action.

The issue of costs[623] incurred for recovering a debt can often exceed the amount being sought. Defendants often rely on this risk when making offers to settle below the awarded amount.[624] It would usually defeat the objective, if the complainant was unable to recover their costs in full, which are generally at the discretion of the Court. The Court is required to allow costs if the award includes a clear reference to "other contingencies".[625] This will/should include *inter alia* the costs for preparing the case, Court fees, attendance at Court, Solicitors, and Counsels fees and general disbursements. The complaint should include a detailed breakdown of anticipated costs and disclose this to the other party prior to the hearing together with an estimate for any further costs.

The Magistrates' Court fee is per Defendant for processing the complaint, irrespective of the amount being recovered. The Magistrates' Court will prepare the summons which the claimants are required to serve upon the defendants. The claimants and the defendants should attend and may be required to give evidence under oath. If the defendant fails to attend the matter can still proceed in their absence. The Court will make the relevant order and will consider any costs on the principle that they are just and reasonable under section 64(1) of the MCA and will be added to the sum stated in the complaint. The MCA requires the complaint to be laid within six months from the date of the Award, miss it and the only option is the County Court. If the six-month window is due to expire and payment has not been received, I suggest that an application is filed within the Magistrates' Court to secure the right to have the matter heard whilst simultaneously making an application for a stay of proceedings to allow settlement negotiations to continue.

---

623 Legal and Surveyors fees.
624 See Chapter 14, subsections 14.4.2 and 14.4.3.
625 Chapter 23, subsections 23.7 & 23.8.

CHAPTER 17

17.0   Section 18 & 19: - Exclusions

All statutory instruments are predicated upon the premise that all things will be made equal following its application, all property owners will and should have the same obligations and rights. It is therefore somewhat astonishing to note that the sole purpose of some sections of the Act exclude certain owners from the statutory legislation. Given that the Act has gone to considerable lengths to define what an owner is within section 20, eyebrows should be raised when considering sections 18 & 19 and why these owners are entitled to an exemption from the very laws that frustrate us mere mortals? Whilst ensuring their ability to earn substantial fees for its application.

17.1   Section 18(1)(a)(b)(c) &(d)

This Act shall not apply to land which is situated in inner London and in which there is an interest belonging to-

(a)	*the Honourable Society of the Inner Temple,*
(b)	*the Honourable Society of the Middle Temple.*
(c)	*the Honourable Society of Lincoln's Inn, or*
(d)	*the Honourable Society of Gray's Inn.*

I am fully appreciative of the UK's wonderfully diverse and archaic built environment that I live and work within. Indeed, on the numerous occasions that I have attended conferences with Counsel, I always endeavour to arrive early to walk around and enjoy the magnificence of the majestic grounds and holidays that surround the barristers' offices colloquially referred to as "chambers." Just having the opportunity to sit in the tranquillity of the Temples gardens is a pleasant and calming experience, but I remain to this day, confused, concerned and bewildered that subsection (a)-(d) exempt these Honourable Societies from vagaries of the Act. I have been unable to find/obtain any rational justification for their exclusion. Given that the Act provides benefits and remedies to property owners one would have thought that these august bodies, given that their very existence (income) is dependent upon the application of such legislation would have wanted to embrace the benefits and protection the Act provides?

17.2   Section 18(2)

The reference in subsection (1) to inner London is to Greater London other than the outer London Boroughs.

This subsection simply adds to the confusion and mystique surrounding the Inner (Greater) London areas and property interests of the Honourable Society of the Inner Temple, the Middle Temple, the Society of Lincoln's Inn; and Grey's Inn being excluded, whilst their colleagues chambers outside these areas are captured under the Act.

17.3   Section 19(1)(a)(b) &(c)

This Act shall apply to land in which there is-

(a)   *an interest belonging to Her Majesty in right of the Crown,*
(b)   *an interest belonging to a government department, or*
(c)   *an interest held in trust for her Majesty for the purposes of any such department.*

and;

Section 19(2)(a) & (b)

This Act shall apply to-

(a)   *land which is vested in, but not occupied by, Her Majesty in right of the Duchy of Lancaster;*
(b)   *land which is vested in, but not occupied by, the possessor for the time being of the Duchy of Cornwall.*

Now if you remain as confused as I am about the intent behind section 18(1) & (2) exclusions, the introduction of this explicit inclusion will leave you further perplexed. The obvious question is why did Parliament include this explicit reference to Her Majesty when the section 20 definitions of owners is explicit? Is the introduction of the words 'interest' and 'occupy' of particular relevance? what qualifies as an interest? what qualifies as occupied? If the crown has an interest in or occupies a building on a lease greater than 12-months, then the section 20 definition of occupier should require them to adopt the legislation, unless it is occupied by HM Queen Elizabeth. Is this occupation defined by a lesser period of time?

CHAPTER 18

18.0   Introduction to basements and special foundations

The construction industry has experienced an unprecedented explosion in subterranean developments (basements) which are now on par, if not exceeding (in volume) loft conversions and traditional extensions. This has been driven by advances in damp proofing technology and innovative engineering designs enabling cost effective subterranean habitable environments to be created. The benefit of building below ground is the avoidance of planning restrictions, although planning departments are becoming better informed and attempting to restrict these works. However, it is important to properly interpret the Act when it applies to a proposed basement because there are potential hazards created by significant divides within the party wall community. Why? This flows from the Acts' inclusion of the special foundation definition[626] and the Section 7(4) veto and how that will or will not determine whether the basement can be constructed across the line of junction i.e., directly beneath the existing party wall.   The conflict has been fuelled by Judge Baileys decision in Chaturachinda, but addressed in the Author's doctoral research.

The inclusion of the section 7(4) veto allows an adjoining owner to withhold written consent preventing special foundations being projected onto their land. This is a significant hurdle that the basement design must overcome, and the 2015 case[627] attempted to set out the way forward by circumventing the Act, with strips/rails introduced beneath the basement. But is it a logical and rational Judgement? The judgement does not sit well within the party wall community, as identified in the authors Doctoral Research[628] where it has demonstrated that the special foundation and the section 7(4) veto is the most common area of conflict[629] experienced within the party wall community, but only when applied to a proposed basement. It would be unrealistic to attempt to include the full extent of the thesis[630] within this book[631] although some elements are included herein to explain why HHJ Bailey judgment is wrong in law.

---

626 See Chapter 8, subsection 8.5.
627 Chaturachinda v Fairholme (2015) TCC County Court at Central London.
628 Antino, P. (2021) "Interpretation of the Party Wall etc. Act 1996 and the Implications for Building Below Ground" Anglia Ruskin University, Ph.D. Thesis.
629 See tables 1 & 2 of the.
630 80,000 word thesis.
631 Dr Anino's Thesis is available from the British Library and/or www.apaproperty.com.

18.1   What is a foundation?

The Building Regulations, Approved Document A1 helpfully defines the function of a foundation: -

> "The building shall be constructed so that the combined dead, imposed, and wind loads are sustained and transmitted by it to the ground: (a) safely, and (b) without causing such deflection or deformation of any part of the building, or such movement of the ground, as will impair the stability of any part of the building".

Section 2(e) of The Building Regulations Approved Document, sets out the various guidelines specifying the minimum thicknesses and depth of foundations etc. But clearly the Approved Document A1 **does not specify, exclude or limit the use of specific materials**, nor does it state that a foundation is restricted to horizontal structures or the lowest point of the building below ground level. The only qualification/function recognised by the Building Regulations is that the foundation must safely transfer the loads onto the ground.

Arguably foundations are singularly the most important component of any structure. If they fail the structure resting thereon will be compromised and, in some cases, subject to catastrophic failure. A foundation's function is to safely support the structure above by transferring the imposed loads safely to the ground. Understanding how these materials/elements perform that function both independently and when joined with another is important, if a cohesive and robust understanding of the function of the foundation (in the context of the Act's special foundation definition) is to be achieved. Each element of the construction process will perform a distinct function that contributes towards the overall structural integrity and dynamics of the structure (see section 18.9.6).

To fall within the Act's section 20 definition,[632] the foundation must satisfy two criteria (1) be the part of the structure that is in direct contact with the ground and (2) upon which the wall rests. When a basement box is constructed beneath the existing foundations it satisfies both criteria (1) and (2) and must therefore

---

632 See Chapter 2, subsection 2.5.1.

by definition be a foundation. There is nothing controversial about that interpretation and application of the definition. [633]

18.2   What is a special foundation?

The Act's section 20 definition (See Figure No 2) does not restrict/limit or require foundations to be horizontal structures, nor indeed does it eliminate vertical elements such as a wall from performing the same function as a foundation. *"Special foundation"* means foundations in which an assemblage of beams or rods is employed for the purpose of distributing any load. Parliament clearly intended the Act to draw a distinction between foundations with and without reinforcement.   Thus, the unique definition of special foundation was included.   The only distinction between the definition and materials used for constructing as 'foundation' and a 'special foundation' is the introduction of "…. an assemblage of beams or rods is used for distributing loads…".   Thus, the Act clearly recognises that reinforcement has a structural function for the distribution of **'any load'**.   The Act's definition does not specify a minimum amount of reinforcement; therefore, the use of any reinforcement will satisfy the definition of a special foundation. Interestingly, the P&T suggest[634] that if the concrete wall is linked to the slab, then the basement is a single structure, which must by definition create the foundation (See Figure No 17). They further opine: *"If a foundation relies on reinforcement for distributing loads, then the whole foundation is likely to be special, even if part of it does not include reinforcement"[635]* which is plainly obvious so why the confusion within the party wall community?

"Special foundation" means foundations in which an assemblage of beams or rods is employed for the purpose of distributing any load.

---

633 Brown, R. W. (1992) "Foundation Behaviour and Repair: Residential and Light Commercial", 2nd edition, McGraw-Hill.
634 Pyramus & Thisbe Club, "Special Foundations: What they are and are not", (2015) P&T Guidance Note No. 12.
635 Pyramus & Thisbe Club, "Special Foundations: What they are and are not", (2015) P&T Guidance Note No. 12.

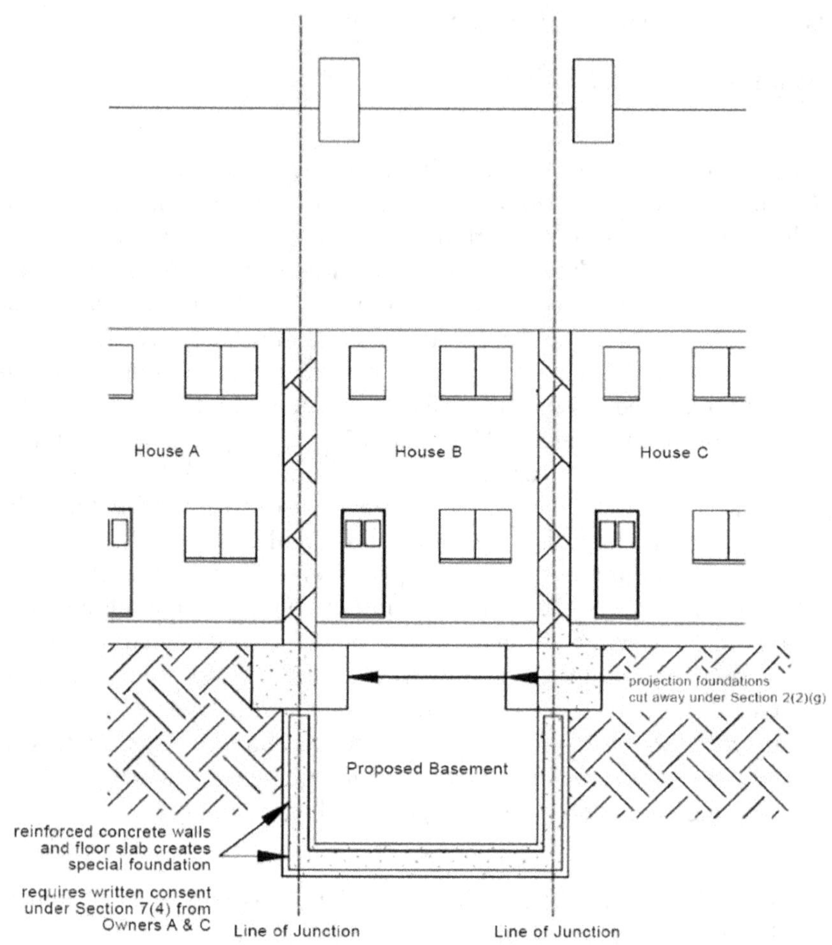

Figure 18 Basement Construction with Special foundations

18.3   The function of a basement box

Buildings are increasingly complex structures and as new regulations come into force to meet more stringent performance criteria,[636] the complexity increases and surveyors must understand and adopt a holistic approach during their assessment. The excavation for a basement box most certainly, as suggested by Bickford-Smith[637] underpin the original foundations, (thus supplanting the

636 Fire, Energy Performance etc.
637 Bickford-Smith, and S, Nicholls, D. and Smith, A. 4th Ed, (2017) "Party Walls: Law and Practice" LexisNexis.

original foundation's function) rendering them redundant (See Section 18.9.6). The preferred method of constructing a basement is to form a reinforced concrete box to create a three-dimensional structure (see Figure No. 17 & 19) for the purposes of transferring any load safely to the ground. The reinforcement links the horizontal and vertical elements of the box creating a single structure/function and should not be assessed as individual elements. Remove any part of the reinforcement from any elements of the basement box and its structural function will fail. A basement's function is defined by: -

1   Positioning beneath the wall, and supplants the original foundations;

2   Is in touch with the ground and forms part of the foundation;[638]

3   The walls are retaining walls transferring the lateral "surcharge" forces created by the adjacent retained soil by directing the loads through the box and onto the ground;

4   The structural integrity of the "box" is determined by the linking of the horizontal and vertical elements;

5   Remove the link and the box loses structural integrity and will fail to support the imposed and dead loads; and

6   The walls of the structure rest upon the base slab.

18.4   The function of a retaining wall

Unsupported soil will move/slip etc. until it achieves natural stability unless it is restrained. In a basement construction, the vertical elements (walls) act as a retaining wall to resist the lateral forces created by the load surcharge applied (See Figure No 19). The reinforced wall must be able to resist the surcharge loads/force applied and to safely transfer them to the ground. This can only be achieved by the inclusion of an assemblage of beams and/or rods (reinforcement) to distribute the loads to the basement box. Thus, satisfy the special foundations' definition. There is nothing controversial in this analysis of the function of a retaining wall. It is also therefore clear that the basement box wall provides the same function as a retaining wall by creating an alternative means of support for the soil.

---

638 Brown, R. W. (1992) "Foundation Behaviour and Repair: Residential and Light Commercial", 2nd edition, McGraw-Hill.

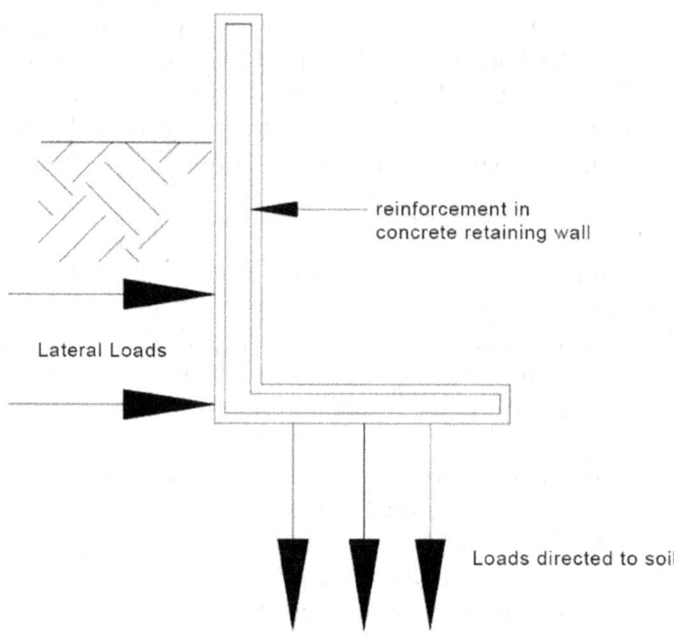

Figure 19 Function of a Retaining Wall

18.5   The function of reinforced concrete

Concrete is weak in tension but strong in compression and by nature requires bulk to achieve its ability to resist forces applied to it. Introduce reinforcement and the need for bulk is removed whilst its ability to resist tensile forces increases allowing the volume of concrete to be reduced, thus becoming more environmentally attractive, economical and structurally sound to construct. The function of reinforced concrete beneath the existing structure must ensure that the structural integrity of the building above is not compromised. The linking of the reinforcement will create a contiguous structure, (contrary to the Chaturachinda judgement), the horizontal and vertical elements of the basement box cannot be considered as having independent functions or definitions. The box acts as one, and ensures that all loads are transferred through the combined vertical and horizontal elements of the box, by resisting the horizontal (lateral) surcharge loads created by the adjacent ground and hydrostatic pressure and any other surcharge loads acting on the basement box/walls.[639]   This is only achievable if the applied loads are distributed through the box as a single entity[640] which is only possible when the concrete has an assemblage of beams and/or rods, for the purposes of distributing **'any load'** and thus will satisfy the Section 20 definition of a special foundation and trigger the Section 7(4) veto.

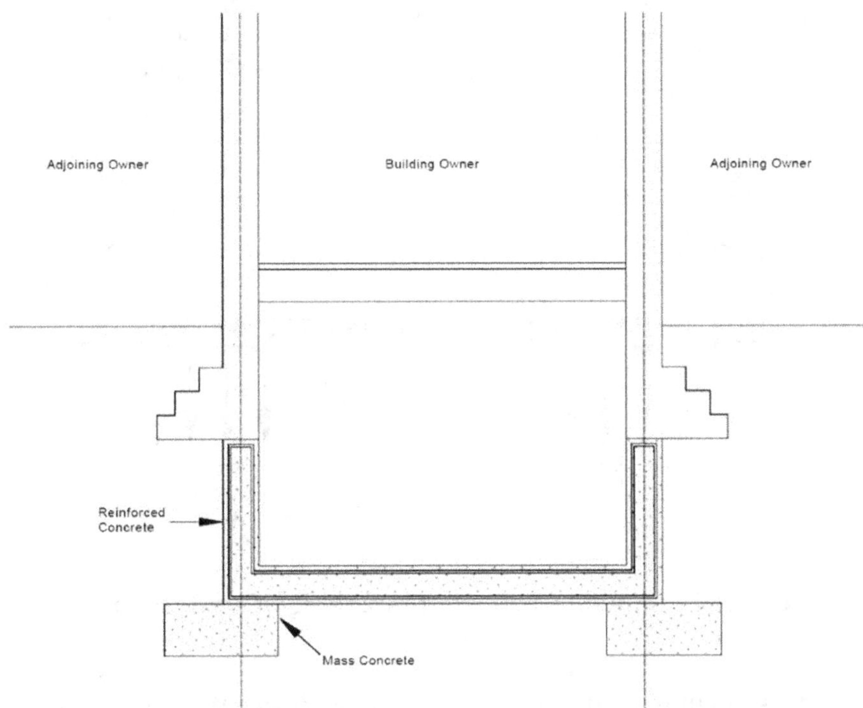

Figure 20 Chaturachinda's Alternative Design Ruled not to be a Special Foundation

The basement box has no other structural function than to distribute loads and is dependent upon the link between the vertical and horizontal elements created by the reinforcement so loads can be safely transmitted to the adjacent soil. Thus, the similarities between the function of a freestanding and retaining wall (See Figure No 19) as recognised by Ambrose[641] and Antino[642] (See Figure No

639 Haslam, S., and O'Connor, L. (2013) "Specialist Domestic: Underpinning and Subsidence ".
640 Horizontally and vertically.
641 Ambrose, J. (1991) Simplified Design of Masonry Structures. New York: John Wiley and Sons, Inc.
642 Antino, P. (2021) "Interpretation of the Party Wall etc. Act 1996 and the Implications for Building Below Ground" Anglia Ruskin University, Ph.D. Thesis.

21) are the same. Furthermore, because the building's original foundations are no longer in touch with the ground, they are no longer the foundation.

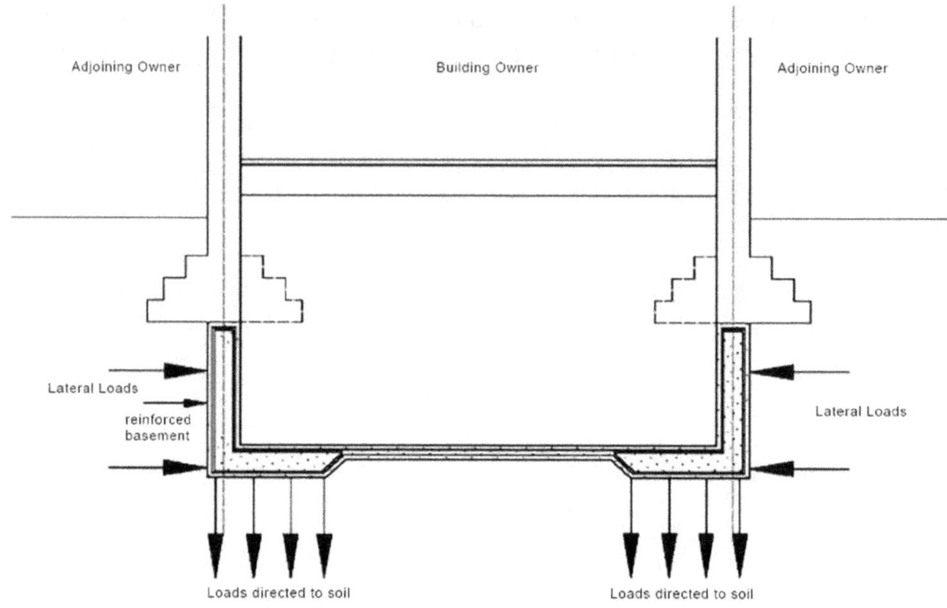

Figure 21 Standard basement Box Design/Construction

18.6   Does raising the party wall downwards create a foundation?

"Under section 2 (2) (a) a building owner shall have the following rights-

(a)   to underpin, thicken **or raise a party structure**, a party fence wall, or an external wall which belongs to the building owner and is built against a party structure fence wall." (Emphasis added).

The inclusion of the word "raise" is not limited or restricted to putting something on top of the wall, and accordingly, it is accepted practice that a party wall can be raised downwards. When we consider the Chaturachinda decision, the third surveyor held that the vertical elements 'wall' (see Figure 20) is only ever a wall and cannot be considered a foundation irrespective of whether it is below ground level. Looking objectively at Mr Redler's position, even when a wall[643] has been extended downwards it remains resting upon the basement (See Figure Nos 27 – 29) slab which by definition is now the foundation (special or otherwise) for the wall, not the rails/strips. Would the material used to construct the vertical elements of the box determine or alter the function? for example if constructed from bricks the issue of the wall being a special foundation falls away, but the function of distributing the loads remains. But it is well established in construction that a wall must/should rest on a foundation in this case the slab upon which the wall rests will become the foundation.

18.7   Special foundations and the section 7(4) veto

Parliament did not explain why it was considered necessary to incorporate two definitions for the foundations or why it appears reasonable to allow the projection of foundations on to the adjoining owner's land without their permission (but not allowing special foundations). The section 7(4) veto is also silent on why the latter is an issue, and the former is not? Analysing the concept should begin with the construction of the specific wording to identify any differing qualifications contained therein: -

*'Foundation, in relation to a wall, means the solid ground or artificially-formed support **resting on solid ground** on which the wall rests.'*

and

*'Special foundation' means foundation in which an assemblage of beams or rods is employed for the purpose of distributing **any load**.'*

The two definitions clearly recognise and emphasise the importance of 'function' which leaves the designer with broad scope to design the foundation in any manner and using any materials necessary to support the structure above so long as they transfer the loads safely to the ground because that is the primary function of any foundation. Therefore, it naturally follows that the only reasonable conclusion that can be reached is that the "function of the assemblage of rods and/or beams" within the basement box is to act as a special foundation.

The following five questions can be used to establish the basements' function and thus, which definition applies. The questions should be asked by the party wall surveyor when considering the design to establish whether or not it is a special foundation.

---

643 See Diagram No. 21.

Table 1 Assessment Questions to Establish if Special Foundations Exist

		YES	NO
(i)	Is the artificially-formed support resting on the ground?		
(ii)	Is the proposed wall resting upon the artificially-formed support?		
(iii)	Is the artificially-formed support transferring any load to the ground upon which it rests?		
(iv)	Does the artificially-formed support contain an assemblage of beams and/or rods for the distribution of any load?		
(v)	Is the artificially-formed support projecting onto the adjoining owner's land?		

If the answer to any of the first three questions (i)–(iii) is "No" then it is not a foundation; if the answer is "Yes" it is a foundation.

If the answer to the first four questions (i)–(iv) is "Yes" then it is a special foundation; and if the answer to (v) is "Yes" the section 7(4) veto applies.

Many basement boxes have been constructed by consent[644] therefore without applying the section 7(4) veto falls away. However, Chaturachinda is the only case that has attempted to address the issue of the section 7(4) veto. The first basement construction design adopted a traditional reinforced concrete box (see Figure No. 21). The adjoining owner's surveyor challenged the design correctly, claiming that it created a special foundation and therefore, under section 7(4), the adjoining owner's written consent had to be obtained before the surveyors could serve their Award. The adjoining owners would not give written consent, and the building owners surveyor did not challenge this interpretation.

The building owners engineer simply amended the basement design and introduced mass concrete rails of nominal (depth and width) beneath the outer perimeter of the box (See Figure No 20) claiming that the strips/rails were the foundation and because these did not contain an assemblage of beams and/or rods for the purposes of distributing any load, the obligation to obtain written consent under section 7(4) was no longer applicable. This proposition was rejected by the adjoining owner's surveyor on the basis that the rails did not satisfy the structural function, i.e., did not safely transfer the loads to the ground, an obvious prerequisite of the function of a foundation. Astonishingly, it was accepted that the rails only purpose was to circumvent the section 7(4) veto. The matter was referred under section 10(11) to the third surveyor who relied upon several cases[645] to explain his approach when coming to his decision:

> "Where a basement is being formed beneath a
> party wall, then it is not necessarily the case
> that the whole structure that is placed beneath
> the existing wall is itself a foundation. This
> was identified in the case of Standard Bank of
> British South America v Stokes [1878] in
> which it was decided that a wall can be raised
> downwards as well as upwards. In my view,
> **the key issue is** the primary **function of the
> structure** in question. A vertical structure

---

644 Often without being advised about the Section 7(4) veto.
645 Standard Bank of British and South America v Stokes (1878) L.R 9 Ch. D. & Gray v Elite Town Management Ltd (2015) County Court at Central London.

formed for the purpose of enclosing an
occupied space is primarily a wall and not a
foundation. The fact that **the load from the
original wall is transmitted through that
structure** and ultimately to the ground does
not make that structure a foundation any more
than a wall above ground is a foundation
simply because it transmits a load form a roof
to the ground." (Emphasis added).

The third surveyor determined that the reinforced concrete basement wall was simply an extension of the original brick wall downwards because he believed that the only function the basement box wall performed was:

"For the purpose of enclosing an occupied
space, and thus, the vertical sections of the
box are walls....."

This is of course non-sensical especially when the walls clearly form part of the basement construction through the link created by the reinforcement and/or function of a retaining wall (See Figure No 19 & 21).

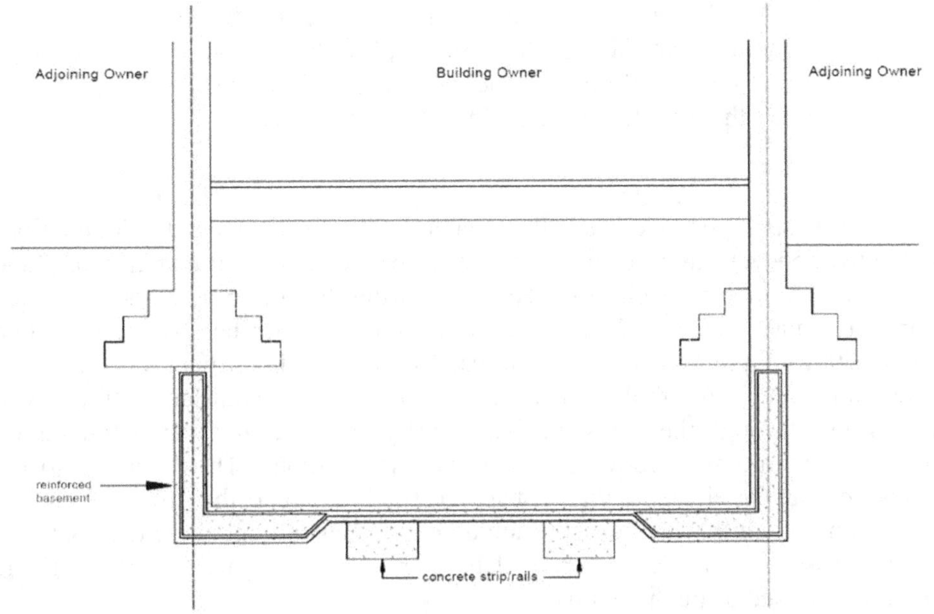

Figure 22 Alternative to Chaturachinda Relocation Strips/Rails does not alter the Function of the Box

Even if we move the rail/strips (See Figure No 20 & 22) inwards the function of the basement box does not alter and therefore the rails/strips cannot under the section 20 definition be a special foundation because they do not transfer the loads to the ground. The box does as a three-dimensional box does.

The third surveyor clearly gave no account or consideration to the basement wall acting as a retaining wall (See Figure No 19 & 21). Accordingly, incorrectly concluding that a concrete wall was only a wall separate from the basement slab which is incorrect. Having reached this decision, he applied section 2(2)(a), and held that a party wall can be raised downwards in reinforced concrete as a wall without requiring written consent under section 7(4) when the wall sits astride the line of junction. The third surveyor also recorded "whilst having taken note of Mr. Wright's contention that the mass concrete foundation is not a necessity…**that may be the case** I do not believe that means it does not succeed in achieving that" (emphasis added).

The question the author asks is. If the rails are not a necessity, then their function to distribute loads falls away and therefore cannot be the foundation, **because a foundation is a necessity**.

> "The rails placed beneath the basement box
> transmit the load from the wall to the ground,
> and therefore it is the rails and nothing else
> that constitute the building's foundations".

The third surveyor accepted that where reinforced concrete foundations extended beneath the party wall, they were on the adjoining owner's land and were by definition a special foundation requiring the adjoining owner's written consent under section 7(4). The third surveyor further suggested that, irrespective of the fact that the original loads from the structure above were now transmitted through the vertical reinforced concrete walls and ultimately to the ground through the box/slab, that still did not make the wall a foundation any more than a wall above ground was a foundation. Thus, coming to the decision that the elements that distributed the loads onto the ground were the mass concrete rails which do not include reinforcement, and were therefore not a special foundation. However, as demonstrated (See Figure No 19 & 21) the loads are passed through the box

Not unsurprising, the third surveyor's Award was appealed, coming before HHJ Bailey (now retired) who recognised that reinforced concrete is in common use in basement designs. At paragraph 46 of the judgment, Bailey obiter dictum:

> "Where it is clear that a person has deployed an
> artifice or device purely to circumvent the clear
> intention of Parliament it is unthinkable that the
> Court will turn a blind eye to such behaviour".

> "While Mr. Pole succeeds in demonstrating that
> there are forces at work, with resultant downward
> loads, other than the (main) downward force
> consequent on the weight of the building, what he
> does not demonstrate is that these forces bear
> down on the Adjoining Owners' land without
> passing through the mass concrete."

How the Judge decided that the appellants had not demonstrated to the Court's satisfaction that any part of the box transmitted loads (See Figure No 19, 21 & 23) onto the adjoining owner's land is absent from the judgment. Although it must be obvious that if the rails were unnecessary, the box is transferring the loads to the ground not the rails. HHJ Bailey is silent on the lateral loads (See Figure No 19) from the adjacent soil and how those loads extend along the full width of the basement slab.

At paragraph 57, HHJ Bailey was clearly persuaded by the respondent's (building owner's) submission obiter dictum: -

> "It matters not where the load is distributed. Simply that the sole consideration is where the wall rests. Therefore, the wall rests on the mass concrete foundation, and as the mass concrete is not a special foundation, it may simply be asserted that the appellant's argument fails, and fails even if it were possible to **demonstrate that the load is distributed to the adjoining owner's** land by the slab without such distribution bearing through the mass concrete." (Emphasis added).

Actually, the wall rests on the slab as demonstrated by the construction process (See Figure No 27 – 31) as shown in Section 18.9.6 HHJ Bailey continued: -

> "In this connection it is plainly not sufficient for the adjoining owner to show that load is distributed to ground alongside the mass concrete on the building owner's side of the foundation. **It is necessary to show that load is distributed to the ground which is directly beneath the party wall,** which includes the basement party wall originally constructed for the basement of 30 Abingdon Villas, and which is to be deepened in the same vertical plane by the Respondents in accordance with Mr. Pringuer-James' design." (Emphasis added).

The Acts definitions of "foundation and special foundation" does not include HHJ Bailey's bizarre interpretation it simply states 'any load'. The function of the box is critical and demonstrates this, further, the Act does not specify any such qualification/requirement. Bizarrely, (if not controversially) HHJ Bailey had previously presided over the earlier Gray case which had incorporated a reinforced concrete basement, and upheld the Award in Gray v Elite judgment (2015) that a basement was a special foundation. This is not the first time HHJ Bailey has expressed conflicting views strikingly similar cases: -

> "It is clear from the plan that the works included reinforced steel foundations and were special foundations for the purposes of section 7(4)." [646]

On comparison of these two cases, it is not clear why or indeed how HHJ Bailey reached two conflicting judgments when: (i) the function of the box remained the same; and (ii) the third surveyor acknowledged that the mass concrete rails made no contribution to the distribution of any loads, when handing down the judgment HHJ Bailey stated:

> "In coming to my decision, I have considered the interpretations [definitions] set out in Section 20 of the Act. This defines a special foundation as 'foundations in which an assemblage of beams or rods is employed for the purpose of distributing **any load**'. It is appropriate to consider reinforced concrete to be a foundation within this definition and therefore a reinforced concrete foundation beneath the party wall that extends across the boundary onto the Adjoining Owner's land would be a special foundation requiring the Adjoining Owner's consent. However, the definition of foundation is 'in relation to a wall, means the solid ground or artificially-formed support resting on solid ground on which the wall rests.' (Emphasis added).

> "Where a basement is being formed beneath a party wall, then it is not necessarily the case that the whole structure that is placed beneath the existing wall is itself a foundation. This incorrect for reasons set out a box is a single structural element with one function). This was identified in the case of Standard Bank of British South America v Stokes [1878] in which it was decided

that a wall can be raised downwards as well as upwards. In my view, the key issue is the primary function of the structure in question. A vertical structure formed for the purpose of enclosing an occupied space is primarily a wall and not a foundation. The fact that the load from the original wall is transmitted through that structure and ultimately to the ground does not make that structure a foundation any more than a wall above ground is a foundation simply because it transmits a load form a roof to the ground. With this design, the feature that transmits the load from the vertical reinforced concrete wall to the ground is the mass concrete strip foundation and as a result there is not a special foundation in this design that requires the Adjoining Owners' consent. I have taken note of Mr. Wright's contention that the mass concrete foundation is not a necessity for the structure being proposed and has been designed to achieve the result of this interpretation. That may be the case but I do not believe that means that it does not succeed in achieving that."

On summary of HHJ Bailey's decision it appears that he held that: -

(i)   The primary function of the box is to form a wall enclosing an occupied space;
(ii) A wall does not form a foundation to the structure above;
(iii) It does not transfer loads onto the ground;
(iv) It did not transfer loads from an adjoining owner's land to the ground;
(v)   The box walls were resting on the mass concrete rails; and
(vi) The mass concrete rails transmit the load to the ground and are therefore the foundation.

This summary is flawed because: -

(i)   The box is a single structure with a single structural function;
(ii) The walls are retaining soil and are a foundation;
(iii) The box transfers the loads to the ground;
(iv) The box walls are not sitting on the concrete rails; and
(v)   The concrete rails do not transmit all of the load to the ground.

221

The authors Ph.D., research demonstrated that the Chaturachinda judgment was wrong. It did not recognise that the basement walls are resting on the basement slab, and not the rails. Neither does it recognise the function of the box to distribute any load. The judgment does address the function of the reinforcement although blame for that may rest with Chaturachinda's counsel for not advancing that as a ground of appeal. Neither does the judgment consider what would occur if the reinforcement **had not** been incorporated and that may also rest with counsel for not arguing the point properly or at all.

18.9 Established basement construction techniques and designs

Not all basement constructions are new works, some involve alterations to existing basements to create usable environments. Whilst, it is unusual for party wall surveyors to have any involvement in the design process or the method of construction, early involvement will provide an opportunity to advise on the design and to remove any possibility that the works may create conflict.

18.9.1 Accepted basement and cellar designs

There are a wide range of accepted basement construction techniques that are used to form the basement walls[647] subject to numerous factors that will influence the design process. Most certainly the geotechnical make-up of the soil and the construction of existing structures will influence the design and are classified as:

> (a) cellar extensions;
> (b) new single level basement; and
> (c) new multi-level basements.

18.9.2 Cellar extensions

Cellars were commonplace in Victorian properties originally designed for the storage of fossil fuels etc. They were not designed for habitation and have low head heights, were devoid of any damp proofing and are the least complex form of construction. These often-used brick spreader foundations which undoubtedly are both a foundation and a retaining wall. Converting a cellar to a basement where brick spreader walls are used as both a foundation and a retaining wall requires cutting away the stepped brickwork to form a vertical

---

647 Butcher, T. (2007) "Risks in Domestic Basement Construction", NHBC Foundation BRE Press.

surface. Followed by the introduction of traditional underpinning foundations to the appropriate depth, around the perimeter of the wall or removal of the brick walls in their entirety and replacing them with reinforced concrete. The underpinning is executed in a series of non-sequential steps and relies on the integrity of the surface wall to share load whilst small sections are progressively undermined.[648] Once the perimeter underpins have been formed, the remaining central bulk of the soil is excavated to the appropriate depth and a new basement floor slab is formed.

Method:

(1) Expose the top of the existing foundation by removing the existing floor construction along the edge of the wall and foundation that is to be underpinned;
(2) Excavate along the existing foundation in a series of small sections typically 1–1.2 m in length but certainly not exceeding 1.2 m. The process adopts a hit and miss approach with the bays being individually excavated non-sequentially;
(3) Position reinforcement (if specified) and pour the concrete;
(4) These pins are left to cure;
(5) The process is then repeated until all of the pins have been formed creating a contiguous foundation; and
(6) it is common practice to insert starter bars horizontally between the pins to bond them together unless reinforcement is specified.

18.9.3 Single level basements

The formation of a new level below an existing footprint where no cellars or voids previously existed. Underpinning the existing structure with a box construction (See Section 18.9.6) is the common method of construction by inserting a reinforced concrete box below the existing walls. Before commencing any underpinning activities, it is appropriate to consider the practical issues that relate to the construction process for retrofit basements. Although the construction process is the same irrespective of whether mass concrete underpins or a reinforced box is formed. Whichever method is adopted, both structures will supplant the original foundations by underpinning them.

---

648 Ove Arup, (2010) "London Borough of Camden: Guidance for Subterranean Developments", Ove Arup and Partners Ltd.

18.9.4 Multi-level basements

This involves creating several levels below the existing footprint and in some circumstances beyond it, which increases the probability of building below the ground water level. This is an additional complication and will increase costs of any basement construction project.[649]

18.9.5 Accepted basement construction designs avoiding Special foundations

There is one significant difference between Figure No 20 and Figure No 21, the latter does not have the concrete rails/strips. The thickened perimeter slab is designed to distribute the loads created by the combined weight of the retained soil and the structure above the basement box through to the ground (See Figure No 21). The use of mass-filled concrete rails directly below the slab (See Figure No 20) suggested by HHJ Bailey et al, allegedly avoids the section 7(4) veto, even when it is accepted that the rails/strips are superfluous to the distribution of loads. If a foundation does not distribute the imposed loads onto the ground, how can it be a foundation?

The following Figures No 21, 22 & 23 demonstrate alternative designs. However, Figure No 21will not avoid the section 7(4) veto. Figure Nos 24 adopts a mass concrete underpin foundation with an independent reinforced concrete floor slab avoiding the Act's definition of a special foundation.

---

649 Haslam, S., and O'Connor, L. (2013) "Specialist Domestic: Underpinning and Subsidence."

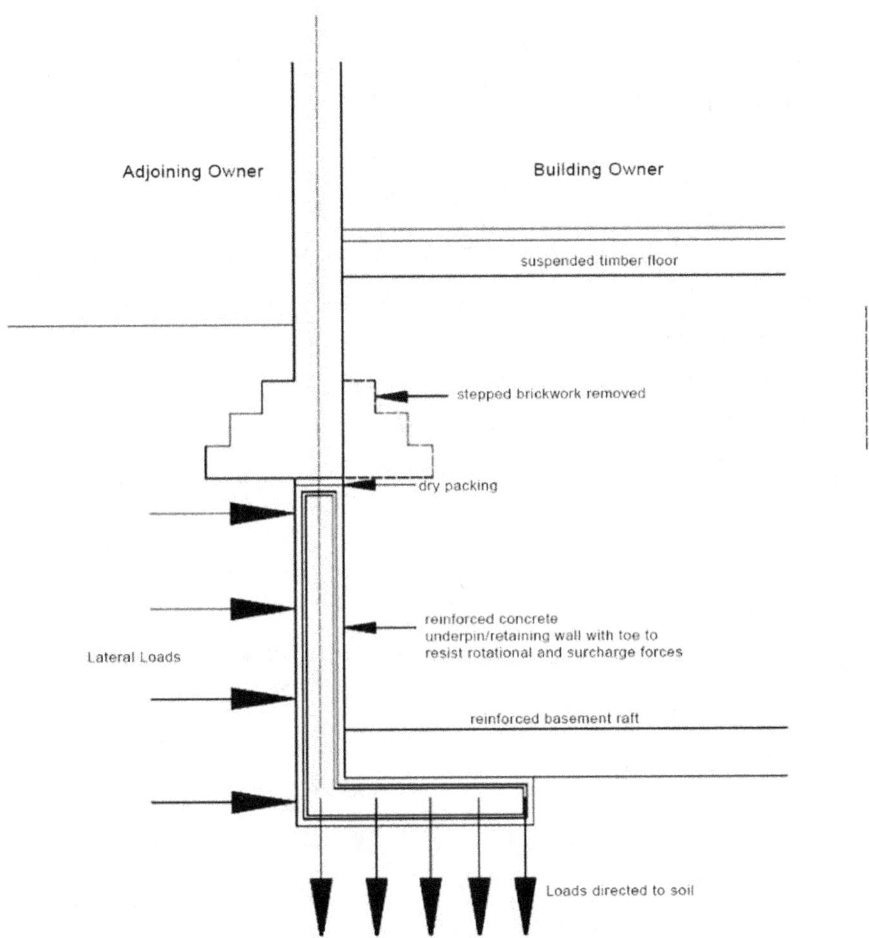

Figure 23 Reinforced Concrete Wall and Toe with Independent Slab

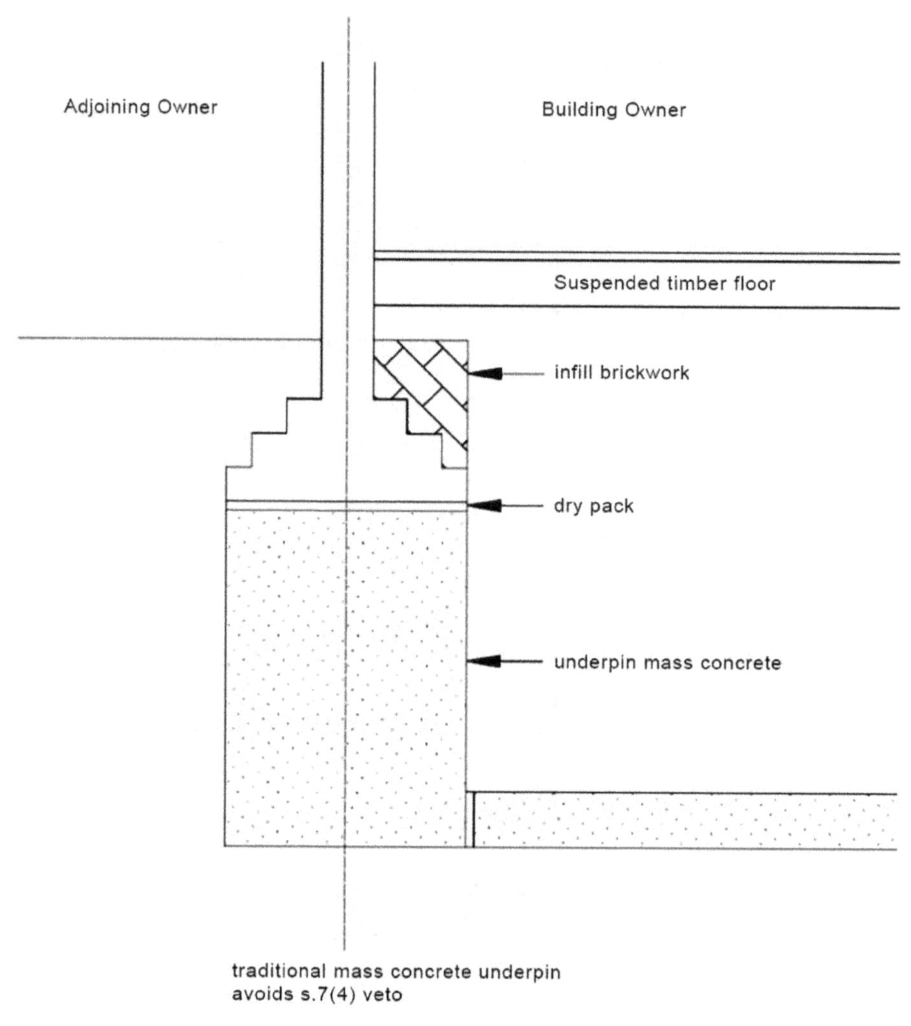

Figure 24 Full Width Concrete Strip Foundation with Independent Slab

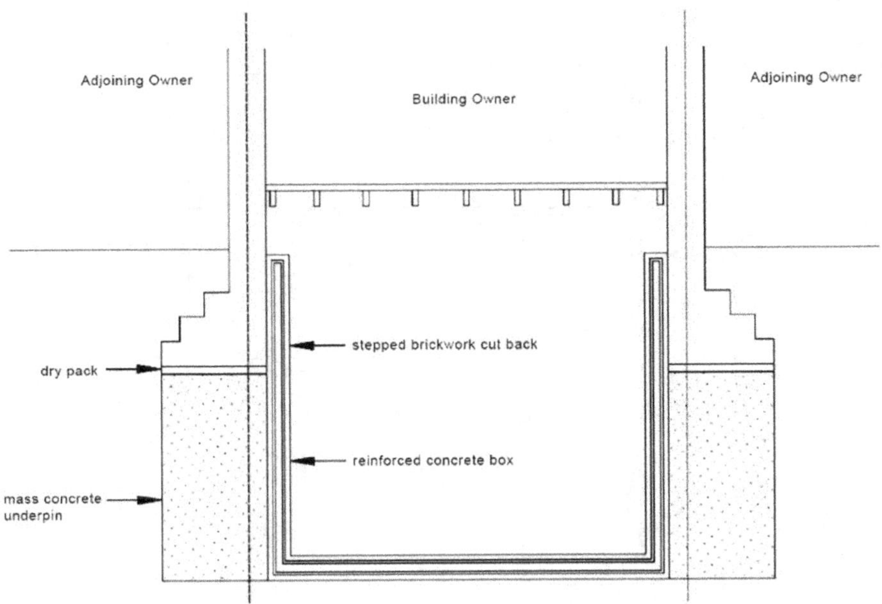

Figure 25 Full Width Concrete Strip Foundation with Reinforced Internal Box

Figures No 24 - 26 will not require written consent under section 7(4) because the mass concrete underpin is not reinforced. However, the mass concrete projects past the width of the party wall and therefore could be challenged as being unnecessary by the adjoining owner.

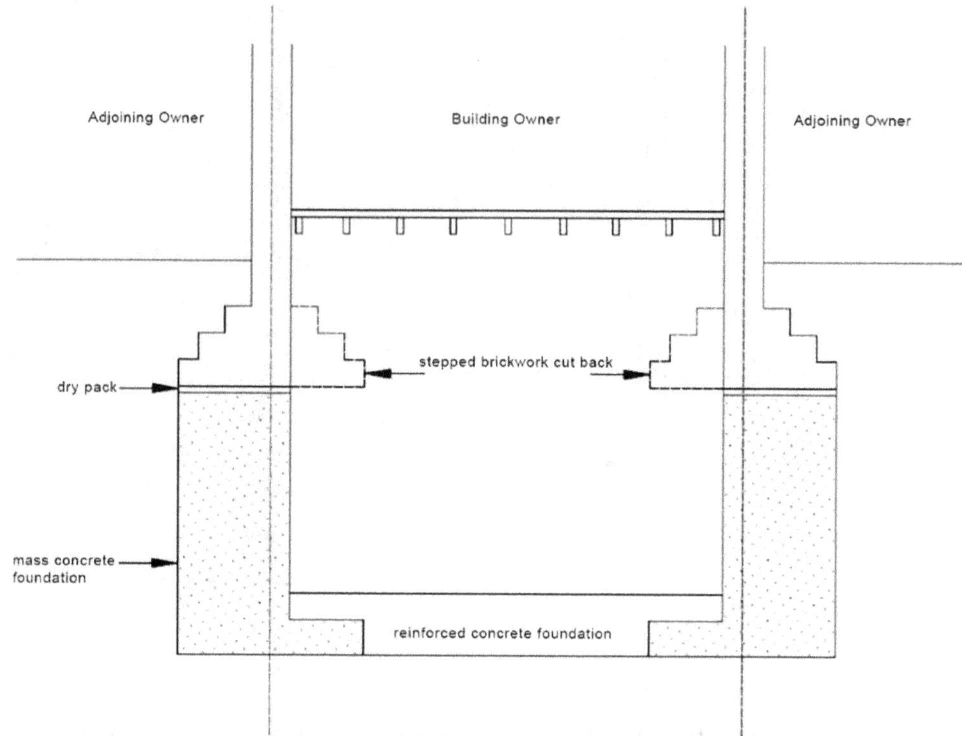

Figure 26 Mass Filled Concrete Foundation with Separate Reinforced Slab (Not Notifiable)

Figure No 23, requires written consent because it incorporates a reinforced concrete underpin foundation/retaining wall with a reinforcement concrete toe. The function of the toe is to prevent rotational movement when lateral forces created by the retained soil are imposed on the concrete retaining wall. The loads are directed downwards through the vertical elements of the underpin and then distributed onto the soil through the toe, which transfers any load to the ground. A reinforced concrete slab is then cast, resting upon but not tied to the retaining wall 'toe' which is clearly a special foundation.

The following table discusses eight accepted basement designs to establish if they are a special foundation, triggering the section 7(4) veto: -

Table 2 Summary of Accepted Basement Designs and Foundation Classification

Figure No	Foundation	Special Foundation	Section 7(4)
17	X	✓	✓
18	✓	✓	✓
19	X	✓	✓
20	X	✓	✓
21	✓	✓	✓
22	✓	X	X
23	✓	X	X
24	✓	✓	✓

18.9.6 Basement Construction Process

Stage I Beginning The process

In the Chaturachinda Judgment, HHJ Bailey accepted Mr Redler's assertion that the wall sits on the concrete strip/rail. Simply following the construction process of a basement box from commencement to completion (See Figure No's 27 - 31) it is abundantly clear that the concrete wall only sits on the reinforced concrete slab. Taking Figure, No 20 the Chaturachinda design had a mass concrete strip/rail beneath the reinforced concrete slab. Yet on comparison with Figure No 28 the wall does not rest on the strip/rail it rests upon the reinforced concrete slab. When the box is completed (see Figure No 29) becomes part of the three-dimensional box.

If we consider the construction process together with the fact that Mr Redler openly accepts that the concrete strip/rails do not distribute the loads whatsoever, whilst quite astonishingly accepted as being introduced only to avoid the Section 7(4) veto. It is astonishing that HHJ Bailey overlooked this obviously blatant attempt to bypass the statutory procedures. Even more so, when one considers that HHJ Bailey accepted that it is unthinkable that the Court would turn a blind eye to such behaviour but that is exactly what HHJ Bailey did.

In very much the same way as the Reeves v Young & Young & Antino case HHJ Bailey in that case, turned a blind eye to the fact that Mr Redler had never been selected in writing[650] as the third surveyor and then we consider his judgment in Gray v Elite Town Management which conflicts with his approach in the Chaturachinda case, his judgment caused greater concern than to resolve.

People go to Court to resolve a dispute and it is not unreasonable for the parties to expect especially where there is a prominent Judge seemingly adopting or engaging with all the cases relating to one specific field such as the Party Wall Act to be consistent in their approach. Disappointingly HHJ Bailey has on a number of occasions given conflicting decisions on cases of similar matters and facts. Unfortunately, that has generated more disputes within the party wall environment then they have resolved.

Notwithstanding, it is my opinion that both HHJ Bailey and Mr Redler decision in Chaturachinda are unsound and simply a misrepresentation/distortion of the appropriate facts and a reinforced basement box is very much a special foundation.

Figure No 27 below is a typical section detail through a traditional masonry-built party wall on spreader brick foundations. In modern buildings there may be a concrete strip foundation beneath the brickwork but the principles for constructing a basement remain unchanged.

---

650 As required under Section 10(2).

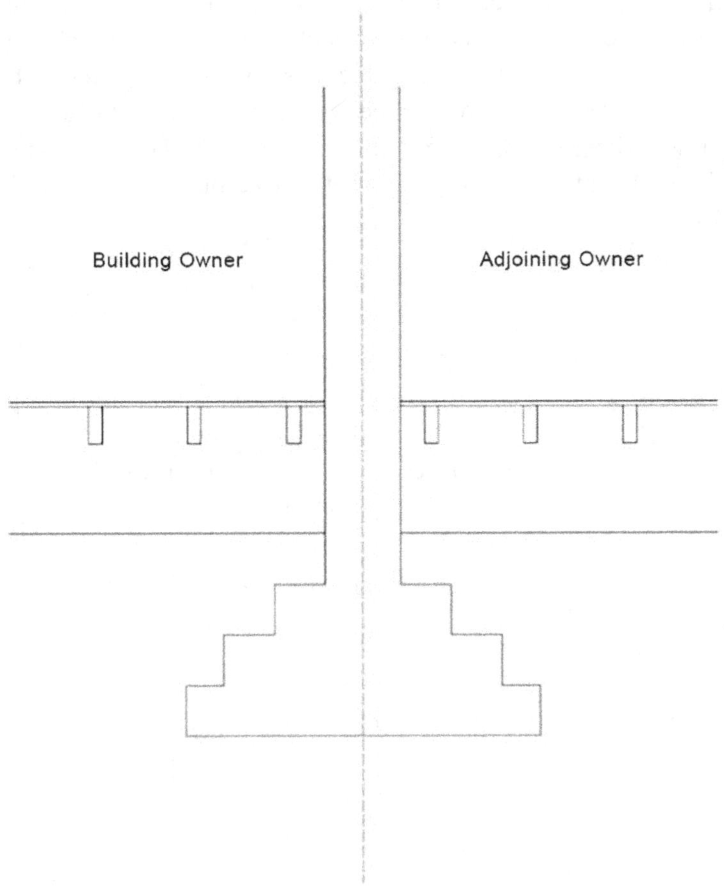

Figure 27 Typical Strip Foundation Beneath Party Wall

Stage I Initial Basement Excavation

The process of excavating below an existing structure (See Figure No 28) is similar to that adopted when underpinning a building. Indeed, the principal function of a basement is in any event to underpin the original structure, whilst creating a habitable/usable subterranean environment. The first stage is to cut an access panel through the floor and to excavate down and underneath the party wall up to but not beyond the face of the party wall on the adjoining owner's side. The excavations will be carried out in nonsequential sections, identical to underpinning with sections being excavated up to 1.2m in width.

A sheet[651] material is then placed against the face of the exposed soil and braced from the other side of the excavated trench. The economical method for building a basement is to increase the thickness of the slab directly below the party wall to act as the foundation for the wall and reduce its thickness where it acts as the flow. Therefore, a stepped foundation as shown (See Figure No 26) is created in anticipation of completing the traditional basement box (See Figure No 19).

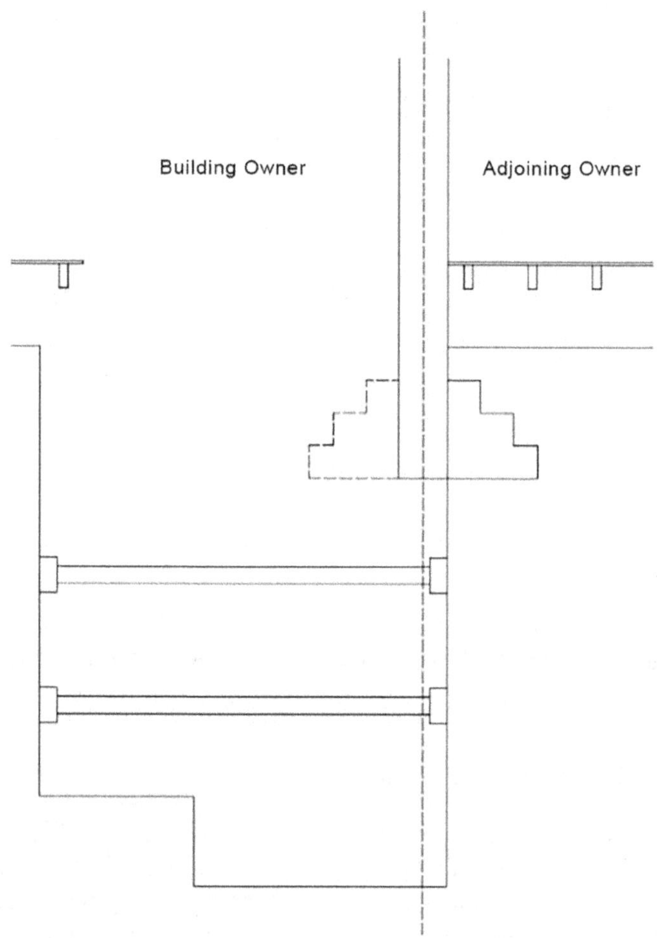

Figure 28 First Stage Excavation for Underpin to Party Wall and Increased Slab Depth

---

651 Steel or Timber.

Stage II Forming the First Element of the Basement

The next stage is to form the reinforcing cage and inserting that into the thickened excavated (void) below the party wall (See Figure No 29) with starter rods projecting horizontally into the unexcavated soil and vertically in order to ultimately tie the reinforcement to all elements of the box. Thus, creating a three-dimensional structure. The lower thickened excavation is then poured with concrete and left to cure. This process is repeated simultaneously with other excavated areas (not sequentially) around the perimeter of the basement.

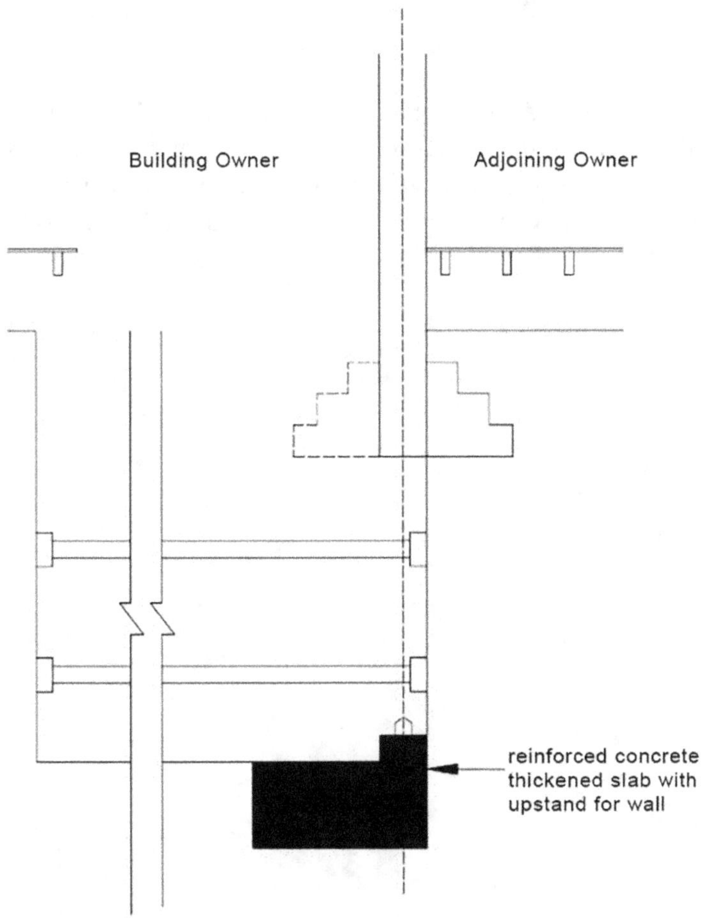

Figure 29 Forming the Thickened Basement Slab

Stage III Forming the Basement Walls and Underpin to Original House

The next stage of the process is to create the reinforcing cage to the vertical elements of the wall insert them into the vertical element (See Figure No 30) tying it to the projecting steel as shown (See Figure No 29) from the base to ensure that the vertical element is bonded and tied to the lower thickened section of slab. Another section of sheet material is formed on the building owners side extending from the thickened base up to but short of the party wall to allow concrete to be poured into the vertical elements. It is then left to cure and on completion and dry pack material is positioned beneath the brick party wall and concrete basement wall.

This process is carried out around the perimeter of the basement area, (not sequentially). Horizontal bars are projected through into the unexcavated soil in preparation of the next excavation following curing and to allow the next section of the vertical element of the basement wall to be tied to the previously poured wall.

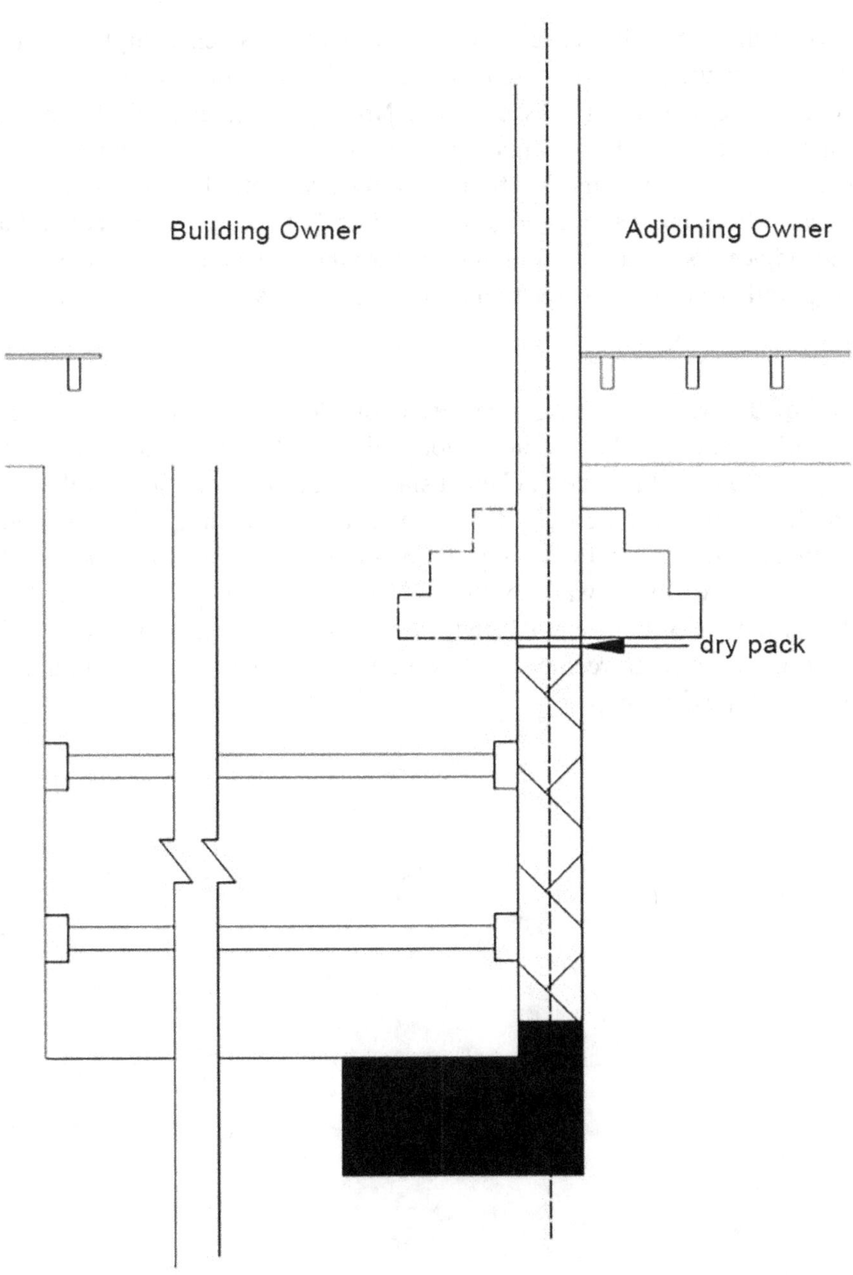

Figure 30 Forming the Underpin and Basement Wall

Stage V Completing the Basement Box

Once all of the underpin vertical elements/walls have been completed around the perimeter of the proposed basement the existing structure is then technically underpinned. On that basis (See Figure No 31) the thickened slab and the vertical element is a traditional underpin because they are the foundation to the original party wall. Its only function to safely distribute the loads imposed on the structure from the wall (see Figure Nos 29 & 30) above and the lateral loads from the adjacent soil safely through to the ground in exactly the same way as a retaining wall performed its function (See Figure No 19).

Once all of the basement walls have been completed and cured the remaining internal soil is excavated again in sections allowing the floor slab to be poured (See Figure No 2) linking the thickened slab (toe's) to the whole box ultimately on completion creating a single three-dimensional structure. The function of the basement structure is to act as a foundation to the original structure (See Figure No 9), retaining wall to the adjacent soil, (See Figure No 3) the foundations and (See Figure No 4) the walls of the basement construction. The introduction of the reinforcement makes the basement box a special foundation without which it will fail.

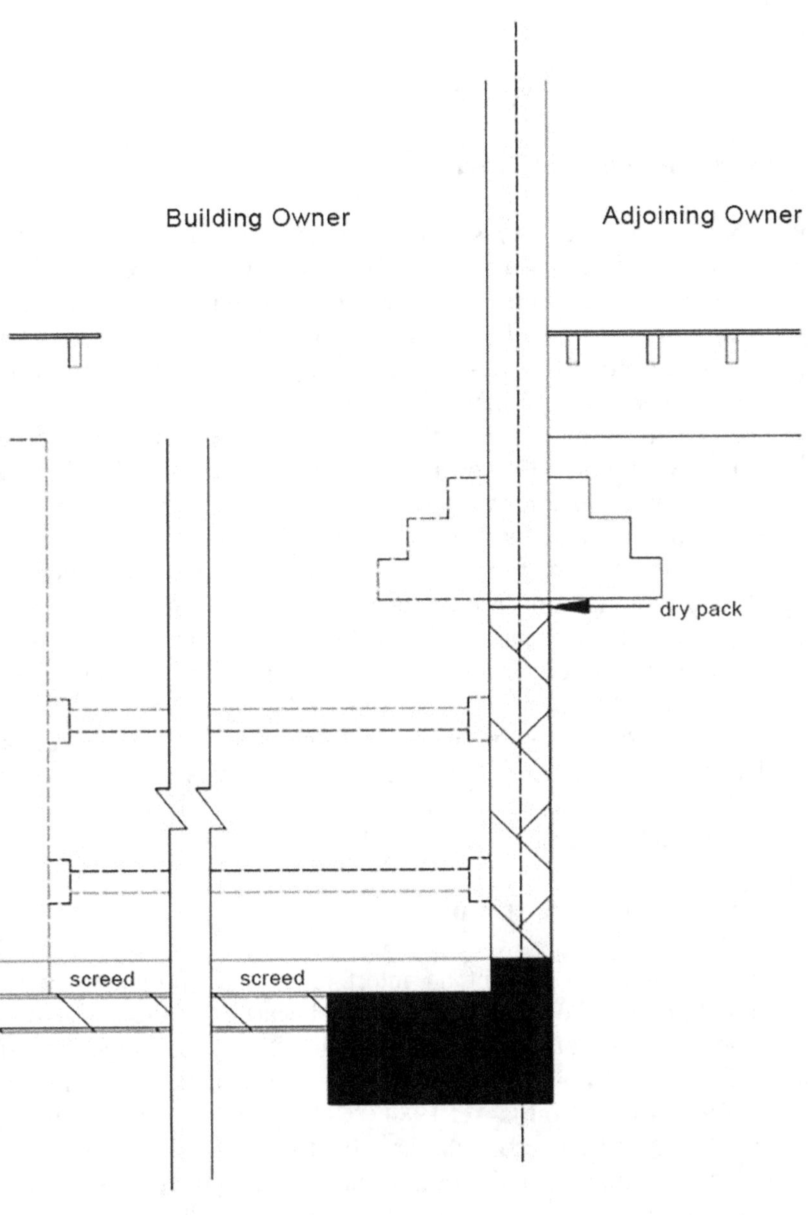

Figure 31 Completing the Basement Box

CHAPTER 19

19.0   Introduction to Injunctions

Neighbourly disputes are very seldom about money or at least primarily.[652] They will usually relate to a variety of historic issues, where the relationship has broken down and as such any further trespass, nuisance, interference and damage, are often interpreted by the aggrieved owner as personal as a personal slight. The dispute often becomes *"a matter of principle"*, however, principals are expensive and party wall disputes where the building owner has failed to serve notice is no different. Reinstating the status entitles the aggrieved owner to seek injunctive relief. However, this is a discretionary legal remedy to ensure not only compliance with the Act, but often breaches of common law. It is a powerful tool that can control the actions of individuals, however there are a variety of injunctions that the Court can grant to restrict a person from undertaking a certain activity 'prohibitor' or force them to do a certain activity 'mandatory'. Whilst the Courts are notoriously reluctant to grant mandatory injunctions, in certain circumstances, an injunction in anticipation of an event *'quia timet'* can be obtained but are very rare. An injunction is also a remedy available for one of the more obscure forms of nuisance now referred to as anti-social behaviour. The purpose of an injunction is to temporarily create an equitable relief and are always at the discretion of the Courts' power conferred by section 37 (1) of the Senior Courts Act 1981 ("SCA").

19.1   Injunctive (interim) relief

The common remedy to prevent an interference with property rights is an interim injunction and should only be sought because an alternative means of resolving the issue is not available or possible[653]. The injunction must be obtained before the notifiable works are completed and should be made under section 38 of the County Courts Act 1984 ("CCA"). Seeking injunctive relief is not for the feint hearted, because the applicant is required to provide a cross-undertaking[654] in damages. This means that if the injunction is successfully rebutted, the applicant must compensate the Defendant for all of their reasonable losses arising out of the injunction. Most injunctions are obtained *ex parte*[655] but apply with immediate effect upon service of the injunction. In older authorities, it was suggested that the Court had no discretion and that a

---

652 Kennedy, K. (2009) 'Neighbour Dispute: Law and Practice' The Law Society, P.105.
653 Conaghan & Conaghan v Abdul (2022) County Court at Edmonton.
654 CPR Part 25 PD.5.1(1).
655 Rusciani v Kumar and Sharma (2012) Chelmsford Count Court.

person was automatically entitled to an injunction against a person. That is no longer the case, but injunctive relief is nonetheless seen as the natural remedy for an interference with property rights[656] especially a breach of statutory obligations.

The Court will hear the application and decide, on the merits, granting a prohibitory interim injunction. The intent is to limit reasonably foreseeable loss or injury to the claimant's property until the matter can be heard in full. The injunction will remain in place until the parties either (i) agree how to resolve the issue or (ii) the parties put their substantive arguments before the Court for a determination at the return date hearing, where the defendant can apply to have the injunction lifted or amended.

The Court will apply the following tests[657] when considering whether to grant an Interim Prohibitory Injunction: -

(i) There must be a serious question to be determined at trial;
(ii) The balance of convenience must lie with the grant of the interim injunction based   upon;
a) Whether damages will be adequate compensation for the claimant at trial for the breach itself, (which weighs against grants of an interim injunction);
b) Whether damages would adequately compensate the defendant if a final injunction was not granted at trial (which supports the grant of an interim injunction); and
c) If the balance of convenience is a fine balance, what is the status quo.

Injunctions are discretionary remedies and not every interference will justify the grant of an injunction. A Judge when dealing with an application should always have regard to the merits of the case and the consequences arising out of the injunction. It is therefore imperative that the claimant provides all the evidence to demonstrate their concerns and the consequences if the injunction is not granted are justified and reasonable. Accordingly, the evidence should include *inter alia* witness statements, expert witness reports, title documents, deeds, plans, photographs and any other information that is necessary to persuade the Court to grant the injunction[658]. If the claimant has delayed seeking injunctive relief and/or the works have been commenced, they will have to firstly apply for an injunction restraining further work from being carried out and possibly a mandatory injunction requiring any buildings constructed where there has been a trespass onto the claimant's land to be demolished.

---

656 Daniel Bromilow Barrister at Law.
657 American Cyanamid v Ethicon Ltd [1975] AC 396.
658 Ferguson Court Residents Association Ltd v Mr. S Fisher (2015) Romford County Court.

There are however instances where the Court have not granted an injunction[659] and[660] where disappointingly the building owners have gone on to cause substantial structural damage to the adjoining owners property. There can be no greater demonstration of the law failing the claimant than in the rejection of injunction.

19.2   Time is of the essence

The Court will treat applications for an injunction as a priority. Therefore, the speed at which an interim injunction is obtained is considered because there is very little value for the aggrieved party if the injunction took several weeks or months to obtain.

It should as a matter of principle be accepted that there are cases where the American Cyanamid test[661] is not required because the facts of the applicant's injunction are sufficiently clear that an injunction is the only remedy necessary.

In Patel v WH Smith[662] Balcombe LJ who gave the leading judgment said: -

> "It seems to me that, first, prima facie a landlord, whose title is not an issue, is entitled to an injunction to restrain trespass on his land whether or not the trespass harms him…..." [??] and the same principle ... applies where the claimants for an interlockary injunction …
>
> If there is no arguable case (on the part of the defendant) as I believe there is not, then questions of balance of convenience, status quo and damages being an adequate remedy do not arise. Prima facie the plaintiffs are entitled to an injunction to stop the trespass on their land."

That was the situation that arose in the Goodmans case.[663] The defendants (Maverstone et al) were undertaking a substantial development which included a basement excavation (see front cover for photograph). In these instances, the defendants did not serve notice under s.6(1) and/or s.6(2). The claimant

---

659 Takhar, Takhar, & Takhar v Mohamed & Mohamed v [2015] County Court at Central London.
660 Macey v Capper & Capper (2019) County Court at Central London F20CL063.
661 American Cyanamid v Ethicon Ltd [1975] AC 396
662 Patel v W.H. Smith (Eziot) Ltd [1987] 1 wlr 853 [2014] EWCA Civ 335.
663 Goodmans Autos Ltd v Maverstone Properties Ltd & Byoot Develop Ltd (2021) County Court at Central London H02CL868

unaware of his rights under the statutory legislation did not do anything about the lack of service of notice. The basement and piled foundations and capping beam were subsequently completed. However, the way in which the defendants were conducting their building works did give cause of concern to the claimant. They were being prevented from operating their business. As one can see from the photograph on the cover there is an access road running along the site hoarding which provides the only ingress and egress to Goodmans garages at the rear.

Goodmans operate a car servicing maintenance and MOT tyre company. They have a high level of traffic flow in and out of the premises as one would expect. The defendants however thought they were entitled to block the access way using that for delivery of concrete, loading, muck away and other building activities necessary for them to do their works. They had no legal rights over the access way.

They chose to use the access way because their site fronted onto a very busy high street of which they had no permission from the local authority to use for loading/unloading.

Faced with a considerable inconvenience which brought the claimants business to a halt they had no option but to seek legal advice. He was referred to the author who immediately inspected noted the obvious breaches of the Party Wall Act but advised him to seek legal advice in respect of injunctive relief to prevent the nuisance from continuing.

19.3   Mandatory Injunction

The Courts are reluctant to grant mandatory injunctions unless the issues are free of ambiguity, however, the claimant can for example, ask the Court to force the defendant to take positive steps to inter alia, serve notice and comply with the Act. These types of injunctions require monitoring and can often lead to additional hearings[664] and costs, for example whether the injunction is being complied with.[665] These are not always well received by the Court, because they prefer to see finality, rather than further delays and hearings.

In Pincus v Singh,[666] the Defendants (Mr Singh) owned a property adjacent to the Claimants. Mr Singh started cutting into and away from parts of the Claimants property. He was asked to stop and confirmed he would. He then continued the next day. He refused to engage in the process and therefore Mr

---

664 Fishenden v. Higgs and Hill Ltd (1935) 153 LT 128.
665 Rusciani v Kumar and Sharma (2012) Chelmsford County Court (unreported).
666 (2022) The High Court of Justice Chancery Division Property, Trust and Probate List (2022) Claim no. PT-2022-000711

Pincus had no option but to obtain an injunction. This is clear evidence that the Court will not facilitate blatant attempts by a property owner to encroach on, damage and/or interfere with another party's legal property rights.

19.4   Prohibitory Injunction

When the injunction is clear cut and requires little monitoring or compliance, a prohibitory injunction is the Courts preferred approach to address the activities of the defendants. It therefore becomes a question of fact as to whether the injunction is being complied with. For example, in respect of a boundary dispute the Court may request as a condition to lifting the injunction a fence to be erected and properly recorded with photographs and measured drawings to establish the exact/correct position of the boundary before lifting the injunction and to avoid future disputes.

19.5   Quia Timet Injunction

This type of injunction is sought where it is anticipated that an intended act or event will interfere with an owner's property rights. A successful application for a 'quia timet' injunction is reliant upon the principle of "reasonably foreseeable" loss and/or damage being caused. For example, there may be an interference with a right of light or interference with the boundary, if certain works are undertaken.

19.6   Freezing Injunction

There may be real concerns that the building owner does not have sufficient funds to pay for the rectification of damages and costs that arise from the injunctive relief, especially where security[667] has not been requested or agreed. Defending a freezing injunction would require sufficient evidence that demonstrates that they have sufficient funds or assets in place to reimburse any damage to avoid a freezing injunction being granted. Obtaining a freezing order will in some instances put pressure on the parties to reach a quick and timely settlement.

19.7   Acquiescence and Estoppel

Acquiescence is the equitable doctrine of laches (pronounced 'lay-cheese'). Laches[668] is defined *as "an old French word for slackness or negligence or not doing"* (Kennedy 2009). Quite simply, this means that a party's failure to act promptly may be interpreted by the Court as having waived their right to seek injunctive relief at a later date. This principal was also recognised in two party wall cases: -

---

667 See Chapter 13, subsection 13.2.
668 Partridge v Partridge [1894] 1 Ch 351.

> "…a party wall surveyor can by his acts or conduct in
> the appropriate circumstances waive a defect in a
> notice or create an estoppel that would bind his
> appointing owner by accepting to act as though the
> notice was valid"[669]

and;

> "It seems to me it is far too late now to argue that they
> can set aside the notice, because the whole process is
> invalid. That cannot be done. You cannot blow hot
> and cold. Where a party is willing to overlook
> deficiencies in the other party's application and it is to
> that other party's advantage that they do so, that other
> party cannot then say when the going gets a bit rough,
> well, that is alright, it is not valid. All the assumptions
> that they have been working under do not apply. That
> cannot be right and the party is asserting that would be
> stopped from saying that the notice is of no effect
> whatsoever"[670].

In these two cases, estoppel prevented the parties from relying on the deficiencies within notices at a later date. As with all litigation, the sensible approach requires the aggrieved party to raise their issues and invite them to be resolved without recourse to the courts[671]. The pre-action letter should include all the relevant information to enable the recipient to understand what they are required to do to avoid an injunction.

19.8   The Shelfer Test

The 'Shelfer test' is designed to avoid encouraging the defendants to take calculated risks. In the Regan case[672], the claimants had not immediately sought an interim injunction, although had raised their objections promptly with the defendants who subsequently ignored their concerns. The Defendants proceeded with the building works having been made aware that the concerns may require the building being pulled down. The Court did not invoke any time constraints on the claimants initiating injunctive relief, because they were able to demonstrate that they acted promptly and the defendants were aware of their concerns. This principle was also applied in an earlier case[673] where the injunction was granted 8 years after the defendants had completed their

---

669 Manu v Euroview Investments Ltd [2008] 1 EGLR 165.
670 Sunsaid Property Company Ltd v Omenaka and Omenaka.
671 Letter before Action.
672 Regan v Paul Properties Ltd [2006[EWCA Civ 1391.
673 Deakins v Hookings [1994] 14 E.G. 133.

building works. However, in the alternative, the Courts also recognise that it may not be equitable (where the injury is small) to grant an injunction. It is almost inevitable that the defendants will argue that damages in lieu of an injunction is the appropriate remedy, because the alternative remedy of demolition would have greater and unreasonable financial implications.

The Shelfer case set out the following principle/rules that were reinforced in a later case.[674]

The Defendant must be able to demonstrate: -

* The Claimant entitled to an injunction;
* The injury to the Claimant small;
* Can the injury be estimated in money;
* Would the Claimant be adequately compensated by a small payment of money; and
* Would it be oppressive to the Defendant to grant an injunction?

Having decided that an award of damages is the appropriate remedy, the Court then has the difficult task of establishing reasonable damages.

19.9   The Tamare's Principles

The core principles are: -

(1)   The Court must attempt to find out what would be a "fair" result of a hypothetical negotiation between the parties;

(2)   The context[675] of the parties conduct scale of interference et al, including the nature, and seriousness of the breach, must be kept in mind;

(3)   The right to prevent a development (or part) gives the owner of the right a significant bargaining position;

(4)   The owner of the right bargaining position will normally expect to receive some part of the likely profit from the development (or relevant part);

(5)   If there is no evidence of the likely size of the profit, the Court can do its best by awarding damages for loss of amenity;

(6)   If there is evidence of the likely size of the profit, the Court should normally award a sum which takes into account a fair percentage of the profit;

(7)   The size of the award should not in any event be so large that the development (or relevant part) would not have taken place had such a

---

674 Jaggard v Sawyer [1995] 1 WLR 269.
675 The parties' actions, reasonableness, scale of the interference.

sum been payable;

(8)   After arriving at a figure which takes into account all the above and any other relevant factors, the Court needs to consider whether the "deal feels right.""

19.10   Enforcing an Injunction

Having obtained an injunction, it is reasonable to expect the recipient to comply as ordered. However, some defendants are not always so inclined[676] and will continue to abuse the law. Whilst an injunction for a breach of the Party Wall Act will relate to notifiable works, the injunction could apply to all work until the matters have been resolved. Any breach of an injunction is a contempt of court[677] and the Court has broad powers to apply further sanctions following non-compliance[678]: -

(i)   Order the party in contempt to pay security to ensure his further compliance: or,

(ii)   Imprisonment up to a maximum of two years.

In addition, the Court will (almost) certainly award the costs of the hearing against the defendants. I have been involved in one party wall matter[679] where the defendants (building owners) breached the injunction on two occasions. Having been fortunate enough to be let off with a verbal warning and nominal costs order for the first breach, the second breach resulted in committal proceedings, however, HHJ Murfitt order that they pay £10,000 to Mr. Rusciani.

Not all breaches will justify an injunction, in some circumstances the interference may be so small that an injunction would be unreasonable and/or oppressive[680] and the Court has the jurisdiction to grant damages in lieu of an injunction[681] if they are considered appropriate.

The Court will take into consideration the transgressing owner's intentions when committing the interference, which may be a critical factor that determines whether the development and/or works go ahead. Some defendants will take a calculated risk and proceed with the interference on the premise that "I shall just buy my way out of this". This approach was anticipated and

---

676 Rusciani v Kumar and Sharma (2012) Chelmsford Count Court (unreported).
677 Contempt of Court Act 1981.
678 Kennedy, K. (2009) 'Neighbour Dispute: Law and Practice' The Law Society.
679 Rusciani v Kumar and Sharma (2012) Chelmsford Count Court (unreported).
680 Shelfer v City of London Electric Lighting Co [1895] 1 Ch 287.
681 Section 50 of the Senior Courts Act 1981 (Supreme Courts Act 1981 as was) and by virtue of section 38 of the County Courts Act 1984.

addressed in the Shelfer decision[682] and effectively stops the 'Big Boys' from walking all over the 'little people'.

The Court will draw a distinction between the remedies; if the Court considers that the defendants had consciously manipulated the circumstances "to fit the Shelfer test" they will be estopped and may be liable to pay damages in lieu of an injunction. The Court considered this to be an important principle and went on to suggest that hurrying up with the building works to avoid an injunction, or otherwise acting with a reckless disregard to the plaintiff was not acceptable. Whilst it should be remembered that the "Shelfer Test" is not cast in stone where the interference is significant[683] the Court will order the demolition of the structure to remove the interference.

The Court's dislike of owners who act with complete disregard to neighbouring owners' rights was demonstrated in a recent case[684] where the developer intended to convert the building into a number of flats. With reckless disregard of the interests of the true owner, Brookwide, shockingly knocked a hole through a party wall and then misappropriated the neighbour's room, because the additional space was critical to the developers' plans.

The High Court referred to Brookside's approach as: -

> "Outright and cynical expropriation of someone else's
> property and its amalgamation within the wrongdoer's
> own property in order that the wrongdoer could make
> a profit out of the use of the combined land".

The Court fully expressed their dissatisfaction when they order damages of £560,000 to "teach Brookwide the necessary lesson that conduct of this type will not be tolerated".

A similar approach was demonstrated in Rusciani v Kumar, when HHJ Murfitt expressed her scathing criticism about the defendants conduct as: -

> "Reprehensible as I consider the Defendants approach
> to have been, to both the requirements of the Party
> Wall Act and to this Court's injunction, I do not
> consider that committal by way of imprisonment or
> fine to be a necessary or proportionate response to that
> wrong given that in the wider context there are other
> more appropriate measures which the Court has
> available to consider to redress the wrong"…."I

---

682 Shelfer v City of London Electric Lighting Co [1895] 1 Ch 287.
683 Regan v Paul Properties Ltd [2006] EWCA Cir 1391.
684 Ramzan v Brookwide Limited [2010] EWHC Civ 2453 (Ch).

recognise that there have been periods when the nuisance has been worse (for example when access has been barred altogether) than at other times when access has been possible and work suspended. However, doing the best I can to be fair I shall award the sum of £10,000 in respect of general damages".

CHAPTER 20

20.0   Navigating the party wall Act

20.1   Flow charts as a road map to navigate the Act

A flowchart is designed to communicate often complex processes in clear, easy-to-understand diagrams. A flowchart identifies the steps and directional links by structuring them in sequential order. It is a generic tool that can be adapted for a wide variety of purposes, and processes, such as education, manufacturing, administration, legislation, construction etc. Typically, a flowchart shows the steps within various shaped boxes (each of which have a specific meaning) and their sequential order by connecting them with arrows to guide the reader though the process and options. Because the purpose of a flow chart is to convey information its construction has to be consistent to avoid a confusion and mis-information in the same way as a road map. Therefore, each shape has a specific meaning within the British Standards[685] as shown in the legend in 20.2 below. This includes limited shapes some of which are not used within the flow charts contained herein and are therefore for information.

---

685 BS 4058:1987, ISO 5807:1985, Specification for data processing flow chart symbols, rules and conventions.

20.2   Flow Chart Legend

The following is a non-exhaustive selection of British Standard flow chart symbols which explain the relevance of various shapes.

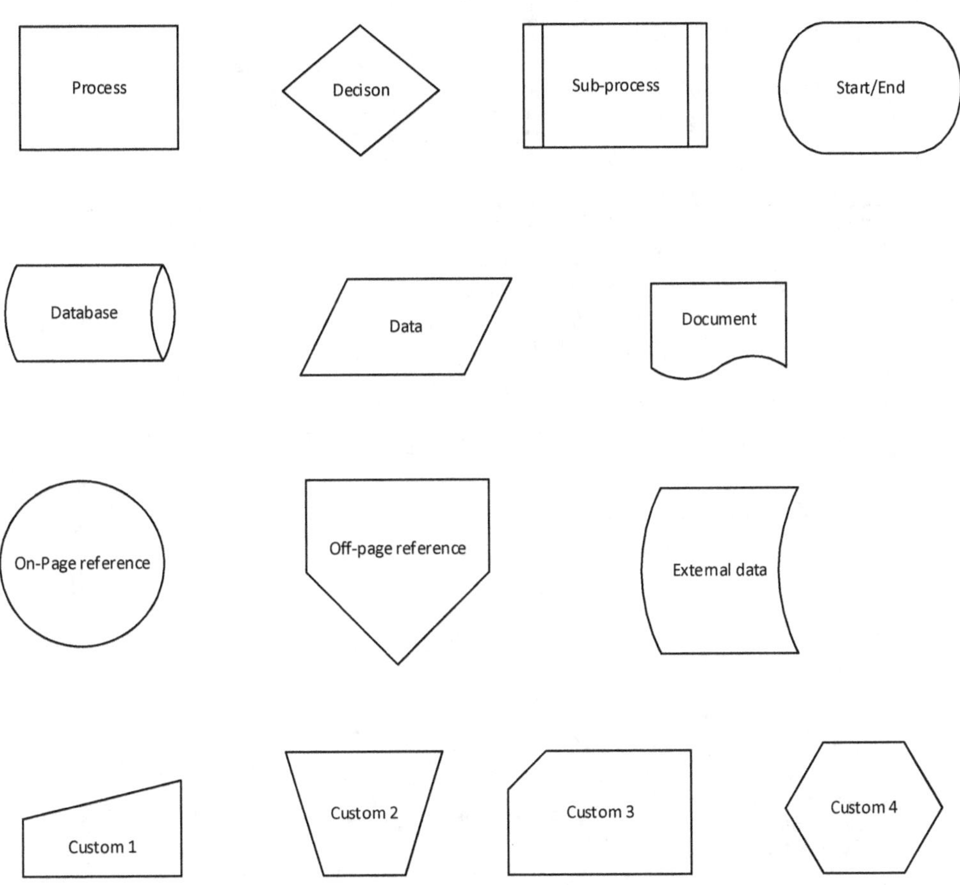

20.3   Section 1(5) Flow Chart

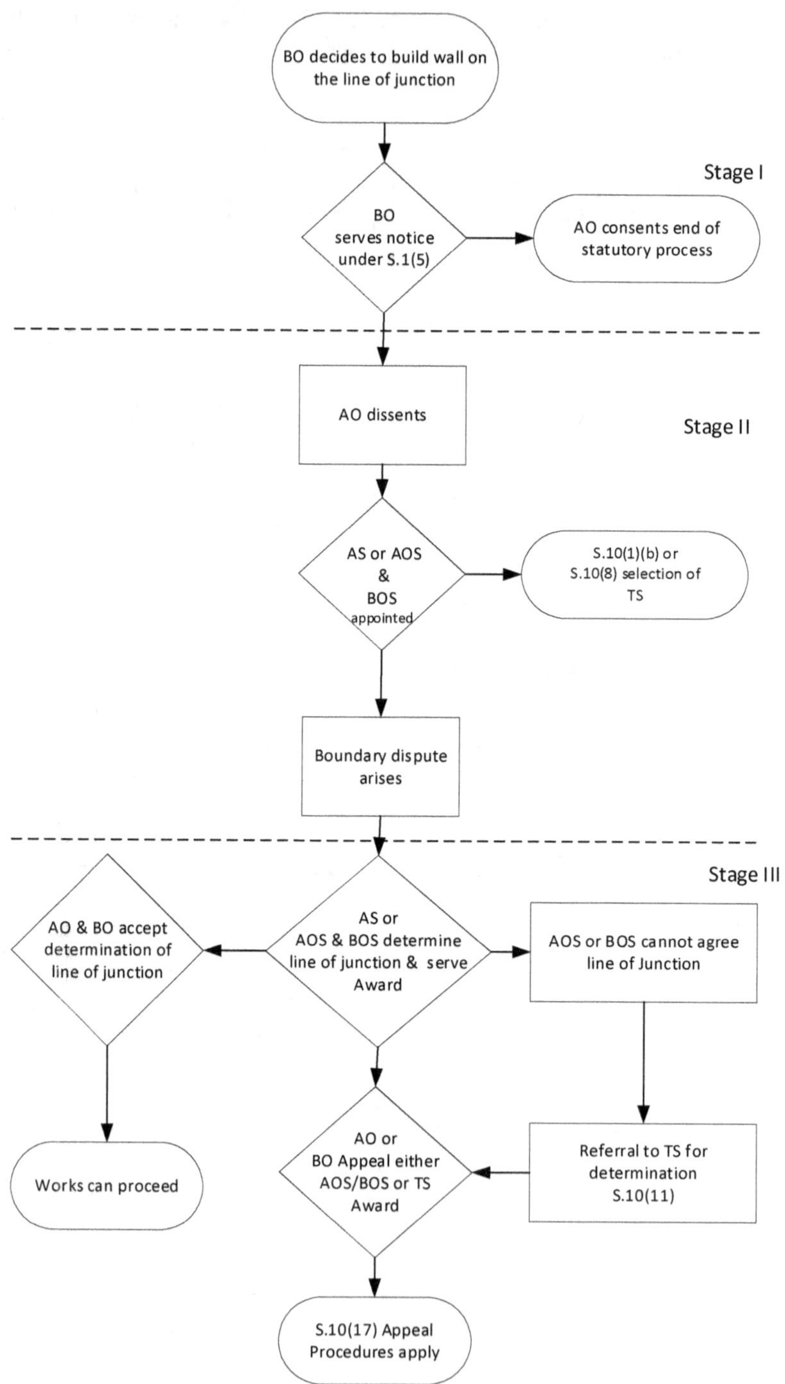

20.4 Section 6(1) Road Map

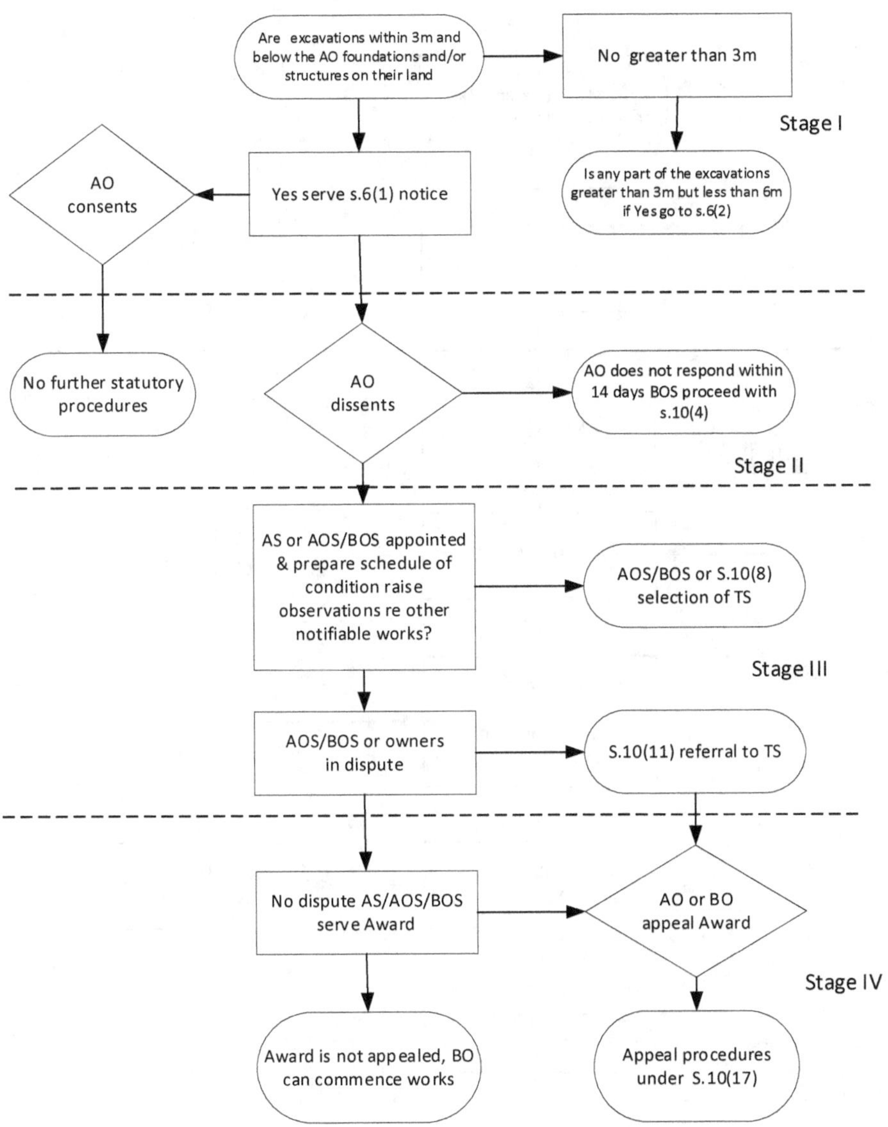

20.5   Section 6(2) Road Map

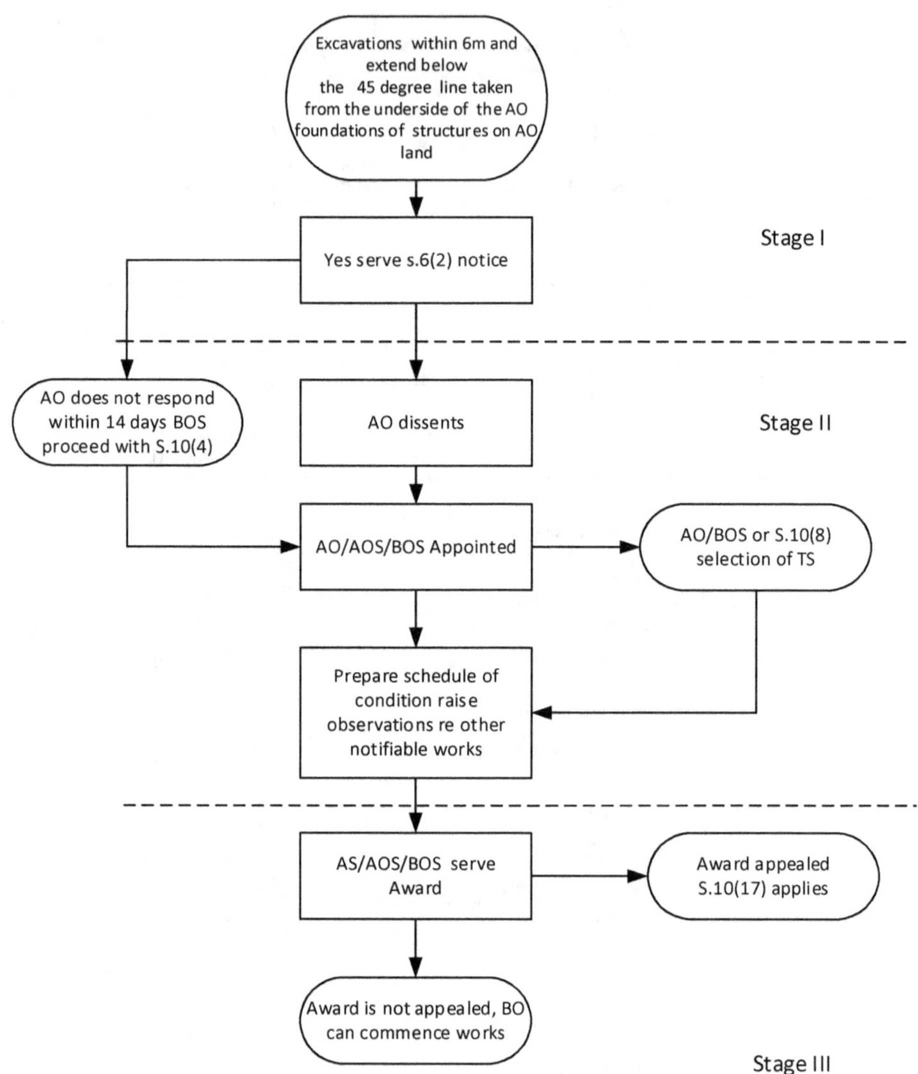

20.6   Section 7 Road Map

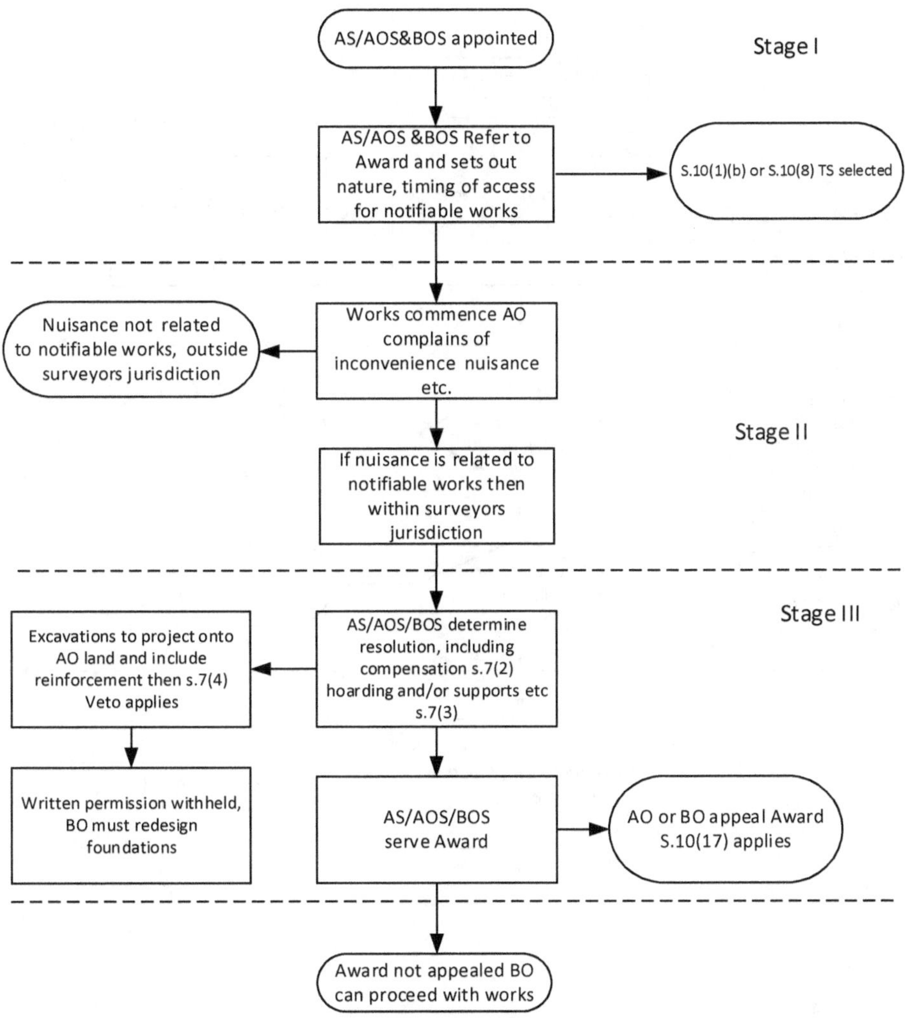

20.7   Section 8 Road Map

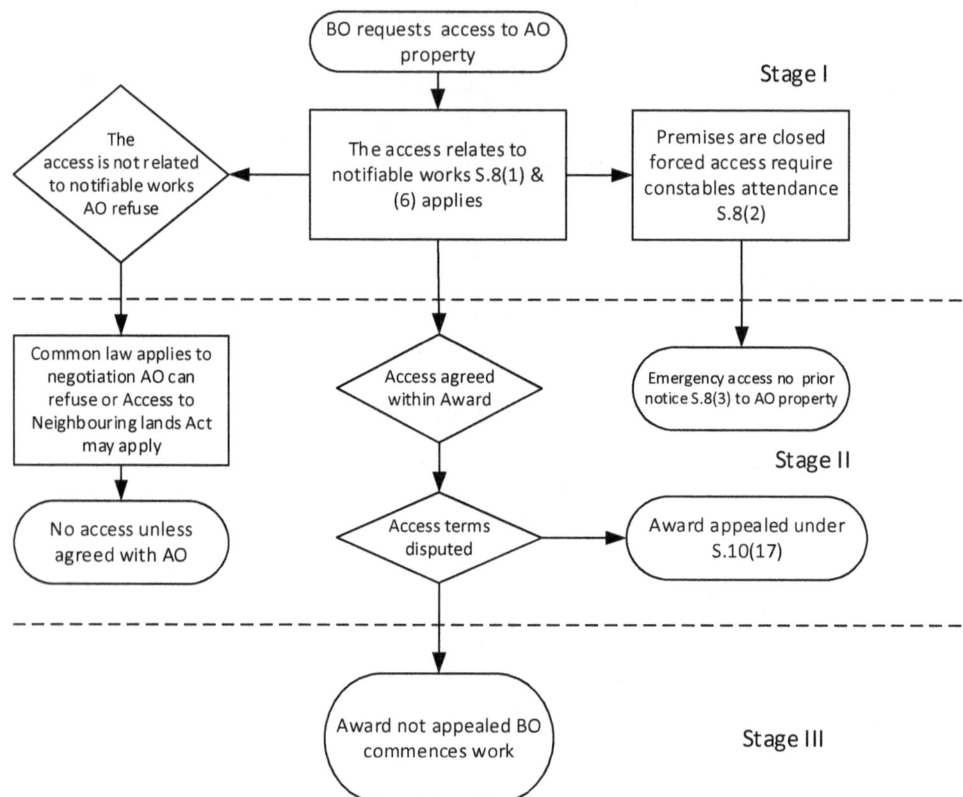

21.8   Section 10(1) Road Map

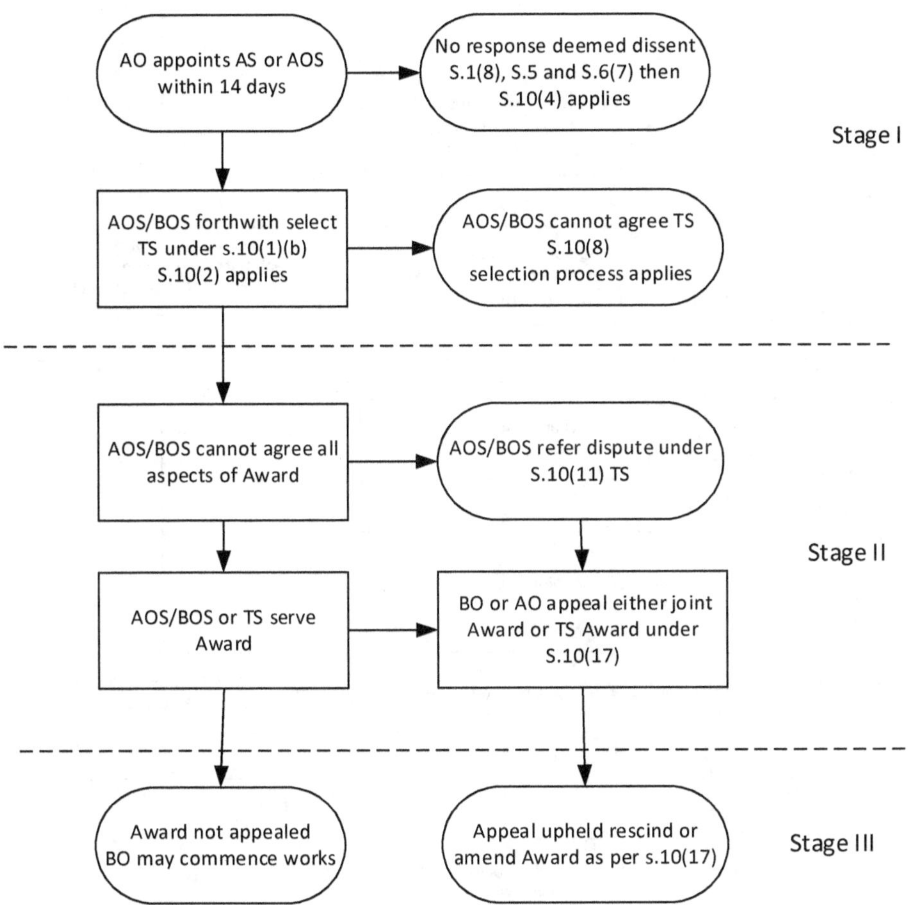

21.9   Section 10(4) Road Map

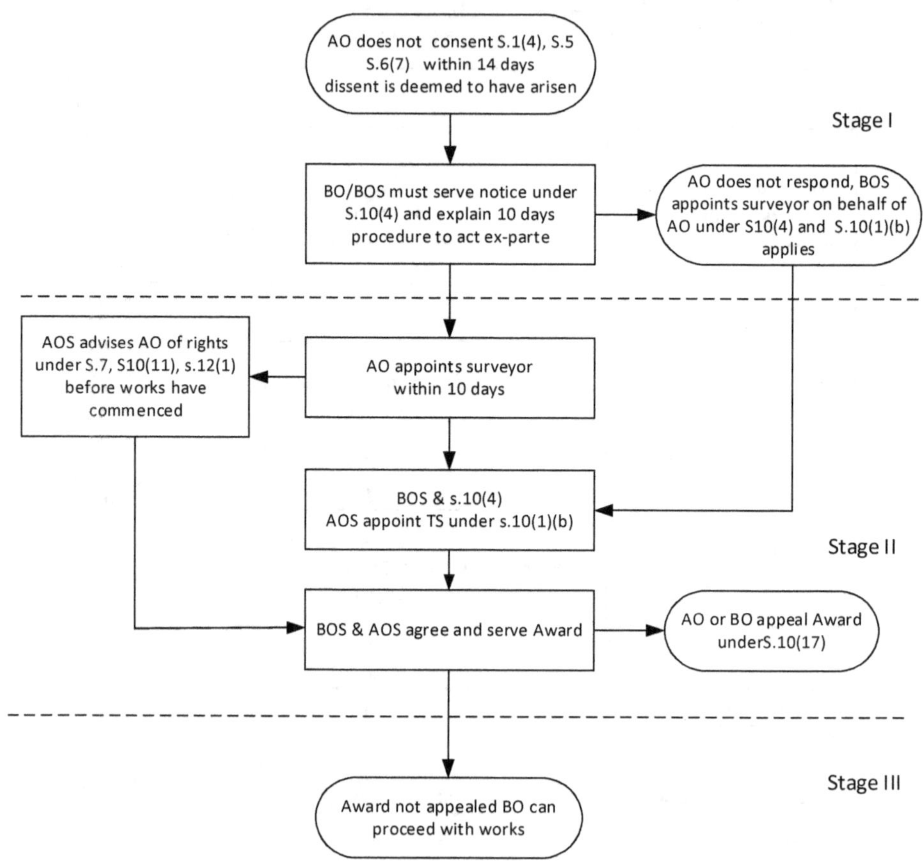

21.10   Section 10(5) and (9) Road Map

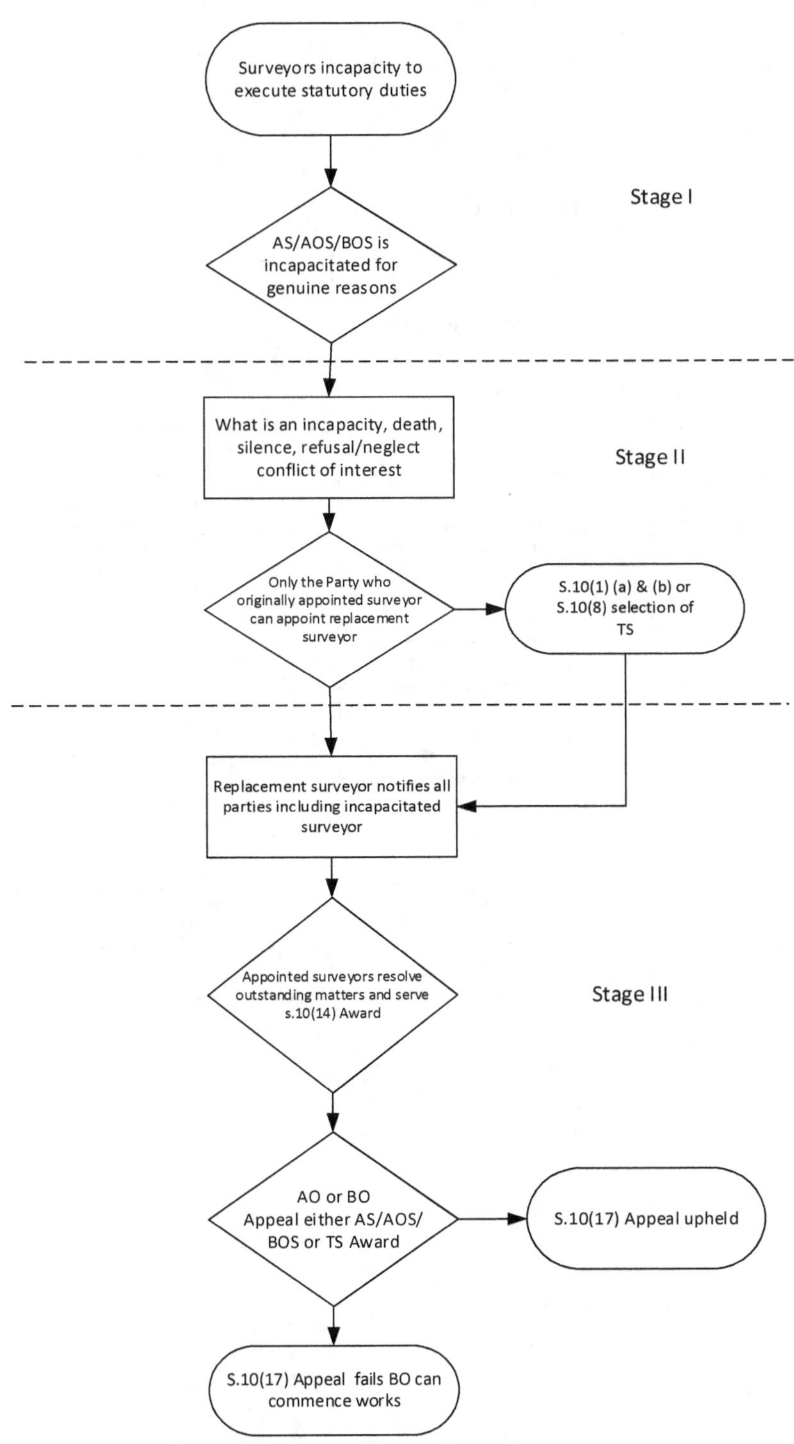

21.11   Section 10(6) Road Map

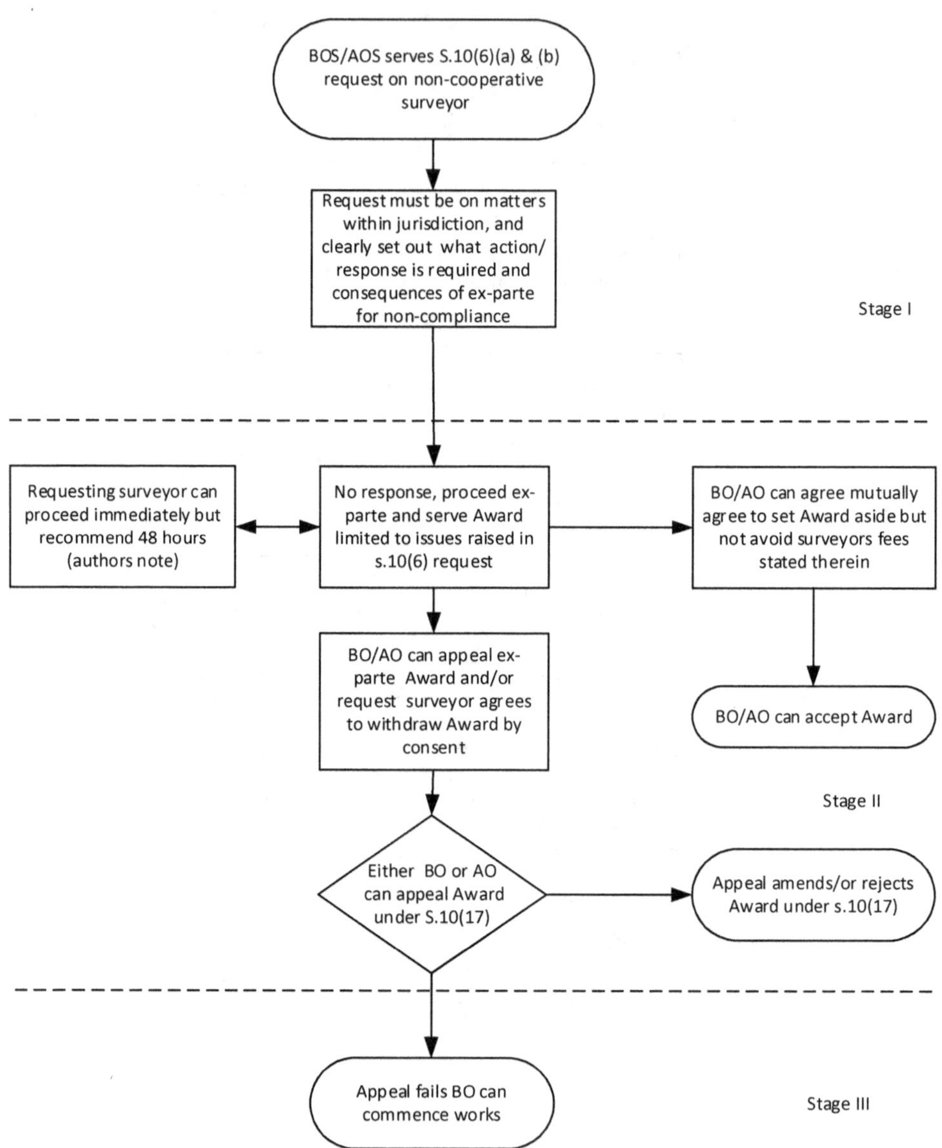

21.12   Section 10(7) Road Map

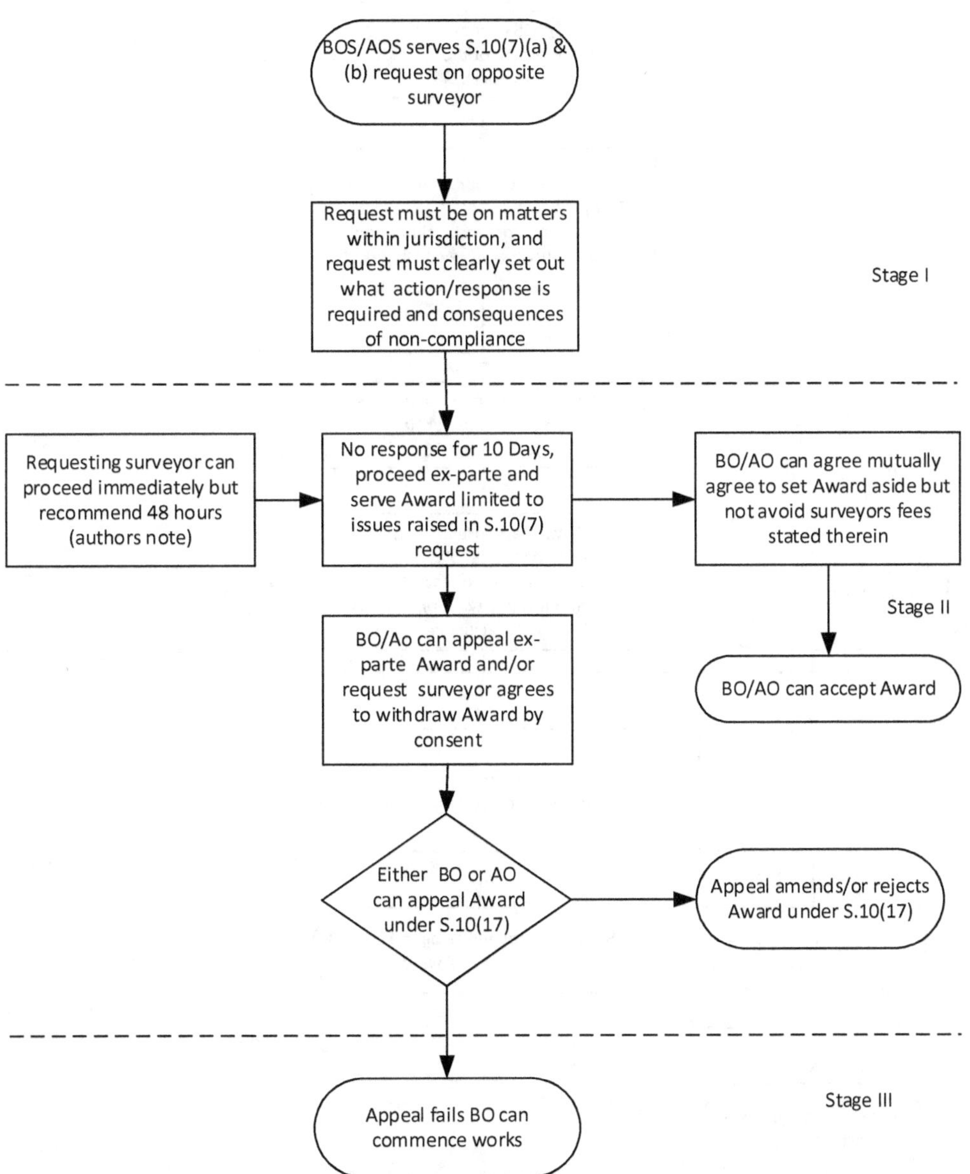

21.13 Section 10(8) Road Map

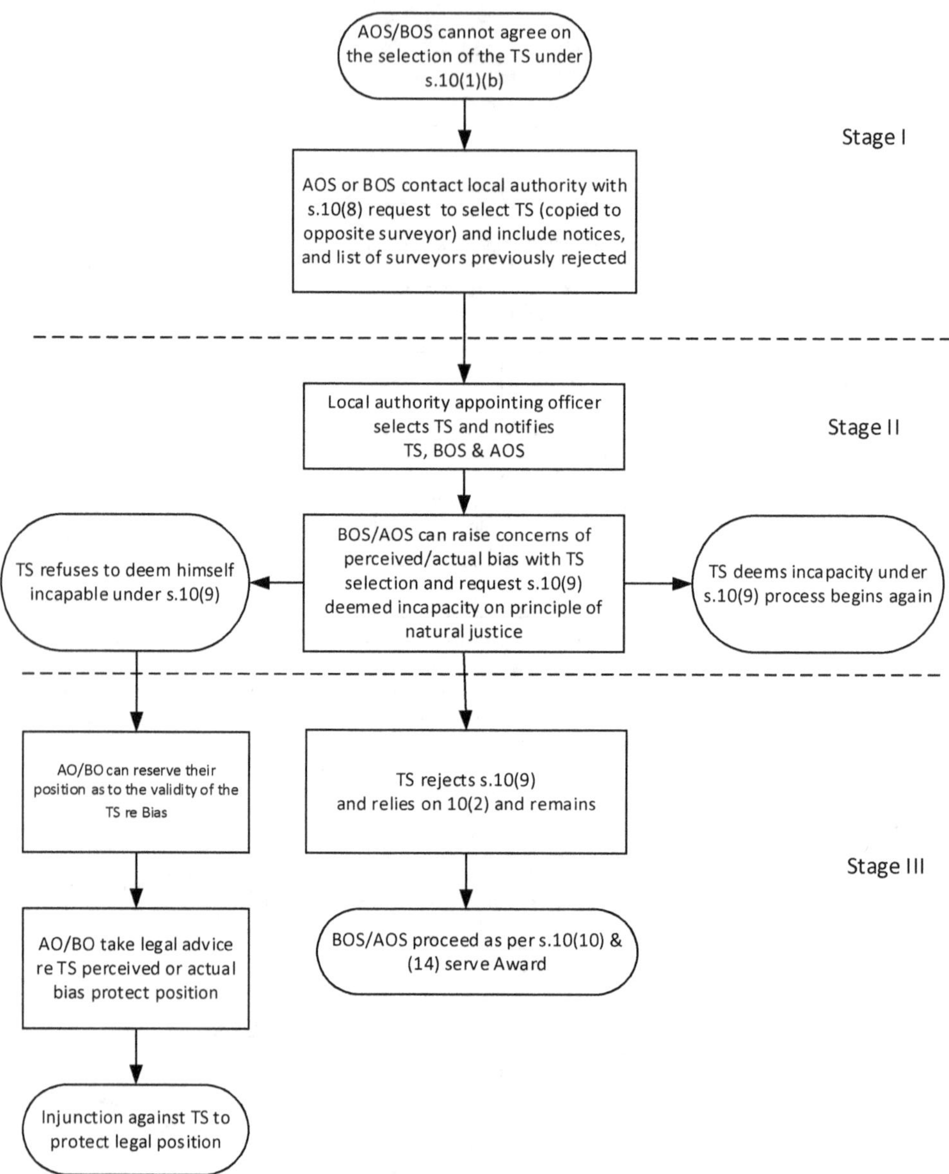

21.14   Section 10(11) Road Map

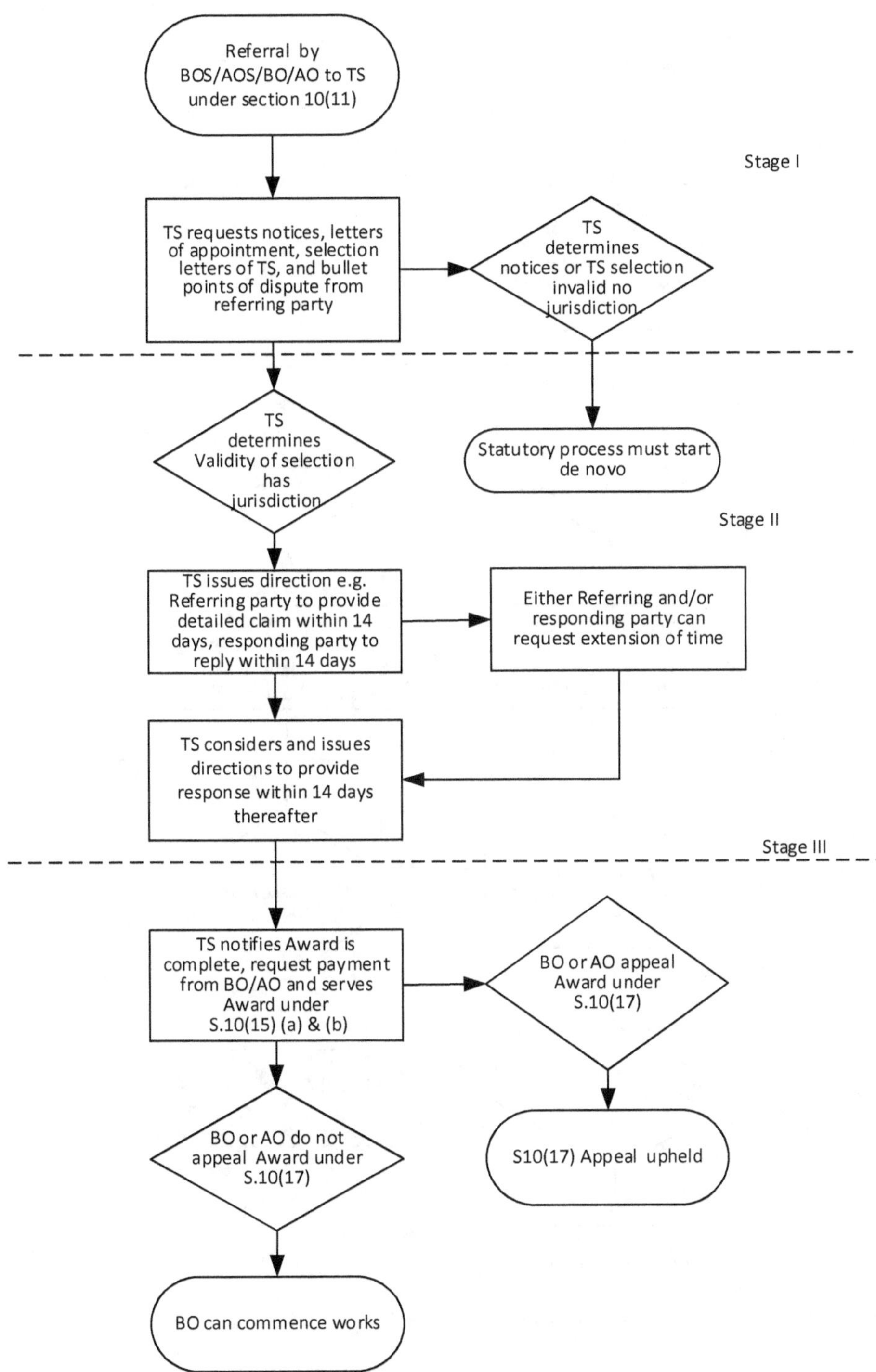

21.17 Section 10(12) Road Map

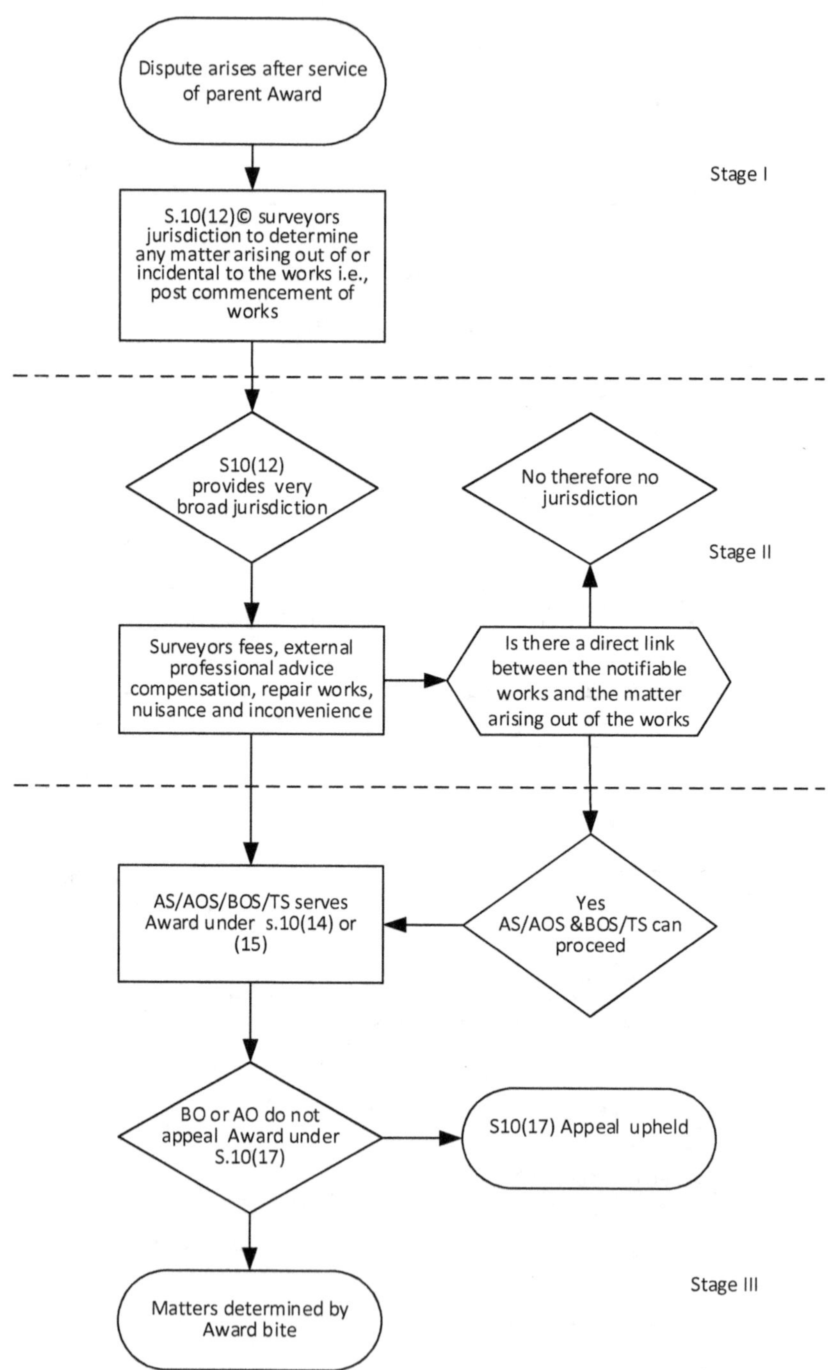

21.18   Section 12(1) Road Map

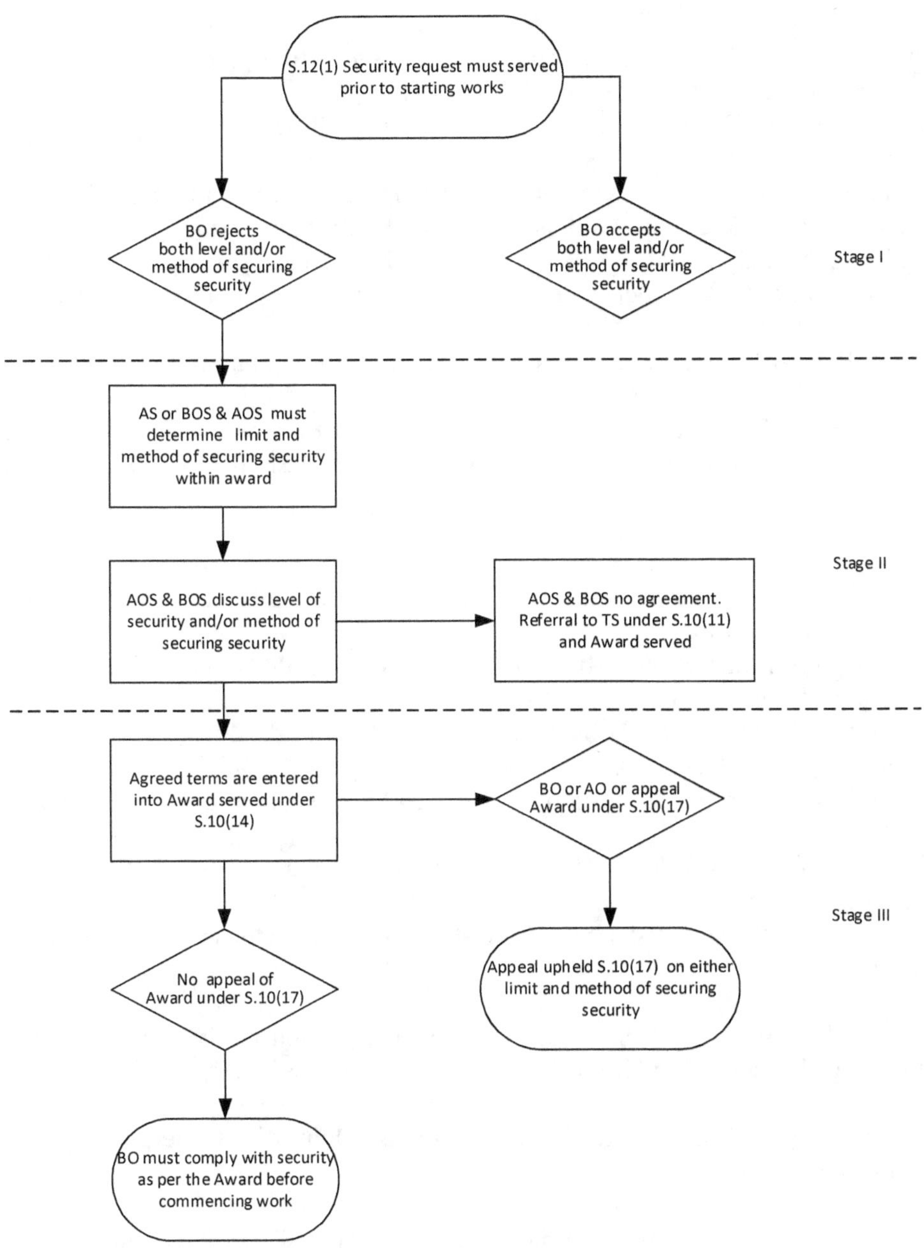

REFERENCES

Ainsworth, R. (2000), "Differences of Opinion Interpreting Section 1," Structural Survey Vol. 18 No 5 pp. 213-217.

Ambrose, J. (1991). Simplified Design of Masonry Structures. New York: John Wiley and Sons, Inc.

Antino, P "Using the Party Wall etc. Act 1996 to gain access to a neighbouring property' Emerald Group Publishing Limited, Structural Survey, Journal of Building Pathology and Refurbishment, Vol. 29 issue No 3 2011 pp. 210-220.

Antino, P. (2012) "A Practitioner's Approach and Interpretation of the Party Wall etc. Act 1996" Xlibris Corporation.

Antino, P. (2012) "A Practitioner's Approach and Interpretation of Neighbourly Matters" Xlibris Corporation.

Antino, P. (2021) "Interpretation of the Party Wall etc. Act 1996 and the Implications for Building Below Ground" Anglia Ruskin University, Ph.D. Thesis.

Bickford-Smith, S. and Sydenham, C. (1997) "Party Walls Law and Practice" Jordan Publishing Ltd.

Bickford-Smith, and S, and Sydenham, C. 3rd Ed, (2009) "Party Walls Law and Practice" Jordan Publishing Ltd.

Bickford-Smith, and S, Nicholls, D. and Smith, A. 4th Ed, (2017) "Party Walls: Law and Practice" LexisNexis.

Bickford-Smith, and S. and Smith, A. (2015) "Special Foundations" Property Law Journal.

BS 4058:1987, ISO 5807:1985, Specification for data processing flow chart symbols, rules and conventions.

Butcher, T. (2007) "Risks in Domestic Basement Construction" NHBC Foundation BRE Press.

Chynoweth, P. (2000) "Unnecessary Inconvenience and compensation within the party wall Legislation" Structural Survey Volume 18 No. 2.

Haslam, S. and O'Connor, L. (2013) "Specialist Domestic: Underpinning and Subsidence.

Isaac, N. (2014) "The law and Practice of Party Walls" Property Publishing.

Murdoch, J. and Hughes, W. (1993) *"Construction contracts: law and Management"* E & FN Spon P.333.

Ove Arup, (2010) *"London Borough of Camden: Guidance for Subterranean Developments"*. Ove Arup and Partners Ltd.

Pyramus & Thisbe *"Special Foundations: What they are and are not"*, (2015) P&T Guidance Note No. 12.

RICS 7th Edition (2020) Guidance Notes "Party Wall Legislation and Procedure"

Samuel, G. (2013) "A Short Introduction to Common Law" Edward Elgar Publishing Limited.

Stones Justices' Manual, Vol.3, 8.26757A.

Whittick, K. G. (2007) "The Party Wall a Short History" Faculty of Party Wall Surveyor

Wood, D. Chynoweth, P. Adshead, A. and Mason, J. (2011) "Law and the Built Environment" Wiley-Blackwell.

APPENDICES

APPENDIX I   LETTER OF APPOINTMENT

Appointing owner's name

Address in full

Date Insert here

Insert Surveyors name and company details here

Dear Insert Surveyors name,

Re: The Party Wall etc. Act 1996 at Insert the address where works are being undertaken

We the building/adjoining owners of **(Insert the address where works are being undertaken** hereby appoint **(Insert Surveyors name and company details here)** as our Party Wall Surveyor and is authorised to sign, serve and/or receive all and any notices and or Awards in connection with the proposed building works and to make all and any necessary appointments on our behalf, that Mr. Antino considers are relevant to the proper application of the procedures under the Party Wall etc. Act 1996.

In the event of a dispute or deemed dispute arising, or having arisen, within the meaning of the Act we hereby appoint the aid Mr. Philip Antino as our surveyor in accordance with section 10(1)(b) of the Act.

For the purposes of compliance with "The Party Wall etc. Act 1996 (Electronic Communications) Order 2016" we are agreeable to receiving notices and/or other documentation including awards by means of electronic communication. We nominate the following email address **(insert email address here)** for all future communications in relation to these party wall matters.

We are entitled to withdraw our agreement to electronic communications but will only do so after giving 7 days' notice. Thereafter, all further communications will be by ordinary post, which will be deemed to be received within 48 hours of the date of posting. We are aware that **(insert the surveyors name here)** appointment cannot under section 10 (2) of the Act be rescinded after the signing of this letter of appointment.

Yours sincerely,

……………………………..   ………………….

Building/adjoining owners' name   Building/adjoining
owners' name

APPENDIX II   ELECTRONIC COMMUNICATIONS

The Party Wall etc. Act 1996 (Electronic Communications) Order 2016

Made   10th March 2016
Laid before Parliament   15th March 2016
Coming into force   6th April 2016

The Secretary of State makes the following Order in exercise of the powers conferred by sections 8 & 9 of the Electronic Communications Act 2000.

The Secretary of State considers that the authorisation of the use of electronic communications by this Order for any purpose is such that the extent (if any) to which records of things done for the purpose will be available will be no less satisfactory where use is made of electronic communications than in other cases.

Citation, commencement and extent.
1.   (1)   This Order may be cited as the Party Wall etc. Act 1996 (Electronic Communications) Order 2016, and comes into force on 6th April 2016.
    (2)   This Order extends to England and Wales.

Amendments to the Party Wall etc. Act 1996

2.   (1)   In section 15 of the Party Wall etc. Act 1996 (service of notices etc) after subsection.
    (1)   Insert –

"(1A)   A notice or other document required or authorised to be served under this Act may also be served on a person ("the recipient") by means of an electronic communication, but only if –

    (a)   The recipient has stated a willingness to receive the notice or document by means of an electronic communication,
    (b)   The statement has not been withdrawn, and
    (c)   The notice or document was transmitted to an electronic address specified by the recipient.

(1B)   A statement under subsection (1A) may be withdrawn by giving a notice to the person to whom the statement was made.

(1C)   for the purposes of subsection (1A) –

"Electronic address" includes any number or address used for the purposes of receiving electronic communications;

"Electronic communication" means an electronic communication within the meaning of the Electronic Communications Act 2000; and "specified" means specified in a statement made for the purposes of subsection (1A)."

Signed by authority of the Secretary of State for Communities and Local Government

James Wharton
Parliamentary Under Secretary of State
Department for Communities and Local Government

10th March 2016

APPENDIX III   DEEMED SERVICE

The Interpretation Act 1978, Section 7 states: -

"Where an Act authorises or requires any document to be served by post (whether the expression "serve" or the expressions "give" or "send" or any other expression is used) then, unless the contrary intention appears, the service is deemed to be effected by properly addressing, pre-paying and posting a letter containing the document and, unless the contrary is proved, to have affected at the time at which the letter would be delivered in the ordinary course of post."

2.0 Practice Direction - Service of Documents - First- and Second-Class Mail

"With effect from 16 April 1985 the Practice Direction issued on 30 July 1968 is hereby revoked and the following is substituted therefore.

1. Under Section 7 of the Interpretation Act 1978 service by post is deemed to have been affected, unless the contrary has been proved, at the time when the letter would be delivered in the ordinary course of post.

2. To avoid uncertainty as to the date of service it will be taken (subject to proof to the contrary) that delivery in the ordinary course of post was effected: -

(a) in the case of first-class mail, on the second working day after posting;
(b) in the case of second-class mail, on the fourth working day after posting.

3. "Working days" are Monday to Friday, excluding any bank holiday.

4. Affidavits of service shall state whether the document was dispatched by first- or second-class   mail. If this information is omitted it will be assumed that   second   class   mail   was   used.

5. This direction is subject to the special provisions of RSC Order 10, rule 1(3) relating to the service of originating process.

J R BICKFORD-SMITH Senior Master
Queen's Bench Division
8 March 1985

APPENDIX IV   SECTION 10 (4) REQUEST

Dear Mr. and Mrs (**insert name**)

Re: Request under section 10(4) of the Party Wall etc Act 1996 in relation to works at (insert address).

Further to the notices dated [**insert date**] you have not appointed a surveyor within the fourteen days as specified under section 5 and therefore dissent is deemed to have arisen. The building owner is entitled to commence his works without unreasonable delay and therefore has now instructed me to serve a section 10(4) notice upon you.

Section 10 (4) (a)&(b)

(4)   If either party to the dispute-

refuses to appoint a surveyor under subsection (1)(b), or

(a)   neglects to appoint a surveyor under subsection (1)(b) for a period of ten days beginning with the day on which the other party serves a request on him,
the other party may make the appointment on his behalf.

This is a request under section 10(4) that you make an appointment within 10-days of the date of this request. If you fail to do so, our appointing owners have instructed me to make an appointment on your behalf.

We sincerely hope that will this will not be necessary and that you will engage with the legislation and appoint a surveyor.

Please do not hesitate to contact the writer if you wish to discuss any aspect of the notifiable works and/or notices.

Yours sincerely,

[**insert surveyors name**]

APPENDIX V   SCAFFOLD LICENCE

This Access Licence is made

BETWEEN

…………………………….. (Hereinafter referred to as the Neighbouring Owners) of ………………………………. who are the freehold/Commonhold/Leasehold owners within the meaning of the **LICENCE** of the premises known as ……………………………………………… shown edged in RED on the attached plan.

AND

…………………………….. (Hereinafter referred to as the Building Owners) of ………………………………… freehold/Commonhold/Leasehold owners within the meaning of the LICENCE of the premises known as ……………………………………………… shown edged in RED on the attached plan.

AND WHEREAS A LICENCE as set out below has been hereby granted

The Neighbouring Owner has appointed

The Building Owner has appointed Mr. ……………………………….of ………………………………………………………………………………………

THE NEIGHBOURING OWNERS DO HEREBY GRANT

1 A Licence and permission for access (subject to the provisions herein set out) to the Building Owners, their agents and/or employers 7 days after the signing of this Licence to:

   1.1 Have access on to the Neighbouring Owners land to execute the works as set out in the attached method statement and detailed on the attached drawing nos. **(INSERT NOS.)** commencing on the **(INSERT DATE).**

1.2 The Building Owners will be responsible for all costs and/or activities necessary for ensuring that the ground surface is sufficient for providing a stable base for the erection of the scaffolding.

1.3 The Access Licence will remain valid for a period of **(INSERT PERIOD)** which includes the required period for the safe dismantling and removing of any scaffolding and the reinstatement of any other works and damage caused to the Neighbouring Owners property.

1.4 If the Building Owner has not commenced the works within the period as set out in 1.3 supra the Licence will expire and the process begins de novo.

1.5 Any sums paid in consideration are forfeited and the Building Owner remains liable for all the costs incurred.

2 Consideration

2.1 The Building Owner will pay within 7 days of the signing of this licence the sum of (INSERT FIGURE) being the consideration for the granting of the scaffolding licence.

2.2 The Building Owner will at all times hereafter indemnify the Neighbouring Owners, their lessees, tenants, visitors and/or employees and/or any other persons entering into and carrying out any lawful activities within the Neighbouring Owners land, for any injury, loss, damage or consequence of anything occurring within and/or falling from the scaffold and/or operatives working therein, on, and within the scaffolding.

2.3 Subject to but without prejudice to clause 2.2 supra, the building owners shall procure and maintain for the period set out under clause 1.3 supra public liability insurance and all necessary indemnities of **(INSERT FIGURE)** for each and every claim and shall supply within 7 days of this licence a copy of the policy and proof of payment of the policy premium.

2.4 The Building Owner shall be responsible for any costs arising out of any interference with any electronic equipment or communication systems operated by and/or stored and/or located within the neighbouring owner(s) property.

3 Ownership

3.1 The granting of this licence does not create an implied or granted relationship of landlord and tenant between the Building Owner and the Neighbouring Owners and/or any statutory legislation which shall apply to such relationship shall not apply to this licence.

3.2 The Neighbouring Owner covenants to procure the licence and/or its terms into any sales and/or lease agreements that it may enter into prior to or during the period set out in clause 1.3 supra.

3.3 The Building Owner cannot assign the benefits of this licence to any other party.

4   Termination and/or cancellation

The Neighbouring Owner may terminate this licence at any time and without any notice if;

4.1 The Building Owner commits a breach of any of the terms of this licence.

5   Variations

5.1 The Building Owner shall provide to the Neighbouring Owners surveyor as set out under the full details of any intended variations 7 days prior to executing the variation and shall not undertake any variations unless the Neighbouring Owners Surveyor provides a written and/or unless the variation is required as a matter of compliance to health and safety requirements, and/or subject to a dangerous structures notice.

5.2 The Neighbouring Owner is entitled to refuse any and/or all variations and is not required to give any explanation.

6   Professional Fees

6.1 That upon the signing of this Licence the Building Owners will pay the Neighbouring Owners Surveyors fee of £ (**INSERT FEE**) plus VAT in connection with the preparation of this LICENCE and including one final inspection. In the event of damage being caused or other contingencies or variations arising, including the pursuing of any sums owed in pursuance of the Act, a further fee shall be payable calculated on an hourly rate of £ (**INSERT FEE**) exclusive of VAT and disbursements.

IN WITNESS WHEREOF I (INSERT NEIGHBOURING OWNERS NAME) have set our hands this .... day of ....
....

Authorised to sign on behalf of the Neighbouring Owners:

Witness:

Occupation:

Address:

Date: **(INSERT DATE)**

IN WITNESS WHEREOF I (INSERT BUILDING OWNERS NAME) have set our hands this .... **day of** ....
....

(INSERT BUILDING OWNERS SURVEYORS NAME) to the Building Owners:

Authorised to sign on behalf of the Building Owners:

Witness:

Occupation:

Address: Date: **(INSERT DATE)**

APPENDIX VI REVOCABLE PERMISSION

[*name*]

[*address*]

our ref: …

your ref: …

Dear Sir[s]

[*location*]: grant of revocable permission to [*grantee*]

We act for [*name*], the owner of [*potential servient tenement*].

We confirm the grant of permission from our client to [*grantee*] [and those authorised by him *or wording as appropriate to cover the circumstances of others carrying out the use*] to [*describe use permitted by grant in broad terms to avoid non-authorised uses continuing*].

Please note that this permission is revocable by our client by further notice.

We should be grateful if you would confirm your acceptance of this revocable permission by counter-signing this letter where we have indicated below. We have enclosed a pre-paid envelope for your use in returning the counter-signed copy of this letter to us.

Yours faithfully

[*firm*]

I accept the permission granted to me by [*grantor*] in this letter.

Signed: ....

[*full name*]

[*date*]

APPENDIX VII UNILATERAL GRANT OF PERMISSION

[*name*]

[*address*]

By hand, by special delivery and
by first class post

our ref: …

your ref: …

Dear Sir[s],

Grant of permission to [*identify use*]

We act for [*name*], the owner of [*potential servient tenement*].

We give you notice that our client grants you permission to [*describe use in broad terms to avoid non-authorised uses continuing*].

Yours faithfully

[*firm*]

APPENDIX VII ANALYSIS OF PATEL & PATEL v LEVY ET AL

Patel & Patel v Peters, Peters, Levy, Fox, Conway & Conway [2014] EWCA Civ 335

8 years on and party wall surveyors still misunderstand/misquote this case.

This was a matter in the Court of Appeal Civil Division on an Appeal from the Central London County Court of a Judgment handed down by HHJ Hand QC (Case No. 2CL20031).

Was the Appeal worth the financial expense?

The dispute was over Mr. Wright's *ex parte* award for his fees of £20,000 and upheld by HHJ Hand. This was challenged in the Court of Appeal where the Patels incurred substantial legal costs.

Who were the winners in this case? Not the adjoining owners and most certainly not Mr. Wright!!

Whilst the Appeal was upheld, the Patels did not recover anywhere near all of their costs. Indeed, the shortfall i.e., the difference between the costs and those awarded against the Respondents adjoining owners exceed Mr. Wrights fees, this was due to the expertise of

Where was the common sense in not trying to reach an agreement somewhere in between possibly? In any event, the Patel's spent considerably more money than they would have done if they had simply paid Mr. Wright in the first instance.

Where is the logic in that?

Were the Patel's correctly advised in the first instance and was it sensible to rely on Mr. Burns and Mr. Frame's assessment of Mr. Wright's fees? Circa £2,500 reasonable?

Given the Building Owners' works involved a complex basement construction where there are six adjoining owners in separate private houses in the Hampstead, were Mr Burns and Mr frame being reasonable in their section 10 (10) award to expect Mr Wright to have completed those works for the £2,500 i.e., £416 per adjoining owner?

<u>**The Appeal**</u>

The Appeal was before Lord Justice Richards, Lord Justice Beatson and Lord Justice Briggs.

Mr. Nicholas Isaac (as he then was) and Ms. Cecily Crampin both of Tanfield Chambers www.tanfieldchambers.co.uk were instructed for the appellants, the six Respondents (adjoining owners) represented themselves through Dr David Levy. The matter was heard on the 17th March 2014, I was in attendance.

Their Lordships judgment sets out in paragraph 2 the central issue of the appeal which related to: -

"Whether or not the Appellants surveyor, Mr. Justin Burns, had refused or neglected to act effectively, upon receipt of a section 10(6) or (7) of the Act request, with the consequence that the Respondents surveyor (Mr Grant Wright) was empowered to act ex parte in issuing an Award in respect of his own fees."

That is the extent of the Judgment and the decision **nothing on costs**.

I have seen correspondence between Mr. Burns, Mr. Frame, and Mr. Wright because I was in fact asked to provide some guidance to Mr. Levy on a number of issues arising out of these party wall matters, and I in fact attended the March hearing.

<u>**The Facts**</u>

Mr. Wright had served a legitimate request under section 10 (7) on the 21st of December thus effectively triggering the 10-day period within which Mr. Burns should have responded to stop any ex parte rights. He did not.

For reasons which are not clear, Mr. Wright stated within the section 10 (7) request that he will not be considering that the 10 days have expired until the public holidays had been adjusted for.

There are no provisions within the Act to adjust any 10-day period for Bank Holidays or weekends. Presumably, Mr. Wright was simply being reasonable, a gentleman and professional in anticipation of Mr Burns doing the same and reaching a reasonable compromise on his fees.

Mr. Wright's decision to adjust for holidays etc. effectively made the section 10 (7) period at large. Because he did not act ex parte within the 10-day period or indeed prior to Mr. Burns email of the 6th January which was served outside of the 10-day period, Mr. Burns was at liberty to reply but it does not make the £2,500 a reasonable sum.

That was a fatal error on Mr. Wright's part, he had left the door open for Mr. Burns to adopt whatever strategy such as a 10(10) referral to Mr. Frame until such time as an ex parte Award had been served.

Mr. Wright's timesheets totalled just under £20,000 which does not in itself seem an exorbitant amount of money when compared to the Appeal costs of six figures. There are 6 adjoining owners and that works out at an average of £4,000 per party wall matter and it was a complex basement in Hampstead.

Mr. Wright assumed that 10-days having passed Mr. Burns was not entitled to respond outside the 10 days and/or that his response was not an effective response and served a *ex parte* Award

Therefore, the Lordships had to deal with two discreet points: -

1)   Whether a failure to comply within 10-days of a section 10 (7) request creates a continuing state of affairs so that the surveyor who neglects to act effectively may still act effectively thereafter, or whether, once the 10-days have expired, it is a "once-and-for-all" power so that later compliance could not remedy the default.

2)   Whether Mr. Burns email of the 6th January 2012 was "acting effectively".

That is the extent of the matters that the Lordships had to consider.

They **did not address the strategy or the technique** that Mr. Burns adopted with Mr. Frame.

That has never been tested in a Court of Law, and most certainly it is wrong for surveyors to claim Mr. Burns and Mr. Frame's strategy as having been supported by the Court.

If Mr. Wright had served an ex parte Award on the 10th day of the section 10 (7) request, being the 31st December or indeed any time before Mr. Burns reply of 6th January 2012 that would have been a valid ex parte Award.

The Patel's only option would have been to appeal the Award and/or to obtain a declaration of invalidity (which it would not be) because it complied with the provisions under section 10 (7) or simply have the fees awarded by Mr. Wright adjusted in accordance with section 10 (7).

<u>**Judgment**</u>

The Appeal decision does not give anything other than guidance on the application of section 10 (7) request and the 10-day period having a continuing state of affairs until an ex parte Award is served.

Their Lordships have determined that whilst the Act specifies a 10-day period that passes before a surveyor can proceed *ex parte* under section 10 (7) that does not preclude the recipient surveyor from responding at a later date providing that response is before any ex parte Award has been served.

The second point that their Lordships decided was whether or not Mr. Burns email of the 6th January albeit outside the 10-day period) was acting effectively. Mr. Wright believed that it was not acting effectively and this is where I disagree with Mr. Wright. Even though I do not accept that Mr. Burns assessment was reasonable he was nonetheless entitled to respond and express his opinion because time was at large due to Mr. Wright having failed to serve an ex parte Award.

Just because a recipient of that response does not agree with it, would not necessarily be a failure to act effectively in general terms, but ultimately that would depend on the response.

A similar situation arose in the Bansal v Myers case in that case as the adjoining owner surveyor I had invited the BOS to respond to my fees under a section 10 (7) request.

The BOS refused to state "you must discuss them with the BO", which clearly was a failure to act effectively, as held by HHJ Platt thus triggering my right under section 10 (7) to act ex parte and to award my fees as I believed them to be reasonable.

The BO appealed and lost. HHJ Platt ruled that my request under section 10 (7) was correct because the BOS response was a refusal to act effectively.

That is the fundamental difference between the Patel & Patel case and the Bansal v Myers case.

<u>**Justin Burns & Alex Frame's approach**</u>

These two surveyors determined that they would reach a conclusion on Mr. Wright's fees without involving him is that reasonable?

Their approach appears to be based on a misconceived assumption that there was a standard (one price fits all) fee for party wall matters. Although they both regularly charge considerably more than £416 for an Award.

Anyone of any experience acting within the Party Wall Act will know that each case turns on its own merits. Indeed, whilst it would appear that Mr. Wright's fees of £20,000 might appear excessive, when broken down into the 6 adjoining owners, that is an average cost of £4,000 per owner, and thus not necessarily THAT excessive or unreasonable.

 Notwithstanding, Mr. Burns' figure of £2,500 for all six Awards WAS BASED on his refusal to even consider Mr. Wright's Time sheets!!!!

How could Mr. Burns' assessment be objective or reasonable?
Is that an appropriate response?
Does it demonstrate impartiality or reasonableness?

If you consider those costs in relation to the six-figure legal costs, is there approach disproportionate to the matter, and indeed it was subsequently found on legal assessment to be an excessive fee.

<u>**Respondents' liability on costs**</u>

 I referred the Respondents to Ms. Avril Ashley of AJA Legal Services www.ajalegal.com an eminent expert on legal costs. She advised and indeed represented the Respondents and successfully argued that (Mr. Isaac and Mr. Hearsum's costs) were excessive and should be reduced.

The balance of legal COSTS paid by the Patels.

Therefore, on reflection were Mr. Wright's fees unreasonable when compared to the legal costs?

What would you, the reasonably-minded independent observer concludes?
Was the building owner's approach misconceived?
These are the important questions that should be answered

APPENDIX VIII SECTION 10(1)(a) AWARD

**AN AWARD UNDER THE PROVISIONS
OF THE PARTY WALL ETC. ACT 1996
TO BE SERVED ON THE
APPOINTING OWNERS UNDER SECTION 10(14)**

WHEREAS [**insert Building Owners name**] (hereinafter referred to as the Building Owners) of [**insert Building Owners current address**] freehold owners within the meaning of the said Act of the premises known as [**insert address relating to works**] did on the [**insert date of notices**] serve upon [**insert Adjoining Owners name**] (hereinafter referred to as the Adjoining Owners) freehold/leaseholder (amend as required) owner within the meaning of the Act of the adjoining premises known as [**insert Adjoining Owners address**] of their intention to exercise the rights given to them by the Party Wall etc Act 1996 under [insert notices].

AND WHEREAS A DISPUTE HAS ARISEN the Building and the Adjoining Owners have appointed [**insert Agreed Surveyors name**] of [**insert Agreed Surveyors address**] to act as the Agreed Surveyor.

NOW I, being the agreed surveyor so appointed, having inspected the said premises DO HEREBY AWARD AND DETERMINE as follows: -

1   (a)   That the proposed works fall within the meaning of [**insert notices**] of the Act.

     (b)   That the Schedule of Condition dated [**insert date if applicable**] attached hereto forms part of this Award and is sufficient for the purposes of the adjoining owner.

     (c)   That drawing Nos. [**insert drawing reference**] and attached hereto and any others which may be disclosed may form part of this Award if the Agreed Surveyor determines so.

2   That fourteen days after the service of the signed Award the Building Owner shall be at liberty if they choose but shall be under no obligation to carry out the following works.

     (a)   [**insert description of works**].

3   That no material deviation from the agreed works shall be made without prior consultation with an agreement by the Agreed Surveyor.

4   That if the Building Owner exercises the above rights, they shall;

(a)   Execute the whole of the aforesaid works at the sole cost of the building owner.

(b)   Take all reasonable precautions and provide all necessary support to protect excavations and the adjoining owner's land and buildings by providing shoring to the trenches until they are backfilled.

(c)   Make good all structural or decorative damage to the adjoining owner's building occasioned by the said works in materials to match existing works to the satisfaction of the agreed surveyor, or if so, required by the adjoining owner make payment in lieu of carrying out the work to make the damage good.

(d)   Shall take all necessary precautions and cover all excavations at the end of working day and provide security fencing to all boundaries where walls/fences that have or may be removed.

(e)   Hold the adjoining owner free from liability for any injury or loss of life to any person or damage to property caused by, or in consequence of, the execution of said works.

(f)   Bear the reasonable costs of the making of any justified claims.

(g)   Carry out the whole of the said works so far as practical from the building owners.

5   That the agreed surveyor shall be permitted reasonable access to the adjoining owner's property from time to time during the progress of the works at reasonable times and after giving notice in accordance with section 8.

6   That the whole of the works referred to in this Award shall be executed in accordance with building regulations, and any other requirements or statutory authorities, and shall be executed in a proper and workmanlike manner in sound and suitable materials in accordance with the terms of this Award to the reasonable satisfaction of the two said surveyors.

7   That the works shall be carried through with reasonable expedition after commencement and so as to avoid any unnecessary inconvenience to the adjoining owners or occupiers. In particular noisy works the subject of this Award shall be restricted to between the hours of 8.00am and 17.00pm on Monday to Friday, Saturday works shall be between 9.00am and 1.00pm, no works on Sundays or Bank Holidays.

8   That upon the signing of this Award the building owners will pay the agreed surveyors fee of **[insert fee]** + **VAT** in connection with the preparation of this Award. In the event of damage being caused or other contingencies or variations arising, including the pursuing of any sums owed in pursuance of the Act, a further fee shall be payable calculated on an hourly rate of **[insert hourly rate optional]** + **VAT** and is exclusive of any/all disbursements.

9   Any costs incurred by either party in settling this matter shall be determined by the Agreed Surveyor in accordance with section 10(12) and (13).

10   That the agreed surveyor reserves the right to issue any further Awards that may be necessary, as provided in said Act

11   That this Award shall be null and void if the permitted works do not commence within 12 months from the date of the notices under section 3(2) and/or 6(8) (amend as required).

12   Nothing in this Award shall be held as conferring, admitting or affecting any right of light or air.

13   That nothing in this Award shall be held as inferring, transferring or ascribing any responsibility to the Agreed Surveyor in regard to Health and Safety matters and particularly in relation to the Construction (Design and Management) Regulations 2007 (if applicable).

14   That either of the owners may within 14 days from receipt of the Award appeal to the County Court under s.10(17).

IN WITNESS WHEREOF I have this **[insert date of signing]** signed and served the Award in compliance with s.10(14).

[insert Surveyors name and signature]

NB: The above is not comprehensive and will require amending to suit the relevant issues.

APPENDIX IX SECTION 10(1)(b) AWARD

AN AWARD UNDER THE PROVISIONS
OF THE PARTY WALL ETC. ACT 1996
TO BE SERVED ON THE
APPOINTING OWNERS UNDER SECTION 10(14)

WHEREAS [**insert Building Owners name**] (hereinafter referred to as the Building Owners) of [**insert Building Owners current address**] freehold owners within the meaning of the said Act of the premises known as [**insert address relating to works**] did on the [**insert date of notices**] serve upon [b] (hereinafter referred to as the Adjoining Owners) freehold/leaseholder (amend as required) owner within the meaning of the Act of the adjoining premises known as [**insert Adjoining Owners address**] of their intention to exercise the rights given to them by the Party Wall etc Act 1996 under [**insert notices**].

AND WHEREAS A DISPUTE HAS ARISEN the Building Owners have appointed [**insert Building Owners Surveyors name**] of [**insert Building Owners Surveyors address**] to act as the Building Owners Surveyor and the Adjoining Owners have appointed [**insert Adjoining Owners Surveyors name**] of [**insert Adjoining Owners Surveyors address**] as their surveyor.

AND WHEREAS they have selected [**insert Third Surveyors name**] of [**insert Third Surveyors address**] to act as Third Surveyor. In the event of his being unable or unwilling to act and there being unable jointly to agree upon a substitute, another Third Surveyor shall be appointed in accordance with Section 10(8) of the said Act.

NOW WE, being the Two Surveyors so appointed, having inspected the said premises DO HEREBY AWARD AND DETERMINE as follows: -

1   (a)   That the proposed works fall within the meaning of [**insert notices**] of the Act (amend as required).

         (b)   That the Schedule of Condition dated [**insert date if applicable**] attached hereto and signed by the said The Two Surveyors forms part of this Award and is sufficient for the purposes of the Adjoining Owner.

(b)   That Drawings Nos. [**insert drawing reference**] and attached hereto and any others which may become relevant and signed by us the said two Surveyors form part of this Award.

2   That fourteen days after the service of the signed Award the Building Owner shall be at liberty if they choose but shall be under no obligation to carry out the following works.

(a)   [**Insert description of works**].

3   That no material deviation from the agreed works shall be made without prior consultation with an agreement by the said two Surveyor's.

4   That if the Building Owner exercises the above rights, they shall;

(h)   Execute the whole of the aforesaid works at the sole cost of the Building Owner.

(i)   Take all reasonable precautions and provide all necessary support to protect excavations and the Adjoining Owner's land and buildings by providing shoring to the trenches until they are backfilled.

(j)   Make good all structural or decorative damage to the Adjoining Owner's building occasioned by the said works in materials to match existing works to the satisfaction of the Appointed Surveyor's, or if so, required by the adjoining owner make payment in lieu of carrying out the work to make the damage good.

(k)   Shall take all necessary precautions and cover all excavations at the end of working day and provide security fencing to all boundaries where walls/fences that have or may be removed.

(l)   Hold the Adjoining Owner free from liability for any injury or loss of life to any person or damage to property caused by, or in consequence of, the execution of said works.

(m)   Bear the reasonable costs of the making of any justified claims.

(n)   Carry out the whole of the said works so far as practical from the building owners.

5   That the surveyors shall be permitted reasonable access to the owner's properties from time to time during the progress of the works at reasonable times and after giving notice in accordance with section 8.

6   That the whole of the works referred to in this Award shall be executed in accordance with Building Regulations, and any other requirements or statutory authorities, and shall be executed in a proper and workmanlike manner in sound and suitable materials in accordance with the terms of this Award to the reasonable satisfaction of the two said surveyors.

7   That the works shall be carried through with reasonable expedition after commencement and so as to avoid any unnecessary inconvenience to the Adjoining Owners or occupiers. In particular noisy works the subject of this Award shall be restricted to between the hours of 8.00am and 17.00pm between monad and Friday, Saturday works 9.00am and 1.00pm, No work son Sundays or bank holidays.

8   That upon the signing of this Award the building owners will pay the adjoining owners Surveyors fee of [**insert Adjoining Owners fee**] + VAT in connection with the preparation of this Award. In the event of damage being caused or other contingencies or variations arising, including the pursuing of any sums owed in pursuance of the Act, a further fee shall be payable calculated on an hourly rate of [**insert hourly rate optional**] and disbursements.

9   Any costs incurred by either party in settling this matter shall be discussed and agreed in accordance with section 10(13)(a)(b)(c) at the agreed rate.

10 That the Appointed Surveyors reserve the right to issue any further Award or Awards that may be necessary, as provided in said Act

11 That this Award shall be null and void if the permitted works do not commence within 12 months from the date of the notices under section 6(8).

12 Nothing in this Award shall be held as conferring, admitting or affecting any right of light or air.

13 That nothing in this Award shall be held as inferring, transferring or ascribing any responsibility to any of the three said Surveyors in regard to Health and Safety matters and particularly in relation to the Construction (Design and Management) Regulations 2007 (if applicable).

14 That either of the owners may within 14 days from receipt of the Award appeal to the County Court under s.10(17).

IN WITNESS WHEREOF We have set our hands this [**insert date**].

[**insert Building Owners Surveyors name**]

Address: [**insert Adjoining Owners Surveyors address**]

[**insert Adjoining Owners Surveyors name**]

Address: [**insert Adjoining Owners Surveyors address**]

NB: The above is not comprehensive and will require amending to suit the relevant issue

www.ingramcontent.com/pod-product-compliance
Lightning Source LLC
Chambersburg PA
CBHW071922150726
47999CB00001B/71